FAMILY LEGACY
AND LEADERSHIP

Preserving True Family Wealth
in Challenging Times

FAMILY LEGACY
AND LEADERSHIP

Preserving True Family Wealth in Challenging Times

MARK HAYNES DANIELL

and

SARA S. HAMILTON
Founder and CEO,
Family Office Exchange

WILEY

John Wiley & Sons (Asia) Pte. Ltd.

Other Wiley Editorial Offices

John Wiley & Sons, 111 River Street, Hoboken, NJ 07030, USA

John Wiley & Sons, The Atrium, Southern Gate, Chichester, West Sussex, P019 8SQ, United Kingdom

John Wiley & Sons (Canada) Ltd., 5353 Dundas Street West, Suite 400, Toronto, Ontario, M9B 6HB, Canada

John Wiley & Sons Australia Ltd., 42 McDougall Street, Milton, Queensland 4064, Australia

Wiley-VCH, Boschstrasse 12, D-69469 Weinheim, Germany

Library of Congress Cataloging-in-Publication Data
ISBN 978–0–470–82571–6

Typeset by MPS Limited, A Macmillan Company, Chennai, India.
Printed in Singapore by Toppan Security Printing Pte. Ltd.
10 9 8 7 6 5 4 3 2 1

*"If we want things to stay as they are,
things will have to change."*

Giuseppe Tomasi, 11th Prince of Lampedusa
(Giuseppe di Lampedusa)
—*Il Gattopardo* (The Leopard) 1958

DEDICATION

This book is dedicated to those who have supported us and inspired us throughout the individual efforts and teamwork required to produce this book. We would like to thank them for their contributions and we fully acknowledge that, without them, this book could never have been written.

Mark Haynes Daniell dedicates this book to the newest member of his family,

Marie-Valerie Celestine Victoria Daniell,

who has brought much joy and already contributed to true family wealth in its fullest definition.

Sara S. Hamilton dedicates this book to two exceptional grandfathers,

James E. Jernigan and Howard W. Hamilton Sr.,

whose conversations around the kitchen table set the stage for a lasting legacy, now in the very capable hands of Nathan Jackson Hamilton.

Together, we would also like to dedicate this book to our fellow members, colleagues, and friends within the Family Office Exchange (FOX) network, an extraordinary collection of families, family office professionals, and advisors who have all contributed, in their own unique ways, to making this book possible. We want to thank these families and experts around the globe, who have generously shared their challenges and successes with us over the past 20 years.

Their willingness to share their own experiences to benefit others is a hallmark of the FOX network that has become a source of knowledge, a community of like-minded families and friends, and our greatest member resource for insights and solutions.

CONTENTS

Appendices

ACKNOWLEDGMENTS

As always, supporting the authors of this work is a team of dedicated individuals without whose sterling efforts no book of this kind could ever be published. We would like to thank those whose names are not on the cover of this book, but whose insights, dedication, and efforts can be found—directly or indirectly—on all of its pages. The collaboration among the members of this team has been one of the most rewarding parts of the process of creating this work.

We would like to thank all the pioneers in the family wealth industry whose ideas have helped shape this body of work. There are far too many to name each one individually, but many have been quoted throughout the work. For their intellectual contributions to this book, and to the field of family and private wealth in general, we are much indebted.

We would like to acknowledge the very substantial contribution—from the beginning to the end of the process of writing this book—made by Jane Flanagan, our true partner in developing the links between family legacy planning, leadership, and risk management. We also would like to thank other colleagues at Family Office Exchange: John Benevides, Ruth Easterling, Mary Jane Fredrickson, David Lincoln, Mariann Mihailidis, Karen Neal, Anna Nichols, and Margaret Vaughan Robinson, whose insights and support through the years have been invaluable in capturing and codifying the most valuable lessons and examples from the world of legacy families.

For her contribution to the many versions of this manuscript we thank Mandy Young at The Cuscaden Group, who, with infinite patience, endless energy, and good humor, added enormously to the content and production process of this book. In Singapore, she is joined by Sarah Chalmers, whose editing skills and calm advice were much appreciated in addressing our many stylistic shortfalls. We also would like to thank and acknowledge Nicolas Oltramare, a savvy investor, selfless friend, wise counselor and true expert on many of the subjects addressed in these pages.

Our heartfelt thanks, as ever, to Karin Sixl-Daniell and Howard W. Hamilton, Jr. for their caring, support, thoughts, editing prowess, and midnight reviews. For seeing us through every stage of this book, and so much more, we cannot thank them enough.

A NOTE ON DISCRETION

In many cases we have used real examples to illustrate the ideas and lessons provided in this book, but protected the actual identities of those involved through the use of pseudonyms (marked with an asterisk) and amended descriptions of the family and the events relevant to the points we make. In so doing we hope to capture the true essence and value of each real example without compromising the confidentiality of any private discussions.

To these families, named and anonymous, we also offer our appreciation.

PROLOGUE

An appreciation of family legacy begins with an understanding that legacy is about far more than the past, and that true family wealth is about far more than money.

Equally, effective family leadership is often more about consensus than directives, leading from within the heart of the family, rather than from the head of the table, and establishing a common direction among relatives with a shared history.

Family wealth is a kind of energy which, correctly applied, can do great good. It is a gift that benefits members of the family, but also extends to those who benefit from the family's philanthropy, business and investment activities, community engagement, and demonstrated personal integrity.

Proper management of family wealth, in all its forms, requires effective leadership, a commitment by all members to the family and its collective future, and a thoughtful approach to managing the risk and change that challenge all family enterprises. This is no small task, and few families overcome the proverb, "riches to rags in three generations." However, there are indeed stories of success, many of which are shared throughout this text. The practices and approaches used by the legacy families who have survived and thrived for generations provide an invaluable guide to all who wish to enhance the legacy and leadership of their own wealthy families.

FAMILY LEGACY

Far too often, family legacy is considered as a concept related only to the past. This backward-looking (and inherently passive) view of legacy fails to capture a much more valuable and dynamic understanding: the essence of family legacy also carries with it the opportunity to shape the future of the family for the better.

Properly understood and acted upon, legacy is a living concept that transcends time and place. While legacy is indeed derived from the past, it is also a connected flow of personal histories, family patterns, events, and memories that exerts a strong influence on the present and shapes the future. Legacy, and effective family leadership building on the content of that legacy, can link the best of a family's past, present and future.

Family legacy encompasses all that a family holds dear and wants to preserve for the future—the history, values, knowledge, and experiences that are just as essential as a family's financial assets.

Legacy families think about the family in the context of the unknown future (i.e. grandchildren's children) and make the necessary investments to provide for those who are yet to come.

Successful multi-generational families have conversations about their reasons for staying together as a family and routinely revisit a set of important questions:

- Why should we stay together in spite of our differences?
- How do we strengthen the ties that bind us together for the greater good of all?
- What is it we want to accomplish together?

Families who stay together for generations benefit from the economies of scale that their combined assets and talents achieve, but also harness the potential of the family to create a community that adds meaning and quality to its members' lives.

Part I of this book identifies the ways that successful families define and enhance their legacies. From documenting their reasons for staying together and investing in the education and training of future family leaders to managing the family with a multi-generational perspective, the lessons learned from legacy families provide a powerful framework for every family leader.

LEADERSHIP IN THE LEGACY FAMILY

What makes a successful legacy family, and what provides the foundation for successful leadership of a family, is the collective commitment by the family members to create and sustain something greater than themselves.

Strong family leaders engage the whole family and move it toward a common set of goals, respecting a shared set of values and guiding principles along the way. They also understand the family history and, in their strategies, behavior, and personal example, reflect the best of the family's current standards and future potential.

Leadership of the wealthy family, while potentially enormously satisfying, is also enormously complex, requiring careful attention and the ability to balance the desire for continuity with the need for (and reality of) change.

Successful family leaders ask the right questions. Thinking about the important questions helps families prepare for the challenges involved in building and sustaining an enduring legacy.

- What is our family legacy, and how does it shape the future of the family?
- What leadership skills are needed, and how can leaders best contribute to the continuity of the family?
- How can we manage effectively the risks that we face, and what leadership skills are needed to face the most critical challenges?

Families who can answer these questions well are more likely to build their own enduring legacies; families who are adequately prepared for these challenges understand the link between family responsibility, family legacy, and financial stewardship. They instill a sense of responsibility within the family and ensure that members are firmly grounded by a set of common values and remain connected as the family tree grows.

The leadership challenges change continually within every family. In times of relative stability, the priority of the family leader may be to ensure that essential operations are managed in an efficient and effective manner, and with a minimum of disruption. Risks are managed, family issues are addressed, and relevant opportunities are identified and exploited.

At other times, dramatic adjustments are needed. Due to changes in the family or in the outside world, there are times when discontinuous change is required, breaking old patterns, pursuing bold new directions, and fundamentally transforming, rather than just transitioning, a family from one state of being to another.

The ability to adapt leadership and strategy to the needs of the times and the specific family situation is essential for success. Part II addresses the challenges of family leadership and identifies the approaches and skills needed for long-term success. Proper planning for succession and an awareness of one's place in the context of the family's generational bridge are important considerations for every family leader.

MANAGING RISK AND CHANGE

Each family emerges from a unique history and faces a unique set of risks and opportunities in a world where the pace of change never slows. A critical role of the family leader is to guide the family through the sea of risks it encounters over time. Risks to the family's wealth and wellbeing range from the financial risk of loss of capital to the human or personal risk of apathy or lack of interest.

One of the greatest challenges that financial families face together is perpetuating the passion and the drive that created the family business and legacy. It is ironic that a successful business generates wealth that makes a family comfortable, and that this comfort often engenders complacency in future generations.

This dynamic is what parents fear the most about leaving wealth to their children. They want their children to experience the pleasures and rewards that result from personal accomplishment; the thought of seeing them lose initiative or never find their calling because they do not need to work is a great concern for many.

Given the fast pace of the twenty-first century, and a society more and more centered on individual and instant gratification, getting a commitment from wealth owners to engage in long-term, intergenerational family legacy planning may be this generation's greatest leadership challenge.

Developing strategies to manage risks and maximize opportunities is the focus of Part III. Risk and change are inevitable, and can be a source of energy and creativity for the family, if they are properly managed.

The role of the network of trusted advisors or "eco-system" as a partner in the wealth management process cannot be underestimated. Families who have a family office often rely on this resource as a powerful manager of risk and change. All can learn from the families who have incorporated effective risk-taking into their family culture.

INVESTMENT IN THE FUTURE

There is, of course, no single "right" answer to the questions of legacy and leadership for any wealthy family. The past and the experience of others, however well understood, do not provide a complete guide to a less certain future. Similarly, the leadership skills needed for future challenges may not be the traditional problem-solving skills of the past.

In an era of constant change, different approaches, new solutions, and a new set of allies and advisors may be required to pursue your family's vision and achieve its supporting goals.

Although each family has its own history and unique destiny, it is our hope that this book will allow leaders of wealthy families, equipped with open minds and the capacity for incisive action, to serve their families with better information, greater insight, diminished risk, and an improved chance to build a lasting family fortune and an enduring family legacy.

PART I

FAMILY LEGACY AND LEGACY PLANNING

1. BUILDING AN ENDURING LEGACY

Every family is heir to a legacy.

Each individual family member, and in particular each member of a family leadership team, plays a part as an heir to his or her family legacy. At the same time, each individual leaves behind a personal legacy for others to inherit that may be positive or negative in content, and great or small in magnitude.

Every family member contributes to the family legacy. The only questions are what will that legacy be, and how will he or she be remembered?

TRUE WEALTH IS MORE THAN MONEY

A legacy may or may not involve substantial financial wealth. It may involve traditional engagement in business, politics, property ownership or art. It may carry with it a famous name, unique values and standards, a special dedication to the larger family or place of family origin, aristocratic lineage, tradition or a respected position in the community. Most family legacies carry with them more than one element that characterizes and shapes a family over time.

To preserve a family's fortunes, financial and nonfinancial alike, example after example of multi-generational success proves that it is essential to understand that true wealth is far more than money. Even the word "wealth" itself is derived from the Old English root words *weal* and *wela*, each with a meaning more akin to wellbeing and general welfare than pure financial wealth. Creating true family wealth and preserving an enduring family legacy thus requires far more than financial investment acumen.

A broad definition of family capital and assets, encompassing the uniqueness of each wealthy family and individual wealth owner, is essential to the concept of legacy. To this end, protecting and building on a true definition of legacy is all about identifying and preserving what the family holds most dear—through time and across generations.

LEGACY MANIFESTED IN MANY FORMS OF FAMILY CAPITAL

True family wealth encompasses financial resources, but also includes family capital that manifests itself in many complementary forms: family harmony, physical wellbeing, a broader sense of legacy and reputation, integrity, spiritual growth, intellectual capital, and the personal happiness of each family member. Not only do these intrinsic states of being determine the quality of family wealth in the broader sense, they also provide the platform from which continuing financial prosperity can best be pursued.

> Definitions of wealth which consider only bank accounts, possessions, and property are wholly inadequate.

As noted family counselor Jeffrey Murrah remarked:

"The challenging question is, 'What is true wealth?' Definitions of wealth which consider only bank accounts, possessions, and property are wholly inadequate."[1]

Family legacy can be a gift that carries with it more than a mere grant or inheritance of name, money, or personal property handed down through the family. It is far more than a static family tree of past births, deaths, and marriages. Legacy is, in its essence, the sum of valued accomplishments, traditions, assets, histories, experiences, lives, places, and memories that flow from the past through the present and into the future.

Family Pride

"All children, and especially the wealthy, benefit from a sense of family pride, and instilling this is another parental responsibility. Wherever the money originally came from, the children want to feel good about it and about the people who made it, managed it, and in whose line they are. What's important is that they grow up feeling that they have a background of which they can be proud and that there are admirable traditions to uphold."

John Levy[2]

---

1 D. Murrah, "The True Meaning of Wealth," Parent University, http://www.pasadenaisd.org/ParentUniversity/parent42.htm.
2 John L. Levy, *Inherited Wealth: Opportunities and Dilemmas* (North Charleston: BookSurge Publishing, 2008), 32.

THE BENEFITS OF LEGACY

Addressing family legacy is not an academic exercise. There is great practical value in managing the elements of legacy and in identifying and establishing an effective model of leadership for the family.

The result of a successful model of legacy and leadership can be a more harmonious family with a greater sense of identity, sharing, and purpose. The entire family can be lifted in stature and accomplishment. Individuals within that larger family can lead richer and more fulfilling lives. Financial wealth is also far more likely to be preserved if a sustainable model of legacy and leadership is in place.

A strong family legacy often provides the emotional glue that keeps the generations motivated to work together.

FAMILY HISTORY: STARTING POINT FOR FAMILY FUTURE

Defining a legacy, which is the beginning of defining the pathway forward for a wealthy family, begins with an understanding of the past. For better or worse, families cannot escape the past entirely, but they can understand and use it to improve the future.

The Value of Family Stories

The ultra-wealthy understand the importance of bequeathing money, property, and other tangible assets. As important as possessions are, there is an even greater, often unrecognized, intangible asset families can bestow to descendents. This asset is the family's story.

"Historians, anthropologists, and psychologists argue that family stories are valued above any material possession."

Judith Kolva[3]

In assembling a usable past that can provide a solid foundation for the future, the importance of family stories cannot be overemphasized. By selecting (and, hopefully, capturing in written form) the stories that mark out a family's evolution, a greater sense of identity, shared family experience, and common family values can be developed. Telling—and retelling as many times as needed—family stories is a key role for all family members.

---

3 Judith Kolva, "Family Stories: An Unrecognized Asset," Fox Resource Library, 2009.

Preserving the Founder's Legacy

"We are proud of the accomplishments and the values of those people who preceded us. My great-grandfather established the company policy of retaining the logged-off lands for the generations to come—at a time when most others chose to cut and run. He worked in the woods as a teamster and respected loggers and their work.

Later, my grandfather carried on these traditions and expanded upon them. He carried the interest of loggers to Olympia, where he became Speaker of the House. He made the town of Shelton (the company's home) a better place to live and work, and he instructed Simpson managers that the future of Shelton must be considered in every business decision and must survive.

My father picked up the mantle from these great leaders. He built the company far beyond the dreams of his predecessors, while maintaining their principles. He looked after the welfare of the company's employees by investing in timberland for future generations."[4]

Family history, however, is not merely an assembly of facts, artifacts, and assets. It is an exercise in understanding, interpretation, and communication. A sense of family history and past accomplishment can enhance an individual's sense of what is possible, strengthen the family's belief in one another, and reinforce the confidence in the family's collective ability to overcome adversity and achieve their collective vision for the future—together.

Successful leaders reflect on shared legacy and values in both historical patterns and guiding principles for the future

- Choose patterns of behavior to carry forward and some to leave behind.
- Identify core values and core competencies as a family.
- Discuss the amount of togetherness that feels appropriate.
- Develop a shared vision of the future together.
- Celebrate the engagement of the family in the enterprise each year.

---

4 Robert Spector, *Family Trees: Simpson's Centennial Story* (Tacoma: Simpson Investment Company, 1990), viii–ix.

The Negative is Often the Most Valuable Not all family stories involve triumph and accomplishment, nor should all family memories be celebrations of past successes. Great entrepreneurs and multigenerational wealthy families may well have struggled, with mixed results, to achieve what they have accomplished.

Negative stories and events in times of adversity are often the most valuable part of history. Positive experiences, at an individual level, merely serve to confirm what is already known. It is the negative experiences that help an individual or a family to grow and to learn, and reinforce the need to apply core values and sustaining principles in trying times.

Awareness of all aspects of a family's history and legacy—good and bad—is the first step toward a better future.

> Awareness of all aspects of a family's history and legacy— good and bad—is the first step toward a better future.

Keeping Secrets and Hiding History Inheriting the valuable stories, lessons, and knowledge provided by family history is a part of life in a successful legacy family. Broad and open discussion of the past is a great forum for reinforcing identity and values. Those stories that are remembered, and how and why they are remembered, remind all members of a family about what counts, and what does not, in being accorded stature and respect beyond the grave.

On the other hand, hiding the truth and the stories that can provide a firm foundation for the future can lead to great risks and costs.

Of all of the values upon which a lasting legacy can be based, honesty and inclusion are among the most important. Excluding family members from important information and misleading them on their actual status can sow seeds of dissent and disillusionment, and set an unfortunate example of family leaders as masters of deceptive manipulation.

Avoiding the costs of such behavior and changing the approach for future generations are important steps forward for leaders of hidden legacies.

DOCUMENTING HISTORY AND LEGACY

The antithesis of hidden secrets is the practice of taking time to document the history and lessons learned for the benefit of future generations of the family. It has become common practice for family leaders to record their memories, either on film or through history maps, to enshrine the history of a legacy family.

When the successful founder takes time to document his or her failures as well as the successes, the value to future generations is immeasurable. Wealth inheritors need to hear their founders' voices, to know that the founders were not afraid of taking risk, and that they experienced hardship and failure along with success.

A Life Story for My Grandchildren

Stuart Moldaw (1927–2008), founder of Ross Stores and financier of Gymboree, spent 40 years as an entrepreneur running private equity ventures and another 20 years running his own family office for the benefit of his wife and two daughters. In Moldaw's book *A Life Story for My Grandchildren*, he writes:

"My greatest happiness came not from money and possessions but from my engagements, accomplishments, challenges, the camaraderie with the people I have met along the way, and the love of my family . . . I hope that my grandchildren will come to understand the joy of helping their less fortunate fellows to fulfill their dreams. We can do so much to make the world a better place.

The advantage of financial wellbeing can make a person indulgent, rob him of the true measure of meaningful accomplishment and allow him to live a shallow life; or it can give him the ability to make a difference in the world that cries out for compassion, action and commitment."[5]

LEADERSHIP, PURPOSE, AND ACCOMPLISHMENT

No one should presume that a family legacy will automatically be maintained. Even with good intentions and honest effort, there is no guarantee of a sustainable outcome.

In fact, the odds are stacked against preserving financial wealth, with family legacy likely to suffer as a result. Far too many families follow the well-worn trail of "rags to riches to rags in three generations," limiting the choices and removing many attractive life

---

5 Stuart Moldaw, quoted in "Stuart Moldaw: Death Notices," *The New York Times*, June 1, 2008.

opportunities for current family members and their succeeding generations.

Although the odds weigh against a successful legacy outcome over the long term, some families, and some family leaders, have managed to create stories of success across generations and through times both testing and triumphant.

These successful wealthy families and their broader legacies are often built, preserved, or evolve through the efforts of a small subset of their members who provide the exceptional energy, insight, leadership, and entrepreneurial spirit to enhance and maintain that legacy.

The broad concepts described here and the specific content of this book are aimed at helping ambitious families to improve their odds of success by developing knowledgeable and capable leaders who understand the importance of a multi-generational legacy strategy.

> Ambitious families improve their odds of success by developing knowledgeable and capable leaders who understand the importance of a multi-generational legacy strategy.

FAMILY LEADER AS CHIEF LEGACY OFFICER

One of the most important roles of the family leader is serving as the Chief Legacy Officer for the family. This is an overarching and visionary role; its success lies in addressing all aspects of legacy in an integrated fashion, while identifying those most important elements of insight and action that can lead to a better and more prosperous future for the collective family.

Leadership of a legacy family requires flexibility and a willingness to fulfill many varied roles to guide the family forward. The most important roles are helping to:

- Preserve the family legacy.
- Capture history and identify the culture of the family.
- Learn from family history (perhaps bringing generations together to map past successes and failures).
- Guide the family process for developing a shared vision for each generation (leaders do not mandate the future vision for the family).

- Understand and address the larger issues and risks that may be challenging the family and its legacy.

- Facilitate the change process while maintaining family continuity.

- Manage the family and its advisors to achieve long-term objectives.

- Identify the roadblocks and ask the right questions.

- Retain assistance from outside advisors as needed.

Obviously, in the struggle to define and maintain an admirable legacy, a sense of purpose and a set of focused activities are essential.

Great legacies are no accident of history. Neither a great legacy nor the fulfillment of a family's higher purpose is the product of passive observation of a family's history, or the disengaged acceptance of whatever choices life presents by way of experience. Ambition, insight, unrelenting effort, tough choices, courage, and personal leadership are all required for a family to reach its full legacy potential.

> Great legacies are no accident of history.

Mere hope is not a strategy, nor a likely pathway to an enduring legacy.

By instilling an understanding and appreciation of family legacy and applying that knowledge at the most critical times, family leaders set the foundation for a more successful future for their families.

Questions for Leaders of Legacy

1. Do you have a written family history that documents the major influences on your family legacy and family wealth?
2. Does your collective family share a common understanding of your family's legacy?
3. What values from the family's history do you want to preserve and pass on to future generations?
4. Do you have a process to help family members understand their own potential contributions to family legacy?
5. What do you need to do to build your own enduring legacy?

Seventh-Generation Thinking

James E. Hughes Jr. is a sixth-generation counselor at law and author of many influential articles on family governance and wealth preservation. He is also the esteemed author of Family Wealth: Keeping It in the Family, *and* Family: The Compact Among Generations, *from which this excerpt is taken.*[6]

Tribes that survive the longest ensure their preservation by practicing what's called "seventh-generation thinking." I believe this type of thinking is essential to the success of a family. I define that success as reaching the fifth generation with its bonds of affinity intact, not just its genealogy, and going on from there to become a tribe. Cultural anthropology explains this evolutionary process: a tribe is no more than an original family of two persons of affinity, which has evolved five or six generations later into an extended human system. But why does success require six generations? Why not four? Simply because reaching the fourth generation may be a matter of luck. But if a family successfully reaches its fifth generation, as a family of affinity, I believe it constitutes a system with real possibilities for long-term success. Luck, while always useful, is no longer likely to be its chief engine for growth.

   To understand the essence of seventh-generation thinking, consider the statement used by the senior Iroquois elder at the beginning of each meeting of the tribe convened in solemn council. I paraphrase: "As we begin our sacred work of tribal decision-making, let us hope that our decisions today as well as the care, deliberation, and wisdom we use in making those decisions, will be honored by and truly beneficial to the members of our tribe seven generations from today, as we today honor the decisions made by our ancestors seven generations ago."

   Such thinking assures the existence of the tribe far into the future and far beyond the lifetime of any living member of the tribe. The elder's words remind us that building a family for long-term success requires vision far beyond any individual's lifetime and far beyond the imagination of any one person. The elder calls on the collective imagination. The elder imagines what the tribe's members will think seven generations from now about the decisions the tribe will make today and asks each tribal member individually to exercise his or her imagination in the same way. The elder gently reminds

(continued)

---

6 Excerpt from *Family: The Compact Among Generations,* 19–20, 2007, by James E. Hughes Jr. Reprinted by permission of Bloomberg Press. All rights reserved.

the tribal family to think back seven generations and to consider how blessed they are by the decisions their forefathers made all those years ago, which permit them to be assembled together so many years later.

Hidden in the elder's wisdom is an admonition that my father, as the elder of our family tribe, frequently offered as we began our work: "Hasten slowly." The tribe practicing seventh-generation thinking understands that without action, entropy and stasis will cause the tribe to disappear as its energy dissipates. But unchecked action that results in chaos will lead just as certainly to the death of the tribe from a surfeit of energy it cannot absorb. Hastening slowly offers the means to use time as a friend, to find time to be a beginner, to be an apprentice, to move on to journeyman, and then to refine the skills for mastery.

To develop and survive, a family, like a tribe, needs to enhance the growth of its members' human and intellectual capital to its highest capacity. Without such enhancement, the family will not have the human assets required to take advantage of the new opportunities the future will offer and to combat the new threats it will pose. Fostering a beginner's mind in combination with seventh-generation thinking affords a family a process and practice that lets its talents and gifts emerge through the increased self-awareness and happiness of its members. It balances the youthful joy and chaos such a process reflects with the elders' ordered sense of the wisdom of time as a friend.

The elder helps leaven the enthusiasm of the beginner's mind with the patience of seventh-generation thinking. Hastening slowly is the path of deliberate, gradual accretion of skills that leads the apprentice to eventual mastery. This is the tried-and-true process of a family's development and enhancement that works best for achieving its successful evolution from family to tribe.

2. DEFINING A CLEAR PHILOSOPHY OF FAMILY WEALTH

Substantial family wealth, either inherited or freshly minted, is a great gift. It offers new avenues for personal experience and growth, along with unprecedented opportunities for the realization of each family member's potential.

Empowered by resources and unencumbered by the stresses of providing for self and family on a daily basis, wealth can be a door to a far more fulfilling life for individual family members. It can also provide the foundation for a positive and lasting legacy for the family as a whole.

However, without a clear philosophy of wealth, financial advantage can trigger conflict and heighten feelings of regret or guilt among inheritors. By defining a philosophy of wealth clearly, potential negative consequences can be avoided.

> Without a clear philosophy of wealth, financial advantage can trigger conflict and heighten feelings of regret or guilt among inheritors.

Long before setting out to invest, spend, or give away wealth, it is essential to clarify the views and philosophy that a family holds toward that wealth. Family leaders will be better prepared to face future challenges if their views are grounded in a solid foundation of shared forward views carefully crafted and communicated by their predecessors.

PROPRIETOR OR STEWARD OF WEALTH?

There are two very different attitudes that family members develop toward inherited wealth. Some family members view themselves as personal proprietors of the wealth (also called "inheritors" by some) who view their inheritance as something passed on to them for their personal use. Proprietors see themselves as fortunate to have received an inheritance, but do not feel obliged to preserve the fortune for future generations or may not believe that a future enterprise is viable for their family. They are comfortable with the fact that the financial legacy may end with their generation, and they may spend down the assets. They see themselves as capable of making this decision without regret or concerns for future generations.

For many others, inheritance is viewed as something to be cared for and passed on to future generations. These owners feel a great responsibility to preserve the wealth during, and even after, their lifetimes. Stewards of wealth often have a broader definition of what they are passing on and a different attitude toward legacy, responsibility, risk, spending disciplines, and education of the next generation.

Obviously, a family or family member who aspires to preserve family wealth for future generations, and acts consistently with that view, is more likely to create a long-term financial and family legacy than one who sees his or her wealth as a short-term resource to be spent or invested with only personal interests in mind.

BALANCING DIFFERENT VIEWS

As experts and family counselors explain, there is nothing right or wrong about these philosophical differences, and most multi-generational families have both types of owners. Each wealth owner needs to be comfortable with his or her own philosophy and not be judgmental about those who feel differently. Troubles often surface when differences in philosophy are not discussed openly as a family.

Second-generation siblings who inherit wealth are almost always told by the founders that it is important to keep the family and the wealth together. They seldom feel that they are in control of the money during their parents' lifetime, so their views on stewardship are typically mandated by their parents and are not challenged during the patriarch's lifetime. With individuals in the third generation or beyond in a family, differing philosophies emerge. The siblings and cousins have more freedom to have different views on spending down or preserving wealth.

> It is essential for families to have a conversation about their philosophies of wealth as they begin to think about legacy and leadership of the family.

It is essential for families to have a conversation about their philosophies of wealth as they begin to think about legacy and leadership of the family. Failure to clarify each owner's basic view about stewardship versus proprietorship may lead to a series of misunderstandings or controversies as families struggle to reconcile differing unstated beliefs.

CONSENSUS AND COEXISTENCE

Proprietors and stewards of family wealth can coexist as long as they respect each other's beliefs and agree on the decisions and actions they need to take that can be mutually beneficial. There is no way to force all family members to adhere to one philosophy. Because every family has a variety of owners, including proprietors, stewards, risk takers, risk avoiders, and consumers, the coexistence of different views is inevitable. Acceptance of these different views is essential for the family to remain together and for legacy to survive.

In most families of substantial wealth, a balanced approach is adopted. Some assets are considered to be personal or "proprietary," with others treated as "heirloom" or "legacy" assets for future generations. Different investment strategies and distribution policies are often in place for the different "buckets" of money. These sophisticated wealth owners see the choice between steward or proprietor as a false choice, since they comfortably embrace both roles with clarity and balance.

If there is a shared pool of family assets or a core operating business, and there are different philosophies about wealth ownership and legacy, there may never be an ability to reach full agreement on all financial alternatives. But setting up a family structure and process that support different philosophies can allow diversity to thrive and the legacy to survive.

A Real World Example

The Aspens* were a third- and fourth-generation family with fundamental philosophical differences about the family wealth. After the sale of the family business, the family met annually to revisit its business history and to discuss the stewardship of the family wealth held in a common trust. Family members struggled to build a shared vision of the future because there were two different philosophies about the purpose for the wealth.

One branch of the family had strong views about being stewards of the wealth for future generations, but other branches saw themselves as the lucky inheritors of a windfall payment with no desire to build or sustain a future family legacy.

After several years of attempting to be compatible, the proprietors voted to leave the family office that had been created for stewardship purposes, and

(continued)

the economics of the family office fell apart. One branch stayed together and selected a common wealth-advisory firm to help them with decisions, while in another branch of the family, each family member made separate decisions about how to manage his or her financial affairs.

This example reflects the potentially great impact a difference of philosophy on wealth can have on a family's unity, an issue that might have been better addressed with an earlier recognition of the differences of view and the implications of those views on the family's future.

One of the most valued roles of a family leader is to help the family balance the needs of both its stewards and proprietors, and to prepare future generations to live with the imbalance in the size of assets to be passed down to them that results from the application of the two different philosophies.

DIFFERENT VISION AND VALUES

Differences in philosophies of wealth and preferences for ownership have substantial implications, and can have a major impact on the family vision, values, legacy plan, organization, and asset structuring. Lack of a common philosophical platform for the future of the family, and varying views on personal involvement, may reduce the chances that the family can stay together. Similarly, a lack of shared values and principles can also contribute to the demise of a legacy family.

ASSET STRUCTURES AND RELATED DOCUMENTS

The vehicles through which stewards and proprietors hold, protect, and transfer their wealth are also profoundly affected by opinions about the philosophy of wealth. Options exist to tie up family financial wealth for many generations, establishing perpetual trusts and guiding them from beyond the grave through a complex set of trust deeds, letters of wishes, and estate documents. Although these documents may be tax efficient in their operation, they are not always positive forces in the lives of the beneficiaries.

Asset structures, properly established and operated, can have a great influence on income tax, capital gains tax, inheritance tax, estate duty, and litigation-related risks (notably marital) that can have a direct impact on the wealth passed on from one generation to the next. A greater share of assets placed in trusts and similar ownership arrangements that are tax efficient can both perpetuate a philosophy of wealth and protect that wealth to a greater extent over the long-term. This approach may be preferred by stewards of family wealth.

On the other hand, proprietors may prefer not to have long-term encumbrances on the management and enjoyment of their wealth. This approach could be characterized by fewer trusts, more partnerships, and a greater use of managed accounts under the direct control of the individuals concerned. In some families, there is a preference to have owners at each generation inherit their wealth through trust vehicles that pay out principal at 30, 35, or 40 years of age. They want each owner to have personal choices that are unencumbered by the rest of the family, believing that this builds healthy, independent relationships at each generation.

INVESTMENT IMPLICATIONS

In terms of investment objectives for family investment portfolios, stewards of wealth and wealth proprietors may well choose very different options for the management and disposition of their wealth.

Wealth stewards, by definition, have a longer-term investment horizon, a greater sensitivity to risk, and a view that looks for solid investments that will do well across many inevitable economic cycles and many generations of varying family circumstances. Wealth stewards may also have a greater propensity to professionalize the investment process, and to establish clear and disciplined investment guidelines.

Wealth proprietors, with their views as "personal inheritors," typically have a very different orientation and resulting approach. They may favor investments with a higher income component and, for some, a greater risk profile. The investment philosophy and the distribution patterns are likely to focus on the provision of unencumbered wealth to invest and spend during the proprietor's lifetime.

Some families strike a balanced approach, with some money considered as expendable inheritance and the remainder as family (stewardship) funds. Many families choose to have multiple investment portfolios or partnerships pursuing separate strategies. One portfolio designed for wealth preservation may have a more conservative orientation and be characterized by low liquidity, a selection of lower risk investments (with lower expected return), a higher proportion of real (inflation-resistant) assets, and a longer-term investment horizon.

Another portfolio, aimed at meeting the spending needs of a proprietor, may be characterized by shorter investment periods, greater liquidity, more income generation and, perhaps, a greater appetite for risk in the search for higher investment return to fund lifestyle expenses in the near future.

Families cannot retain their wealth over multiple generations when their members spend more than they contribute to the pool of family assets. Even large family fortunes can disappear if unsustainable distribution and spending patterns become the norm across generations.

> "Time to go on a 'money diet' until we are in better financial shape."

One well-known entrepreneur in the media world, famed for his great wit and ability to write snappy one-liners as well

---

Killing the Golden Goose

The Willows,* a prominent fifth-generation business-owning family, living on three continents and frequently captured on the society pages of the world's tabloids, stand as an example of how even the most robust business franchises can be threatened by a series of generations running the business with a proprietor's perspective.

Each of the past three generations of the family has tried to live better (and often far more in the public eye) than their parents. The result, in a family business where each member of the family over the age of 21 has a vote on the direction of the business and on the distribution policies of the family, has been to place enormous pressure on the operating business and to deplete the family's liquid reserves.

A beleaguered head of the family, more capable than his fellow family members of understanding where the selfish policies would lead, foresaw a future where the family's views would lead to a "slow liquidation of the family fortune" and an inevitable decline in the dominant position of the family business; pressures for dividends far exceeded the demands for sustaining investment and farsighted financial management of the operating business.

Even with an exceptionally talented investor as head of the family office, who doubled the family wealth in the bull markets before the recession of 2008, the family leadership team is forced to look at a sharp dropoff in individual wealth and family stature in coming generations.

The family-wide view of wealth as a source of funds for consumption, and related short-term thinking, is in the process of running down one of Europe's more scintillating family dynasties.

as his business acumen, announced to his extravagant wife, in the wake of a past economic crisis, that wealth preservation was important, making it "time to go on a 'money diet' until we are in better financial shape."

Without the discipline of a sustainable rate of withdrawal, even a large trust or family wealth corpus will be diminished over time, especially in a family expanding exponentially in size at each generation.

A Sustainable Rate of Withdrawal In the past, a rule of thumb[1] for sustainable distribution over many years would have been in the range of 2 to 4 percent of family assets. J.P. Morgan's research demonstrated that most portfolios with average risk should have generated 6 to 8 percent per annum over a decade, considering economic cycles both positive and negative. Taking a conservative 7 percent average investment return, a typical portfolio might show that wealth management fees require 1 percent of assets per year, tax and transfer costs absorb another 1 percent of assets (when averaged over a generation), and inflation accounts for a 3 percent reduction on average, leaving only 2 percent for distribution to retain the purchasing power of the wealth.

This calculation reflects the economics of the past half-century, rather than the most recent decade. In the past, a relatively safe income could be had from fixed income, and reliable gains were generated by core equity, equity-related, and real estate investments. These provided solid returns above inflation, with income also generated for spending or retention in a future distribution reserve to be released in leaner times. They served to both preserve and enhance capital value.

In the years after the millennium, many sources of income, capital value appreciation, and risk returns have dropped in reliability and return (as did inflation), making significant distributions in a time of sharply declining value a fading fancy and a lively topic of discussion for many wealthy families, their investment managers, and their trustees.

PHILOSOPHY AND FORTUNE

It is clear that the choice of a wealth philosophy and its consequent structuring of investment alternatives can have a major impact on family fortune and legacy.

---

1 "Wealth Preservation: The Spending Rate Matters More Than The Asset Allocation," J.P. Morgan Private Bank White Paper, 2006.

Whether following a philosophy of proprietorship, stewardship or a mixture of both, wealthy families and their leaders benefit from clarifying their views on sustaining wealth.

By understanding their philosophies, aligning their actions as best possible, and seeking to find consensus on important matters, family leaders are far more likely to keep both family and fortune intact and in harmony across the generations.

Questions for Leaders of Legacy

1. Have you clarified your philosophy of wealth with all members of the family and the impact of that philosophy on both the family and individual owners?
2. Have you found a way to accommodate the needs of proprietors and stewards within the family?
3. Have you confirmed that all documents, procedures, and asset structuring vehicles are aligned with your philosophy?
4. Is it time for your family to consider going on a "money diet?"
5. Do you have a process and a structure for operating compatibly in the pooling of assets for investment purposes?

First-Generation Wealth and the $64 Million Question

What do you do, and how do you begin, when you have received (through investment, business sale, income, or inheritance), free and clear of any obligation, a vast quantity of liquid wealth?

This quandary is surprisingly common among those who have created or inherited, but not yet figured out how to manage for the long-term, a great financial fortune. Once posed most often by new wealth owners in developed markets, this question is now being raised in increasingly prosperous emerging markets as well.

The answers to this question may not be immediately obvious to many newly wealthy families. Many successful business owners across the world have not had the time, training, and exposure to put together a clear legacy plan for themselves and their families. Others may not have had the interest or aptitude to develop the skills necessary to learn how to manage a lasting financial fortune, much less an enduring family legacy.

To preserve wealth, protect the family, and realize a set of objectives for the future, wealth owners need to design and implement a well-structured legacy plan. Only by addressing challenges on an integrated basis, and looking forward across multiple future generations, can the leaders and members of a family come close to realizing their aspirations for the future.

What goes into a legacy plan for a first-generation wealth owner and his or her family?

The approach proven to be most successful over time contains the following elements (all of which are expanded upon in the various chapters and sections of this book):

- **Define your vision of the future and personal philosophy of wealth:** Wealth owners need to decide what they want to accomplish in the future and who they want to become, and then set the vision, values and guiding principles that they and their family will respect along the way. Essential here is a clear statement of a philosophy of wealth and its implications for investment and distribution.
- **Organize and educate the family:** With so much at stake, it is essential to organize the family, select trustworthy advisors, establish effective governance (boards, processes, systems, etc.), and design and implement an effective leadership model. This requires drafting or amending all relevant documents (trust deeds, wills, legacy plans, strategic plans, succession plans, and all other necessary short- and long-term documents).

(continued)

Among the key activities here are to codify the Family Promise and draft a Family Constitution. An educational program needs to be set for each family member and for all family leaders.

- **Identify and manage opportunities and risks:** From the outset, wealth owners need to identify and manage the greatest opportunities for growth (in the broadest sense) and the greatest risks to their current and continuing wealth and prosperity. An appropriate family risk profile, risk management principles and process, and family risk-taking culture need to be established.

- **Decide upon your wealth transfer and philanthropic goals and strategies:** New wealth owners have to wrestle with how much wealth to pass on to future generations, which for some owners is the most difficult question of all. They also have a blank slate upon which to design their approaches to philanthropy, social entrepreneurship, and community engagement; with well-conceived philanthropic initiatives, they are able to have a major positive impact on both their communities and their families.

- **Structure, invest, and manage your wealth to meet clear objectives**: The asset structures (trusts, corporations, partnerships, private trust companies, and other entities) and investment strategies need to be developed and carefully implemented on a fully coordinated basis. These policies should be clearly spelled out for implementation during the wealth creator's lifetime and beyond. The full strategy and management plans for any family business(es) are part of an integrated approach to family enterprise management.

- **Build a supporting eco-system**: High-quality advice, financial oversight, and implementation support are essential to support the realization of a long-term vision, as is tapping into the various sources of ideas and opportunities available for investing and preserving wealth. Designing and aligning the appropriate eco-system, including an effective family office or its equivalent, and selecting and managing the most qualified advisors (who are both expert and trustworthy) are necessary parts of any successful legacy plan.

- **Define success and monitor progress**: Describing what would constitute success (or failure) of a legacy plan and its constituent parts can define what needs to be measured and managed along the way. Systems of reporting, control, custody, and compensation for all staff and advisors are part of a solid foundation for legacy planning and execution. Monitoring and measuring the value and progress of the legacy plan are an important part of an effective family process.

With this simple framework in hand, wealth owners can plan for the future and act today to achieve the best possible outcome over multiple, deserving generations of their legacy families.

3. THE FAMILY PROMISE, THE CONSTITUTION, AND RESPONSIBLE OWNERSHIP

An enduring family legacy can only be built by family members who are in agreement about a basic set of principles that reflect and support their beliefs, attitudes, and behaviors. The agreement needs to be viewed as a compact among the family members about their future together, and the terms of this compact need to be consensual, equitable, and transparent to all.

This solemn compact is known as the Family Promise.

THE FAMILY PROMISE

A Family Promise is the sum of the commitments a family makes to its members and to those with whom the family interacts. It is based on a foundation of trust and establishes a shared set of objectives, values, and principles, which define who the family is, what binds the family together, and what it wants to accomplish together.

The spirit of the Family Promise can be captured in written documents developed by the family, which include the history, aspirations, principles, and agreements that underpin the legacy of a family.

While a written Constitution is one of the most important documents, the Family Promise includes other formal documents and principles governing the family, as well as informal and unspoken commitments upon which family members can rely.

The Family Promise begins with a definition of who is a member of the family, identifying the people to whom the Promise is made and from whom a reciprocal commitment is expected. It includes a statement of vision (purpose and objectives), values (ethics and abstract ideas), participation principles (age, branch, and generation, prior experience, selection process, etc.), and governance principles (specific rules). The Promise is a compact addressed both to family members and those who interact with the family, reflecting at all times the family's greater values and aspirations.

A well-formulated Promise describes the legitimate expectations family members should have for themselves, their children, and succeeding generations. Among the most important are participation in family activities, decisions, businesses, and wealth distributions.

The reciprocal side of the Promise may require family members to respect certain values, agree to establish governance principles, adhere to set standards of responsible behavior, and ensure that they are all living up to the Family Promise as it applies to interactions with non-members of the family.

Content of a Family Promise

- Definition of family
- Family vision
- Family values seen in actions
- Bill of rights and responsibilities
- Statement of commitment and engagement
- Guiding principles
- Principles of education
- Leadership selection criteria
- Skills inventories and capability assessments
- Career development plans
- Letters of wishes or trustee guidance
- Family meeting ground rules
- Dispute resolution system
- Principles of review

DEFINING FAMILY MEMBERSHIP

Although the impact and scope of a Family Promise extend beyond the borders of the family, any family guidance needs to begin with an understanding of who are the members of the family to be governed by the Promise.

As a first step, leaders need to ensure that they have a working definition of family membership. Is it a standard bloodline definition of descendants from a defined individual? Does it include in-laws or stepchildren? Do men and women have equal rights? And does it extend to the broader sets of cousins and other relatives who perhaps should not be left out of the benefits of family wealth?

The answers to these questions need to be specified in order to understand the full set of participants and the implications for each in the governance of the family and participation in the management and distribution of family wealth.

FAMILY VISION

Having defined who a family is and where it has come from (based upon an understanding of family history), a successful leader must work with the greater family to decide *where* the family needs to go, setting a clear goal and defining a path toward that longer-term vision. The vision outlines the full extent and content of a family's aspirations, influencing the future of each individual as well as the collective family entity.

Setting out a course for the future is not just about governance, business, and family money. It is about setting a balanced approach to a future that addresses all aspects of family capital: moral, intellectual, spiritual, charitable, social, physical, and financial. These related types of family capital manifest themselves in both family values and accomplishments, creating an overall family ethos of integrity, hard work, and generosity, hopefully leading to a healthy and balanced life as well as continuing financial prosperity.

The vision is the overarching objective, the "timeless goal over the horizon," toward which a family can orient itself for many generations. The family vision statement should be general in nature, enduring in relevance, and applicable to the diverse needs of family members. A vision such as "enhance and protect the lifestyle options of our descendants so that each succeeding generation can live as well as the last, and make an increasing contribution to society" may serve as a solid, long-term, aspirational vision for many generations of the same family.

In setting out the overarching goals and long-term commitments of the family, leaders need to consider the preservation and enhancement of the non-financial elements that make up family capital, as well as preserving and distributing material wealth fairly.

FAMILY VALUES SEEN IN ACTIONS

In addition to specifying in which direction they wish to lead the family, family leaders need to define *how* the family will travel along its journey, specifying which values and guiding principles need to be respected along the way. In so doing, family leaders can shape the future of the family and its members on a coherent basis. Actions speak louder than words; through their demonstrated priorities, philosophies, decisions, and actions, legacy families define far more who they are and what they aspire to be than through the words captured in their formal statements.

> True values, reflected in character and demonstrated in action, are the cause of legacies prospering or declining over time.

Is the family truly a well-organized family with clear legacy rights and responsibilities oriented toward achieving a certain set of goals in a certain manner, or is it, in action, an unstructured entity that enables its individual members to do what they please as and when they please?

True values, reflected in character and demonstrated in action, are the cause of legacies prospering or declining over time.

Situational versus Secular Values Deeply held values should not change from one situation to the next. Values that stand for all time and in all situations are often described as "secular" values, describing those principles that do not change with any one situation or view of short-term self-interest, and do not vary in application from one member or generation of the family to another.

Such core values are an integral part of the family's identity and Family Promise and are the opposite of "situational" values that are short-term and, over time, usually inconsistent.

Internal and External Alignment Families, to be true and consistent, need to have a full alignment at all times behind a single set of values and common guiding principles that establish family identity and demonstrate what a family believes in and stands for.

Just as values should not change from one situation to the next, a family's way of operating should be consistent internally and externally. The same principles of honesty, courtesy, and professionalism that underpin interactions between family members should also govern the interactions between family members and family employees and parties outside the family and the family enterprise.

Without deeply held family values, wealthy families can make the error of pursuing money as a sole and complete goal in itself, and thus lose sight of the many other goals and attributes that make up a full legacy.

Some values may be as basic as "we will treat with respect, and be respected by, every person and firm who comes into contact with our family." Others are more abstract ideals that guide a family's actions and underpin its ethics and identity.

Such values as "demonstrate caring in our community and commitment to corporate social responsibility" provide guidance in the definition and execution of a long-term legacy plan, can underpin family and family business strategies, and contribute to the agenda of family meetings, performance reviews, and business tactics.

A summary of selected values, with commentary, may also be integrated into an Ethical Will, Family Mission Statement, Family Constitution, or other similar documents.

An example of such a statement of values from an ethical will is set out in the following box.

Reflections on Life Values

"While there have been far too many experiences, and far too much valuable learning in my long life to fit into one brief document, I would like to commend the following list of values and reflections to family members for their own contemplation.

Love and happiness: Of all things to pursue in life, love and happiness are the highest goals. My greatest happiness came from marrying the woman I loved, pursuing the career in business and public service which was my great passion and to which I was always fully committed, and in creating the large family I always wanted, a wonderful family that grew up in a loving and caring environment.

Honor and ethics: Being true to one's word, speaking frankly and acting with integrity are the bedrock of a life worth living. Without honor and a profound sense of what is right, and acting upon that belief, the quality of any one life is vastly diminished.

(continued)

It may not be easy taking the high road. There will always be people try-ing to drag down those who are following the better path, and there is often a personal cost to maintaining a life of integrity. It will always be worth reminding our children and their children that the higher road is often the more difficult pathway to follow, but it always leads to a far better place.

Expertise and excellence: I have found out, over the years, that it is not what someone does that makes for a full life, but how they do it that makes all the difference. An attention to quality, a high level of effort, striving to achieve excellence in whatever field of endeavor is chosen, and seeking out experience, expertise and knowledge from those more skilled or capable than I has always made a great contribution to the quality of my own life. I commend this attitude to others and hope that it has the same beneficial effect on your life that it did on mine.

When I failed to live up to these standards, the results spoke for them-selves in ways I am not happy to remember, but which served as a constant reminder of how much better it is to do a good job—and live by the right values—in whatever we choose to do."[1]

REALITY CHECK ON FAMILY VALUES STATEMENTS

In thinking about family values and legacy, it is essential not to be misled by facile or superficial values statements, even those drawn up by so-called outside experts.

All too often, these sorts of self-congratulatory summaries are drawn up to make a family feel good about itself or confirm what a family would like to be, without testing in any way to see what the reality of val-ues-related behavior is, or what a fami-ly's true beliefs are.

> True family values are seen in action, not in words.

True family values are seen in action, not in words.

One essential exercise in mak-ing a values statement meaningful is to test each value listed against a barometer of real and objectively defined behaviors. If a family prizes hard work, do members of the younger generations put in more than an eight-hour day, with a focus on preserving or

---

1 Mark H. Daniell, *Strategy for the Wealthy Family: Seven Principles to Assure Riches to Riches Across Generations* (Singapore: John Wiley & Sons (Asia), 2008), 472–3.

enhancing their family wealth and legacy? If a family aspires to be generous, have family members in fact, given 10 percent or more of their money to charity on a regular basis? If caring is an element of a family's values, do family members know the names of the spouses and children of the people in their family office, and spend time with staff, friends, and family if injured or ill?

This kind of "values gap" analysis, testing real world actions against aspiration and the formal words selected, can put some real teeth into a values statement and sharpen the cutting edge of a family's legacy plan.

Family vision and values statements should also pass the "thumb test," in which the family name is covered and the remaining words can still be seen to be uniquely well suited to a specific family—and far more than a general statement applicable to most families.

GUIDING PRINCIPLES

Guiding principles are more specific than either vision or values statements. A vision can orient a family's decision-makers in countless situations to navigate toward a shared long-term goal. Values can define an individual's character and guide action at a high level, exhorting family members to act in a "sensible," "harmonious," or "ethical" fashion.

While vision and values are more abstract and aspirational in content, guiding principles are the specific principles and standards of behavior that define the boundaries of acceptable—and unacceptable—family behaviors. Such principles may include "never invest in gaming, alcohol, and tobacco shares" or "install professional management in every business by the third generation." They can provide clear and firm guidance within the context of laudable, but less clearly defined in action, values.

Guiding principles inform and limit actions. In some cases, a statement of values does not provide a definitive guide to help family leaders make decisions in line with past family principles. Such principles as "we will only enter new markets with a proven local partner" or "we will only allow members to take up leadership positions in our family business after 10 years of a successful career outside our family business" are explicit rules based upon a family's history and best understanding of how family enterprises and business legacies can be protected and fostered.

THE FAMILY CONSTITUTION

To support the Family Promise and enable the family's leaders to operate within a defined and agreed system of governance, a number of documents and processes need to be in place.

This system of organization and governance, primarily (but not entirely) captured in a written Family Constitution, consists of structures, processes, and principles that are best set out with precision and prior thought.

The Family Constitution, similar in many ways to national constitutions, spells out the rights, responsibilities, and governance of the family. As with national constitutions, family structures and procedures, even well crafted and well balanced, are not enough to give full guidance to family members. Appending a specific Bill of Rights (as many national constitutions have done) and a matching Bill of Responsibilities (as many nations should have done but did not) can be a major addition to the Constitution.

WRITTEN VERSUS UNWRITTEN CONSTITUTION

Well-governed legacy families with capable leaders have both an integrated and written Constitution and a clear set of supporting documents to reinforce the greater Family Promise.

Families may have a collection of documents that contain some of the content of a Constitution: a family credo or vision or mission statement, an approach to organization and family participation, a statement of family values, operating guidelines for family participation, articles of association and bylaws, shareholders agreements, and memoranda of association.

Best practice would inform leaders that it is advisable to have a written Constitution that integrates and addresses as many issues as possible. Having a clearly-worded and fully-agreed single statement of purpose, membership, direction, values, governance, dispute resolution, rights, and responsibilities clarifies how a family can and should operate. This increases the chances of harmony and legacy being preserved without constant review and discussion.

In particular with regard to money matters, an understanding of specific rights and responsibilities, along with agreement on a dispute resolution mechanism, can go a long way toward limiting misunderstanding and reducing legacy-threatening conflict.

THE PROCESS OF DRAFTING AND AMENDMENT

Needless to say, the process of drafting any foundation document is as important as the eventual content. Setting out a process that is inclusive, well-paced (slow enough to obtain needed consensus but fast enough to keep up necessary momentum), and transparent will go a long way toward obtaining final buy in on its terms and future adherence to its content.

The same is true for the process of review and amendment. While making changes should be possible to make room for family evolution, learning, and adaptation, the inclusive review and amendment process should not be too frequent or flimsy, reflecting the nature of the document as an enduring social compact and a lasting individual covenant.

RESPONSIBLE OWNERSHIP

Responsible individual owners of wealth are the building blocks of a family's legacy. The legacy will rise and fall with the decisions and actions of its family members, leaders included.

Agreement on the definition of "responsible ownership" is important for families who want to enhance the likelihood of individual decisions and actions being consistent with the long-term best interest of the greater family. By supporting beliefs, actions, and behaviors with a clear understanding of "owner responsibilities," the collective and individual family members can take a giant step toward the preservation of their legacy.

> Responsible individual owners of wealth are the building blocks of a family's legacy.

This concept applies equally to wealth stewards and proprietors.

NO RIGHTS WITHOUT RESPONSIBILITIES

One Middle Eastern family, with a first generation comprising many brothers working together, realized the need to formalize a friendly but disorganized approach to family governance and family values. Realizing that their children had different views of their respective rights and responsibilities, they agreed with their lead advisor to attach as part of their new Family Constitution very explicit language that captured their shared view that along with rights come specific responsibilities, which needed to be understood by all concerned. The words they chose were as follows:

FAMILY BILL OF RIGHTS

- Be informed of all important matters relating to the family and participate in the family meeting.

- Obtain access to any information provided to other family members.

- Be heard at family meetings in accordance with the appropriate procedures.

- Vote as a member of the family, in proportion to shareholding, on family business matters and as an individual in non-business matters.

- Be considered for roles in family governance and management, based on ability and willingness to fill those positions, subject to meeting the criteria established in this document, and as set out separately by the family governing board.

- Leave the family without penalty, subject to appropriate succession planning, transition, and other actions.

- Receive a market rate of compensation if selected for an active management role in the family business.

FAMILY BILL OF RESPONSIBILITIES

- Learn and understand the family history.
- Support the Family Promise and the Constitution.
- Respect and live the Family Values.
- Work hard at school and in employment within and outside the family enterprise, to pursue a high level of achievement and to set an example for family business employees.

- Work constructively within the family structures and operating principles defined herein.

- Strive to ensure that family capital of all types is in better shape when passed on than when received.

BELIEFS, ATTITUDES, AND BEHAVIORS

A Family Promise is all about ensuring a better future by building trust, defining beliefs, shaping attitudes, and influencing behavior. A Family Promise does not arise in a vacuum. Psychologists argue that beliefs lead to attitudes, which lead to behaviors, and that all three need to be fully aligned if behaviors are to change—or to remain within a consistent and acceptable set of outcomes.

There are clear linkages between attitudes and certain types of behavior, and the goal is to establish those connections in the minds of young owners early on, so that appropriate behavior becomes second nature for them. Figure 3.1 shows several examples of these important links.

Figure 3.1: Linkages between Ownership Attitudes and Behaviors[2]

Ownership Attitudes	Ownership Behaviors
Belief in the future of the family	➡ Willingness to invest time training future generations
Preservation of history and legacy	➡ Telling stories of success and failure
Entrepreneurship in future efforts together	➡ Endorsing and experimenting with change and innovation
Clear definition of "belonging"	➡ Stating a clear policy on in-laws communication to in-laws about their roles
Belief that we are stronger if we stay together	➡ Creating governance structures to ensure trust among owners and reasonable exit strategies

---

2 Sara Hamilton and Joline Godfrey, "*Preparing the Next Generation for the Responsibilities of Ownership*" (Family Office Exchange White Paper, 2007), 15.

ACTIVE VERSUS PASSIVE OWNERSHIP

Every family member has an opportunity to contribute to the family legacy in some meaningful way, but each family member must decide how engaged he or she wants to be with the larger family and its legacy, and how he or she plans to contribute to the collective whole. Often, when family disagreements arise, at the heart of the problem is the issue of active versus passive engagement in family matters.

Some family members may feel strongly that it is important to stay active in the affairs previously managed by their parents, while other owners may feel uncomfortable taking on so much responsibility, given their lack of experience or capability in business matters. What is critical for the collective health of the family is that active and passive owners are able to choose the appropriate level of involvement that fits their personalities, capabilities, philosophies, and interests.

As younger generations become involved, they should be counseled about whether they will take an active or a passive role in the family enterprise. Siblings should be allowed to change their level of involvement as circumstances change, and as interest in family matters increases or decreases during different life stages.

The essential question to be discussed together is, what role does each owner want to play in the oversight and management of the family enterprise?

Active Owners

- ❏ Provide guidance and direction for the family enterprise regarding goals, objectives, and performance expectations.
- ❏ Attend regular meetings with managers and make decisions on issues not delegated to managers.
- ❏ Actively participate in business meetings, contributing ideas and suggestions, and asking questions.
- ❏ Hire management staff and develop personal performance goals for managers.
- ❏ Review and understand all ownership documents—ask questions about structures and operating agreements.
- ❏ Review all business documents before family meetings and make a list of questions for discussion.
- ❏ Proactively think of ways to enhance the value of the family enterprise.
- ❏ Actively engage in educational programs each year to increase knowledge and insight about financial, business, and family matters.
- ❏ Ask for feedback from family members and professional advisors to increase self-awareness and effectiveness.

Once siblings and cousins agree on the level of commitment being made by each owner, they must work together to create a reasonable decision-making process and governance structure for their shared legacy and shared ownership of assets. This process can take many years of discussion to reach agreement, but the family cannot move forward toward an aspirational future legacy without having these agreements in place.

HONORING THE PROMISE, BUILDING A LEGACY

Like any other solemn commitment, a Family Promise should be kept.

This "compact among generations"[3] is a deep and abiding agreement that provides the mortar between the bricks of a family legacy. It is the trust-based agreement that provides a foundation for all the other connections, decisions, and activities of the greater legacy family.

> Like any other solemn commitment, a Family Promise should be kept.

Each major transaction and family transition, and the career of each family leader, should respect and reinforce governance, reflect a responsible

Passive Owners

- ❏ Help make decisions on future direction for the enterprise and which family members will serve as leaders.
- ❏ Vote on family delegates to represent interests on governing board and support their decisions.
- ❏ Attend annual family business meetings, and ask questions when appropriate to enhance understanding.
- ❏ Stay informed about what is going on through quarterly written communication.
- ❏ Respond to email requests in a timely manner.
- ❏ Support active owners and admit any lack of understanding regarding business matters.
- ❏ Understand their own personal skills and interests and how they impact the continuation of the family enterprise.
- ❏ Provide constructive suggestions and feedback to family leaders and senior managers on an as-needed basis.
- ❏ Receive regular financial summaries and performance results.

---

3 James E. Hughes Jr., comments made at FOX Global Family Council, Zurich, 2005.

approach to ownership, and honor and reinforce the Family Promise within and across generations, in a shared effort to build a laudable and enduring legacy.

Questions for Leaders of Legacy

1. Do all family members understand the idea and content of the Family Promise?
2. Do you have a Constitution containing an agreed statement of family vision, values, and guiding principles, preferably captured in a single written document?
3. What is your working definition of family membership, and at what trigger points (age or accomplishment) do members undertake their roles and responsibilities?
4. What responsible beliefs, attitudes, and behaviors support your Family Promise?
5. Is there a sense of commitment to honor the content of the Family Promise in the future—within the family and in relationships with others?

A Family Roadmap for Responsible Ownership

Successful wealthy families take the time and effort to map out a series of activities which help them to guide their families to preserve family wealth and harmony across many succeeding generations.

One of these is a seventh-generation New Zealand family who have set out a very clear roadmap to link together their history and future vision for the family as a whole and for each individual family member. That proven roadmap can provide a useful guide and framework for other families and their leaders who aspire to long-term prosperity. The family were kind enough to share their approach and the guiding documents created by the family's fifth generation cousins, which follow below:

Family Roadmap

Use your family roadmap and decide where you want the journey to take you and what role you can choose to play in supporting the family.

Personally Commit to the Success of the Family

- Read and reflect on:
  - ❏ The Family's Core Values
  - ❏ The Family Vision Statement
  - ❏ The Family Mission Statement
- Become a Participant of the Family Charter and attend the Family Assembly
- Dedicate personal time and energy to support the family's success
- Actively participate in the decision-making process for the Family
- Have honest and active communication processes
- Respect different opinions among Family members
- Ensure processes for healthy disagreement and resolution
- Celebrate the Family history and preserve the philanthropic legacy

Core Values

The values that are held by the Family can be identified as:

- A continuing recognition of the Family's heritage
- Enterprise, hard work, providence and determination
- Ethical conduct and protection of privacy

(continued)

- Generosity of spirit, and care for and contribution to our community
- Belief in the values of Family harmony, a community of interest, encouragement of personal achievement and the realization of individual potential

Vision Statement

"To perpetuate the success of the Family."

Mission Statement

"To act as stewards of the Family's heritage and values, while ensuring preservation of wealth and continued prosperity for present and future generations."

Utilize the Resources Provided for Family Members

- Make use of the resources provided by the Council and the Financial Services Division
- Family History and Legacy
  - Family tree
  - Kinship report
  - Family archives
  - Family history books
- Participate in Social Activities
- Receive and actively contribute to the family newsletter
- Utilize the Family Office website
- Understand the fundamentals of portfolio and investment construction
- Make use of mentoring opportunities and internships
- Observe at Council meetings
- Attend educational courses and seminars
  - Introduction to the Family Business
  - Understanding the Constitution
  - Seminars and Courses
    - Fundamentals of Portfolio Construction
    - Estate Planning, Trusts, Wills, Enduring Powers of Attorney
    - Property Relationship
  - Communication Courses
  - Philanthropy Workshops
  - Due Diligence Courses
  - The Institute for Strategic Leadership Courses
  - Institute of Directors Course
  - Other e.g. Accountancy, Governance, Risk Management, HR, etc.
- Use the Family Library Resource

(continued)

Serve on the Family Council

The Family Council will undertake:
a) To uphold the Family Vision and Mission Statements
b) To ensure responsible, committed and enthused stewardship of Family assets
c) To review the performance of the Family Office
d) To identify, discuss and resolve Family issues
e) To promote recognition of Family values in Family businesses
f) To promote and encourage education and leadership programs for Family members
g) To encourage the development and preparation of potential Family successors for Family interests
h) To provide a communication link between Family and the Family businesses
i) To oversee the Philanthropic activities of the Family

Some attributes of Council members may include:
- Commitment to their role
- Commitment to upholding and promoting the objectives and values enshrined in the Charter
- Enthusiasm
- Vocalize their own ideas and beliefs
- Have the courage of their own convictions
- Actively engage in discussions
- Good listening and communication skills
- Disseminate information back to those they represent and enter into dialog with that group to promote collective engagement
- Passion for Family unity

Demonstrate the Skills and Authority of a True Leader

Family members wishing to contribute in leadership roles for family interests may possess the following skills:
- Demonstration of the skills and the authority of a true leader
- Demonstration of financial literacy
- Demonstration of successful commercial experience
- Possible sector experience
- Demonstration of competent strategic and analytical skills
- Knowledge of Family businesses
- Knowledge of Family history and values
- Knowledge of corporate governance and the role of management

(continued)

- Understanding of the New Zealand legal environment
- Understanding of the New Zealand Human Resource environment
- Ability to work as a team with management, independent, and Family Directors

Roles available may include:
- Family Trustee
- The Family Philanthropic Trust
- The Family Philanthropic Foundation
- The Family Corporation

Become a Mentor for Future Generations

- Invest in the education and vocations of the next generation
- Demonstrate the importance of valuable work and service
- Develop the human and intellectual capital on the Family balance sheet
- Foster an entrepreneurial spirit
- Establish a Family model for responsible ownership behaviors

4. PREPARING CHILDREN FOR THE RESPONSIBILITIES OF WEALTH

Thoughtful, intentional preparation of children and grandchildren for the responsibilities of ownership is the most critical component for sustaining a family legacy for generations.

While much has been invested in improving the financial advice that is essential for preserving wealth, less emphasis has been placed on developing responsible owners who share a broader vision for their future and the future of their capital. Sustaining family wealth and legacy through the generations requires a partnership between responsible owners and superior advisors based on a solid understanding of the responsibilities of wealth.

> Thoughtful, intentional preparation of children and grandchildren for the responsibilities of ownership is the most critical component for sustaining a family legacy.

EDUCATING THE NEXT GENERATION

Educating members of a wealthy family involves learning about the family's history, values, and its philosophy of wealth. Setting goals

---

Educating Wealth Owners

"A family seeking to preserve its wealth must understand the need for all of its members to be thoroughly educated on how to be owners rather than managers of the family enterprise, so that its family members will be competent to make risk-taking decisions as owners together."

James Hughes[1]

---

1 James E. Hughes Jr., "A Reflection on the Roles and Responsibilities of Each Family Member as an Owner of the Family Enterprise in a Family Governance System," unpublished online article, http://64.71.40.26/jamesehu/Articles/Owner.pdf.

collectively for the future and learning how to work with a team of siblings or cousins to make decisions and achieve goals are key responsibilities for owners.

Education that begins at an early age and continues through adulthood (in age-appropriate stages) is a worthy investment in the future of the family.

It is no surprise to learn that educated family members make better owners, and that continuing education is essential for growing the human, financial, and philanthropic capital of families around the world.

An informal study[2] of some of the most experienced U.S. family offices yielded the following insights about the process of preparing the next generation to be successful owners.

- The creation of an education strategy for the responsibilities of ownership must be a partnership between owners (as leaders who define vision and boundaries) and their advisors. Education is the responsibility of all family stakeholders, not just the principals.

- Education aimed at developing human capital in the family must be engaging, and even entertaining, to sustain the interest of multiple generations and to build bonds that reinforce shared visions, values, and learning.

- Owners' educational journeys may occur at varying developmental stages and in a variety of ways. Respect for individual readiness, learning styles, and unique needs helps ensure success for family learning and legacy.

- Readiness for the responsibilities of ownership is a process, not an event. Meeting once or twice a year with owners without a sustained, coherent framework of learning goals and clear outcomes is not sufficient. Educational opportunities need to be consciously threaded throughout the activities of the family and the family office (if there is one) as a persistent, cumulative learning process.

> Educating the next generation is a family responsibility that cannot be delegated.

One overarching theme resounds: educating the next generation is a family responsibility that cannot be delegated. Only a strong partnership between

---

2 Sara Hamilton and Joline Godfrey, "*Preparing the Next Generation for the Responsibilities of Ownership*" (Family Office Exchange White Paper, 2007), 17–18.

the family and its advisors with a fully engaged family, yields successful results.

WITH WEALTH COMES RESPONSIBILITY

Professors Craig Aronoff and John Ward, experienced advisors in family education, believe the first step in preparing for wealth and enterprise ownership is a commitment to become a good owner.

This preparation is particularly challenging in the twenty-first century. Contributing personal time and energy to the family enterprise can seem like a sacrifice for family members whose lives are surrounded by other opportunities and responsibilities. The hectic pace of modern life and travel only makes it more difficult.

Being a Good Owner

"When you prepare yourself to be a good owner, you are creating the opportunity for yourself to contribute. You are finding the way to earn what you own by being a good steward of it—preserving and building it for the next generation, for employees, and for the community."

Craig E. Aronoff and John L. Ward[3]

Asking family members to invest in an uncertain, long-term vision of the future may be a difficult thing for them to accept; it takes a far-sighted, patient owner to embrace this challenge.

Family leaders identify and take into intelligent consideration some of the common challenges they face when trying to engage the next generation in the education process:

- Lack of motivation
  "I have a trust fund, why should I bother to work?"
- Lack of time
  "We live too far from the rest of the family and are too busy."
- A sense of entitlement
  "This is our due, not something we have to re-earn, sustain, or nurture."

---

3 Craig E. Aronoff and John L. Ward, *Family Business Ownership: How to Be an Effective Shareholder* (Marietta, GA: Family Enterprise Publishers, 2001), 39.

- Fear of the loss of wealth
  "I don't know what I'd do if I lost my inheritance; it's too awful to contemplate."

- Guilt
  "I'm too embarrassed by the benefits that my friends don't have."

- Subsidy of adult children
  "I love my kids and don't want them to face financial distress."

- Desire to maintain and perpetuate a lifestyle
  "This is my money; the next generation is on their own."

- Reluctance to accept financial responsibilities
  "I really don't want to think about the management of our money; that's the family office's job anyway."

- Reluctance to admit to financial issues
  "We don't have any financial issues; the family office has it all under control."

- The impact of new relationships or new spouses
  "I see the world differently now that I'm married; I am rethinking my loyalties and responsibilities."

No matter how well intentioned a family may be about educating for ownership, good intentions can be neutralized by entrenched attitudes, apathy, anxiety, denial, fear, or simply competing activities, events, visions, and goals.

EDUCATED TO BE A GREAT OWNER

Learning to be a great owner is not easy, and it is not something one can go to school to learn. Nor is the education—technical and emotional—of the next generation something that can be fully delegated to third parties or outside institutions. Under the cover of an expensive infrastructure, surrogates in the form of nannies, tutors, maids, and even boarding schools may be used to replace the far more valuable and appreciated assets of parental guidance and attention.

"Strong parenting is the best estate planning tool."

Ellen Perry[4]

Starting on Time

Many of these issues can be found in the story of Martin,* the conscientious son of a successful real estate developer. Martin's father recently sold part of his business and tapped Martin to set up a financial structure to support the founder and the future needs of all three of his sons. Because Martin had an accounting background, he understood the financial complexities created by his father's advisors and how they would affect his relations with his two brothers in the future.

Martin spent time getting a solid education about family financial matters, organized all the financial decisions for review, and asked other family members to get involved in the future of the family enterprise. Their response was less than enthusiastic.

It was at this stage that Martin discovered one of the greatest challenges facing every financial family: some owners do not feel comfortable taking responsibility when they should for their part of the financial picture. They avoid or delay active participation because they are not motivated to be involved in something they do not control, and for which they do not feel entitled.

But how, he wondered, would they ever learn what they needed to know to be smart owners in the future if they did not get involved in learning at a sufficiently early stage in the process?

As time passed and family leadership transferred to the brothers' generation, the timely—or not—commitment of the new owners turned out to be an important determinant in the family's ability to stay together and sustain its wealth.

Unfortunately, there is no surrogate for the leaders of the nuclear family in the education of their children, an investment that can yield generations of high returns.

Once parents, and often grandparents who have seen the benefits of an appropriate education for their own children, decide to get involved in educating the next generation, it becomes increasingly clear what they need to do.

Merely getting started may be their biggest hurdle to overcome.

---

4 Ellen Perry, Wealthbridge Partners, excerpt from comments made at FOX Fall Forum, Chicago, October 20–22, 2009.

Experts note that families can encourage responsible ownership through the following methods: build an education program
that teaches family virtues, values, and history; require every owner
to complete a basic financial education and to read and understand

the legal duties conferred by the legal
documents supporting each owner; teach

Merely getting started
may be their biggest
hurdle to overcome.

owners how to make competent decisions
in tandem with their financial advisors,
and encourage active participation in
all family meetings related to their ownership roles.

WHEN TO TELL THE CHILDREN

Clear and open communication between parent and child from an
early age is one of the cornerstones of an effective education. Most
family leaders say that it is important for families to understand and
discuss the issues surrounding family financial wealth from an early
age, while the discussion about the actual sums and more complex
financial issues comes later.

The right time to have a detailed conversation about the family's
wealth varies, depending on the individual's level of education and
maturity. Some families set an age of between 21 and 30 for such
conversations. Others begin discussions at the end of formal education or upon attainment of full participating rights in the affairs
of the family. Parents who share confidential financial information
with their children at an appropriate age are sending a strong message of trustworthiness to the children, who often value trust more
than the financial information itself.

"The Conversation"

"The tradition when I was growing up was that you went to a meeting at the
family law firm in Boston, and the family lawyer would explain the terms of
the trust you were going to live on for the rest of your life and that was it,"
Aldrich says. "There was no education. You took the back seat to your advisers and trust experts. It was just madness. We had zero training."

Nelson Aldrich Jr.[5]

What is most important about the conversation is that it takes place in an environment where there is adequate time to outline the full picture, to describe the implications and challenges inherent in the family's overall situation, and to respond to any questions or concerns about the family's situation.

It is often helpful to begin the discussion with a brief review of the family history, the Family Constitution, and, possibly, an overview of the family's legacy and vision for the future.

Many wealthy parents have found giving children a regular allowance that they must manage for themselves can be a beneficial part of the educational process, often in relation to the completion of a defined set of family chores. As a valuable variation on the theme, other parents work with their children to divide an appropriate allowance into three equal portions: one-third for charity, one-third for saving, and one-third for discretionary spending.

Encouraging children to keep—and balance weekly—a small accounts book can help to teach the value of tracking and controlling their money as well.

It is important to ensure that family members are provided with the necessary preparation regarding their wealth. Figure 4.1 outlines the critical information that proven leaders believe should be provided at each stage of development.

CREATIVE WAYS TO ENGAGE THE NEXT GENERATION

To be successful, an education program should be age-appropriate and designed to engage the participants. The best experiences are often those where participants learn by doing.[6] One family pays new board members a training stipend to meet regularly with the family office CEO to become familiar with topics discussed at board meetings. Another family holds breakfast briefings with parents of teenagers and an outside advisor to coach them on how to discuss important family financial issues in a manner that both achieves the objective and feels comfortable for the parents.

---

5 In Robert Frank, *Richistan: A Journey through the 21st Century Wealth Boom and the Lives of the New Rich* (London: Piatkus Books, 2008), 226.

6 Sara Hamilton and Joline Godfrey, *"Preparing the Next Generation for the Responsibilities of Ownership"* (Family Office Exchange White Paper, 2007), 22–23.

Figure 4.1: Critical Knowledge by Age Group

STAGE I	STAGE II	STAGE III	STAGE IV
What our values are	How to earn money	How our wealth is owned	How to raise a family with strong values
How we value money	How we spend, save, and share our hard-earned money	How to get a job and live on our earnings	How to balance work and family
How we choose to spend our money	How to live on a budget	How to develop a personal budget and balance sheet	How to be a part of a community
What the family business means to the family	What it costs to borrow money	How to purchase a car and insurance	How to live financially within our means
How we choose to give back to our community	How to repay our debts	How to get a mortgage on a house	How to make the right career choices for our skill set
	How to share with those who are less fortunate	How to contribute to philanthropic causes in a meaningful way	How to provide leadership for important causes
0–10 years old	11–20 years old	21–30 years old	31–40 years old

Several families rely on summer camps or programs to provide younger family members with opportunities to learn with their siblings and cousins. One family designs and hosts a "reality readiness camp" for a week each summer. For the past seven years, this group has traveled together for social service projects, such as home construction for Habitat for Humanity, and visits to Costa Rica to witness environmental distress. Another family organized a one-week bare-boat sailing adventure for the 14- to 18-year-olds; this family learned that nothing built teamwork skills among their teenagers like learning to sail together.

It can be challenging to keep the younger generation interested. Relying on creative solutions, such as a financial Monopoly game designed by one family, holds the attention of younger family members while teaching important financial concepts. Another family started a fourth-generation investment committee with responsibility for directing family funds into private equity investments in order to learn about venture capital opportunities and to teach important skills about business, investing, and decision making. Each year, a member of the investment committee presents the results at the annual family meeting; the third generation has been very impressed with the professionalism of the younger investors.

OVERCOMING THE DARK SIDE OF WEALTH

Children from families of wealth and privilege can be both beneficiaries and victims of their inheritance.

Investing in a phased program of education, exposure and experience to support the process of family education and inheritance is a positive step toward the preparation of the next generation.

> Children from families of wealth and privilege can be both beneficiaries and victims of their inheritance.

Preparing the next generation requires building on the positive and constructive, as well as being aware of and protecting against the "dark side" of wealth, where a life of privilege can, sadly, all too often lead to self-destructive views, habits, and lifestyles.

A Different World

"Ultimately, the reality is that heirs grow up not in an easier world but a different world. They do not have to make it on their own financially, but they must rise to the challenge of navigating a family and a business world already populated with a diverse and colorful cast.

They will fail if they don't develop the skills, sensitivity and personal identity needed to balance the existing demands with their own contribution. They succeed if they have a solid foundation in personality, intelligent financial skills, and good support for leadership in adulthood."[7]

---

7 Dennis T. Jaffe and James A. Grubman, "Acquirers' and Inheritors' Dilemma," *The Journal of Wealth Management* 10 (Fall 2007), 20–44.

Those who fail to master both the potential opportunities and problems wealth presents risk wounding their children as well. By giving children too much too early, and by failing to educate them on the broader issues of wealth, effort, and individual self-reliance, parents can deprive them of the joys of anticipation, effort, and reward.

In *Inherited Wealth*,[8] John Levy points out many of the psychological sources of problems associated with wealth that can create threats to the enjoyment of a substantive and fulfilling individual life, and can trigger emotional problems of substantial magnitude.

Among other concerns are delayed or limited development, insufficient understanding, limited experience, diminished work ethic, inability to sustain attention and effort, incomplete relationships, and other fundamental causes of personal dissatisfaction and, potentially, an empty and unfulfilled life.

Levy points to Erik Erikson, a renowned psychoanalyst and authority on the process of human development, who identifies critical tasks that need to be mastered in order for a person to develop into a reasonably whole human being: basic trust, autonomy, initiative, industry, and identity. Each of these is experienced as a crisis that, if resolved, leads to healthy development.

Erikson identified basic trust as the first of these developmental tasks and considered it a prerequisite for all of the others. Failure to achieve basic trust, which can be defined as " . . . reasonable trustfulness as far as oneself is concerned," typically results in an attitude of mistrust. The decision to trust another person involves risk. The experience may result in pain or disappointment, or may yield rewards sufficient to ensure that such a risk is worth taking. The example that parents provide in their willingness to take these risks, by trusting their children, friends, and advisors, is profound and can serve as a powerful precedent.

POSITIVE PARENTING

"80 percent of parents believe that their children are being taught personal money matters in school, yet 90 percent of high school students and 87 percent of college students say that whatever they know about money they learn from their parents."[9]

---

8 John L. Levy, *Inherited Wealth: Opportunities and Dilemmas* (Charleston, SC: BookSurge Publishing, 2008).
9 Jumpstart Coalition, "Kids and Money Facts," http://www.kidswealth.com/kids_money_facts.php.

It is far better to begin to educate the next generation from a very early age than to try to correct a pattern later in life. How can parents do a better job of raising responsible adults and family leaders from an early age and avoid the dark side of wealth?

Experienced family leaders have pointed out the value of several possible approaches.

- Look for ways to allow children to think and act for themselves, and be willing to let them make mistakes.

- Provide opportunities for children to interact with all kinds of people (e.g. one family requires family members to spend at least one year in a foreign culture or a disadvantaged area of their own country).

- Have children work for pay early on. Learning to live on a budget gives young people a sense of how to manage money, understand its value, and be accountable for one's actions.

- Help children achieve a sense of identity that is separate from the family. One way to achieve this is to allow the young person to go to school in another community or country where the family name is less familiar.

- Allow young adults to find a job without the assistance or intervention of the family. Being chosen for a position on one's own merits is an important experience.

- Ensure that work experience is challenging and allows the young owner to learn in the face of adversity.

- Enlist the assistance of a mentor who can help develop leadership capabilities and assess potential leaders.

THIRD-PARTY ASSISTANCE

Given the importance of the issue for members of the next generation and for the collective family and its legacy, finding and engaging only the very best educators makes a world of difference.

Many families invite external experts from disciplines ranging from investments to consensus-building to speak at family meetings. Aunts, uncles, or long-term, trusted advisors often make excellent mentors for younger family members. Members of like-minded families, many of whom struggle with similar issues, are invaluable sources of similar challenges, personal stories, and tried-and-true strategies.

LIFELONG LEARNING

Of course, education and learning do not begin at the age of 21 or end upon taking up a role in the family enterprise.

Successful family leaders tend to be lifelong learners. Within a family enterprise there are opportunities for learning lessons in leadership, investment, economics, business skills, working in teams, organizing an effective approach to philanthropy, enhancing personal creativity and growth, and much more. An investment in formal education and informal learning can improve the quality and impact of any one life, and translate into substantial family legacy benefits as well.

> **Successful family leaders tend to be lifelong learners.**

Questions for Leaders of Legacy

1. How have members of your family been prepared to be responsible owners of wealth, and how could that preparation be improved?
2. How do children in your family learn about family wealth?
3. How do members of the family learn together?
4. What strategies do your family use to avoid the dark side of wealth?
5. What education, experience, and specific training would be helpful for all of your family members? For your family's current and future leaders?

Second-Generation Challenges

Children who live with a take-charge, controlling business founder may feel insecure or inadequate by comparison. Because they do not get opportunities to test their own talents and gain the experiences and competencies needed to be in charge, they often do not develop the capabilities or the confidence needed to manage what they will inherit.

This insecurity causes them to avoid taking active roles in the family enterprise, or, in some cases, active roles are not offered to the younger generation for a variety of reasons, so they never develop an interest in the business and financial endeavors of the family. Once the younger generation disengages from the family, it becomes very difficult to persuade them to re-engage in family affairs.

Uncommon solutions

Reorienting Family Members: In some cultures, leadership is shared equally among all siblings after the death of the patriarch. The siblings understand from childhood that they are being trained for ownership and leadership, but they are not often prepared for shared control by the father while he is alive. Developing ground rules and accountability among siblings is a delicate balancing act for business-owning families.

In one family, the matriarch served as the peacekeeper and arbitrator after the death of the patriarch, sorting out the skills of each son and the potential leadership talent of each. The matriarch recognized that "fair and equal" was not a good strategy for the family business, and she made the tough decision to anoint the most capable among the sons while she was still in control. The other sons were directed toward other business ventures that were satellites to the core operating business. By all advisors' accounts, the restructuring of leadership was able to save the family business from the disagreements that could have destroyed it.

Engaging the Second Generation: Several families have been successful at re-engaging the second generation by using a skills assessment process with a career coach, who is able to help the future owners sort out their interests, talents, personal goals, and fears. Another useful exercise is to have owners who are becoming involved in the enterprise fill out a Personal Engagement Profile,[10] which identifies their level of commitment to the family enterprise and their desired level of involvement. This process

(continued)

---

10 This tool was created by Margaret Vaughan Robinson of MVR Consulting.

shows the talent available in the family, identifies the missing skills needed in the enterprise, and helps identify the type of advisors needed to fill gaps and mentor the younger generation.

Key Role of Non-family Members: In some cases, where talent or interest is absent, the family may rely on a non-family member to lead the family governance process for a period of time. The role of this non-family chairperson can be fourfold: to represent the interests of the "collective family"; to identify and mentor future family leaders; to facilitate open and honest conversation among shareholders; and to arbitrate between branches or individuals when disputes arise.

In this model, the chairperson provides continuity that can help stabilize the family's delayed leadership transitions. The chairperson must be well respected by the family and able to serve as an objective voice regarding what best benefits the entire family.

5. PHILANTHROPY AS A CORNERSTONE OF LEGACY

Legacies of generosity and sharing are often the greatest legacies of all.

> Legacies of generosity and sharing are often the greatest legacies of all.

For many families, their philanthropic activities are the most important source of their identity, unity, and personal reward. In responding to the question "what makes your family different from others?" the philanthropic side of family life frequently comes first in a description of what makes a larger family both unique and special.

For family leaders, philanthropy is an obvious avenue for pursuing a number of concurrent objectives. It can provide a link to the past, bring all members of a family together in the present, and can provide useful lessons in values, family meaning, and identity for the future.

Philanthropy is as much about who a family is, as what that family does.

A PLATFORM TO UNITE THE FAMILY ACROSS GENERATIONS AND GENDERS

Philanthropic activity can play many roles, including providing a link to the founder of the family fortune and his or her vision of the charitable focus of the family legacy. Preserving the donor's intent in the work of the family's philanthropy links past and future with great effect.

In addition to linking the family with its past, philanthropic activity can tie a family more closely within and across generations. Either by bringing together different generations on a charitable board or by allocating a sum to be directed by members of the same generation sitting on their own board, families have found philanthropy to be an ideal platform to unite members of the family behind a common cause and to create a sense of shared accomplishment.

In many cultures, a family foundation or philanthropic initiative is one of the few activities in which women can play an equal, or even a leading role to their male counterparts. Although this limiting definition of women's roles is eroding quickly, the involvement of female family members in philanthropy can bridge the gender gap as effectively as it bridges the generation gap.

A PLATFORM TO CONVEY VALUES AND PHILOSOPHIES

By donating or investing family funds, time, and reputation to a chosen cause, family leaders are demonstrating to the members of the family and to the greater world that the family is about much more than financial wealth; charitable activity can be a highly visible aspect of the Family Promise and living proof of the family values that demonstrate a real commitment to the greater world.

Every family has the same opportunity to develop its own charitable programs, no matter what the scale of the family wealth. For most people, being part of a family means learning the family culture and passing the family's values through the generations. If philanthropy is part of a family's ethos and identity, most parents agree that there are many ways to incorporate the concept, as well as the practice, of giving in day-to-day life.

"The best way to raise responsible children with wealth may be to first make sure we are responsible adults with wealth."[1]

TRADITIONS AND REASONS FOR GIVING

The establishment of a culture of generosity in a family can be a major accomplishment and is also likely to be consistent with many of the elements of both family history and the future-oriented Family Promise. The ethical virtues of giving and the impact such generosity can have on a family's stature, sense of common purpose, unity, and wellbeing can make philanthropy a valuable part of any legacy planning exercise.

Although religion is fading as an influence on many wealthy families, the personal history of the family wealth creator and

---

1 Jaffe and Grumban, "Acquirers' and Inheritors' Dilemma," *The Journal of Wealth Management* 10 (Fall 2007), 37.

the ethic that created the original wealth often have religious or cultural origins that can be honored by sharing the wealth these origins provided.

Most systems of belief make specific mention of the value and virtue of generosity toward the less fortunate: the Christian religion exalts faith, hope, and charity as supreme virtues, with charity the most highly valued; the practice of generosity, *zakat*, is one of the five pillars of Islam; and charity is one of the transcendent virtues in Buddhism.

> "If anyone has material possessions and sees his brother in need but has no pity on him, how can the love of God be in him? Dear children, let us not love with words or tongue but with actions and in truth."[2]

It is not the quantum of giving that counts. It is more the spirit, intention, and impact. Families with wealth of any magnitude can establish a legacy of giving and contribution at any level; different families will be comfortable with different levels and forms of philanthropy.

HOW MUCH TO GIVE

There is, of course, no fixed target or social agreement on the amount that any individual or family should give to charity. The Mormon Church requires tithes of 10 percent of after-tax income, and the Jewish tradition of *tzedakah* recommends a 10- to 20-percent donation of after-tax income. Islamic principles mandate 2.5 percent of savings and valuables to be set aside as an appropriate amount.

The Church of England is less precise, encouraging its members to give between 1 and 5 percent of their income to charitable causes, but also recommending a contribution of up to 10 percent. One endorsement for a 10-percent target comes from the Reverend Thomas Binney, who wrote in his 1865 collection of sermons:

---

2 John 3:17–8.

". . . If anyone lays down for himself the rule of devoting a tenth of his income to God, he does well . . . It is to be remembered, however, that for some, a tenth of their income would be too much, while for others it would be far too little."

HOW TO GIVE

Alongside the question of how much to give is the question of how to give.

One of the most informative guides to giving dates back to 1201, and is captured in the works of Spanish doctor-philosopher Maimonides. In his treatise *The Book of Seeds*, he noted that a hierarchy of approaches to giving should be used as a guide to the inherent virtue of the giver.

In ascending order of merit, the eight levels of charity described by Maimonides were:

The Hierarchy of Giving

- Giving with resentment at the costs of filling an obligation.
- Giving without resentment, even happily, but at a much lower level than one should, given the economic situation of the giver.
- Giving, but only in response to a specific request.
- Giving on a proactive basis, before being asked.
- Giving to anonymous beneficiaries in situations where the giver is known to his or her beneficiaries.
- Giving in a situation where the beneficiaries are known, but where the giver remains anonymous.
- Giving in a situation of mutual anonymity, where neither benefactor nor beneficiary is known to the other.
- Giving in a manner to enable the beneficiaries to become independent and capable of giving greater *tzedakah* himself or herself, acts which have been described as "teaching someone to fish" rather than "giving fish to a hungry person."[3]

---

3 In Ephraim Frisch, *An Historical Survey of Jewish Philanthropy* (New York, Macmillan, 1924), 62–3.

Today, more and more wealthy families are choosing social philanthropy, investing in a sustainable manner for long-term, maximum positive impact.

They are also following the route of "giving while living," taking on an active role in their philanthropy during their lifetimes, rather than solely leaving a generous bequest as part of an estate. They are also starting to give at a younger age, instead of becoming involved after retirement from the business community, and are often choosing to do it together with the other members of the family, spouses included.

From Principles to Practice The following activities, which can supplement the three-part savings approach for children (saving, spending and charity), are drawn from The Philanthropic Initiative's White Paper "Raising Children with Philanthropic Values." The TPI article suggests the following action strategies to get the younger generations involved:

- Develop family giving rituals in which children can participate. Perhaps "adopt" a needy family for the winter holidays. Many homeless shelters offer this program, which affords great opportunities for kids to get involved.

- To engage young children, consider joining a parent–child philanthropy club. Some parent–child book clubs have even begun to include a giving component. Perhaps a local book club—or another group to which you and your child belong—would consider adding philanthropy to its activities.

- Create an informal "family fund" or "grandchildren fund" and invite children to nominate their favorite charities.

- Volunteer with children in ways that align with their interests. Take them on foundation site visits, and ask them to write a brief report on the work of current or potential grantees.

- If time is limited, consider using birthdays or holidays to get them excited about giving. Give them a book with a philanthropic message, or make a donation in their name. Talk to them about what philanthropy means to the family. Share examples of why the family supports particular causes or institutions.[4]

---

4 The Philanthropic Initiative, "Raising Children With Philanthropic Values", February 2009, http://www.tpi.org/resources/primer/raising_children_with_philanthropic.aspx.

EARLY INVOLVEMENT AND LASTING IMPACT

Philanthropy is an activity that can be developed from an early age. Even very young children can understand that helping others is a good thing to do. Starting early on something that can be understood and shared across generations provides one of the major building blocks in a family's shared sense of purpose, identity, and legacy. Legacies of generosity can be started while children are young to develop a more cohesive, caring, and lasting family bond.

The management of funds for a philanthropic purpose can also be a solid learning experience for younger members of the family. Because the needs of a foundation can be planned out many years in advance, the portfolio management process provides an education for those who eventually move on to the management of more substantial family funds.

Philanthropy is not just about giving or investing money. Families can also give their time and physical energy to improve the communities in which they live and work. By adding a very personal stamp of approval to community-based activities, wealthy families can both contribute to the education of their younger members and reap the rewards of meaningful family initiatives and individual effort.

AMERICAN GENEROSITY

While the size of charitable activities is not the key determinant of legacy value, it is worth noting that some of the United States' most respected families have an established tradition of giving. The charitable foundations established by the wealthiest families, and the many acts of generosity from families with lesser, but still substantial, means, have led to the creation of the U.S. public library system and the founding of many hospitals, universities, museums, concert halls, schools, churches, and other integral parts of the American cultural, educational, and health care infrastructure. In total, there are about 37,500 family foundations in the United States today, all distributing at least 5 percent of their asset value each year to the non-profit community.

In order of size and market value of assets,[5] the largest of these funds are the Bill & Melinda Gates Foundation, the Ford Foundation, the J. Paul Getty Trust, the William and Flora Hewlett Foundation, and the David and Lucile Packard Foundation.

These philanthropic stalwarts have been joined by Warren Buffett and many, many others in making substantial contributions to the charitable world.

EUROPEAN COUSINS

The vaunted families of Europe have been similarly generous, and without the tax incentives provided to their American counterparts. Some have left substantial ownership stakes in operating businesses, and even total ownership, to their charitable foundations.

Some of the largest European foundations bear the famous names of their founding families. They include the Wellcome Trust, Fondazione Hans Wilsdorf (Montres ROLEX) Genève, Robert Bosch Stiftung, Bertelsmann Stiftung, Sandoz—Fondation de Famille, and the Calouste Gulbenkian Foundation. All are multibillion-dollar bequests, with the Wellcome Trust alone exceeding US$15 billion in value.

STRENGTH IN NUMBERS

By combining funds, Warren Buffett and Bill and Melinda Gates have been able to launch a fund of some US$40 billion in assets, largely focused on improving health and reducing poverty in the developing world. Such a mega fund is expected to have a huge impact in areas such as helping to eradicate polio and reduce cases of AIDS and malaria.

Unlike families such as the Rockefellers, whose foundation has endured over many generations, the Gates family has chosen to go for maximum impact now, and have said that the Foundation will end 50 years after the death of the last current board member. With shrinking endowments following the recession, many other families are choosing the same path.

---

5 Foundation Center Database, November 2009, www.foundationcenter.org.

NEW APPROACHES TO PHILANTHROPY

Consistent with the highest level of giving in Maimonides' hierarchy of giving, newer philanthropy is more about venture philanthropy or social entrepreneurship than old-fashioned checkbook charity.

By seeking out ways to maximize the impact of philanthropic endeavors and stretch the value of funds available, philanthropic families in this new era are looking to blend grants, loans, and equity investments, with some targeted at achieving financial profits as well as positive social impact.

The Skoll Foundation

The generosity and creativity of The Skoll Foundation stands out as a model for creative social entrepreneurship and of high-impact funding.

Jeff Skoll, the Canadian-born former president of eBay, has endowed a large foundation that contributes to a mix of activities including:

- Providing funds for movies through an arm called Participant Media, a venture that has funded high-impact films such as *An Inconvenient Truth* with Al Gore and *Syriana* with George Clooney.
- Funding a global forum at Oxford University on social entrepreneurship.
- Establishing a series of global awards to reward social entrepreneurs with particularly attractive ideas.

Distinguished by the magnitude of the giving and the creativity of the young principal, the Skoll Foundation reflects an active intellectual engagement and the application of personal attention, which is more and more common among young entrepreneurs from the technology sector active in philanthropy.

Also known as mission-related philanthropy, many families are now considering using more of their assets than just the percentage set aside for philanthropy to invest in businesses or projects that have a positive social or environmental impact. The FB Heron Foundation is an industry leader in this field and reports that its investment strategy has resulted in better-than-average portfolio performance as well as increased social impact.[6]

---

6 Institute for Philanthropy, "Giving in the Recession: Tough Times Call for Smart Giving," June 2009, http://www.instituteforphilanthropy.org/cms/pages/documents/Giving_in_the_Recession.pdf.

Not Your Father's Foundation: Giving More With Less

Her grandfather, Max M. Fisher, founded the Speedway gasoline station chain and gave millions to big causes such as the Detroit Symphony Orchestra and the United Jewish Appeal.

Caroline Cummings Rafferty, 29 years old, is being groomed to help run the US$235 million Max M. and Marjorie S. Fisher Foundation in Southfield, Michigan. But for now, she is running a tiny US$1 million foundation and making gifts of a few thousand dollars to charitable organizations.

Cummings Rafferty reflects the struggles facing family philanthropists—one old problem and one new: How do parents foster proper stewardship of family foundations among their children? And with an economic downturn depressing charitable giving, how do heirs manage to do more with less?

U.S. foundations lost nearly US$150 billion in assets in 2008, or almost as much as they had given away during the four years prior, according to the Foundation Center, which tracks information. Nearly one in five foundations cut back their funding in 2009 and expects to give less in the next few years.

Facing a brutal environment, parents have to be especially diligent in imparting skills their children need to carry on the philanthropic tradition. Some, like Ms. Cummings Rafferty's family, set up minifoundations with smaller amounts of money for their heirs to manage. Some parents direct 70 percent of foundation grants while the remaining 30 percent go to charities that the kids choose. Other families are forming junior boards of directors or foundation committees, where children are put in charge of individual tasks such as developing a foundation Web site.

"The best way to pass down a philanthropic legacy or a family's value system is to give children a seat at the table," says Melanie Schnoll Begun, managing director of Morgan Stanley Smith Barney Philanthropic Services. "Take the time while you are alive to explain what motivates you, what issues are important and then involve your children in these decisions."

The economy also is forcing younger philanthropists to be creative. They find that by pooling their resources, they can start bigger programs than they could on their own. For example, nearly 200 donors in their 20s and 30s gave 1 percent of their annual income to charity through an organization called the One Percent Foundation, an online giving circle for young philanthropists started by 30-year-old Daniel Kaufman in 2007. Donors get a say in where the money goes.

"If every American in their 20s and 30s did this, we'd have US$16 billion to give away a year, which is bigger than Bill Gates," Kaufman says.

(continued)

> This new crop of philanthropists say they view donations as investments that can be measured with quantifiable results, such the number of people served. The better the investment performs, the more money donors will direct to the cause.[7]

IMPACT OF NEW PHILANTHROPISTS ON OLD FAMILY LEGACIES

Ironically, a greater individual assertiveness in staking out a position in the family's philanthropic and social activities can have a very positive impact on a family's collective legacy. In setting out on a new and more personally engaging path, the new philanthropists and social entrepreneurs are both redefining the role of philanthropy and assuring that family philanthropic activities are kept fresh and as aligned as possible with the values and ideas of its current members.

By challenging old approaches, refreshing thinking, and testing new models, enterprising leaders in family philanthropic activities can keep their charitable and community activities vibrant and engaging for the family as a whole. This regeneration of a philanthropic spirit in the family can be the source of greater impact, broader family engagement in thinking and action, and, ultimately, a more valuable philanthropic legacy.

Questions for Leaders of Legacy

1. What has been your family philosophy and history with regard to philanthropy?
2. How can charitable activities support the family's broader legacy goals?
3. Who in the family is best suited to lead and support the family's philanthropy?
4. Does the family have an agreed (documented and organized) approach to giving and a strategy to maximize the impact of your philanthropy?
5. Does the family have younger family members who would describe themselves as "new philanthropists" and are you able to expand the current philanthropic framework to include their goals and aspirations?

---

7 Shelly Banjo, *Wall Street Journal*, April 10, 2010. Reprinted by permission of the *Wall Street Journal*, Copyright © 2010 Dow Jones & Company, Inc. All Rights Reserved Worldwide. License number 2413211287483.

The Birth of the New Philanthropist

Rachel Newton Bellow and Suzanne Muchin are partners in ROI Ventures, LLC www.roinspiration.com, a strategy firm and development lab that works on projects with market opportunity and the potential for social impact.

It's always risky to look at a set of trends or indicators of change and declare a fundamental shift in an industry. Trends ebb and flow. Indicators don't reveal their meaning until after the fact. And yet, we're confident that the patterns of change in American philanthropy demonstrate many of the key features we look for when distinguishing transitory variations from longer term significant transformation:[8]

- The behaviors of current players are changing
- New actors are entering the space
- New tools are being used
- The cultural connotations of the industry itself are changing dramatically

From these patterns of change are emerging two new groups of participants in philanthropic and social activities within wealthy families. These patterns emerge from a gradual fusion of the communities and ideas of wealthy families, social activists, and entrepreneurs. This fusion has created two new options for wealthy individuals and families seeking a new way forward in using their wealth and influence to make a mark on the greater world.

One (the most visible) is the social entrepreneur—the problem solver who uses innovative methods and market thinking to make measurable headway in solving seemingly intractable social problems. The other (far less visible) is what we might call the "new philanthropist."

What makes the "new philanthropist" new? Four critical characteristics come together to create a new model of philanthropy and a model of new philanthropists:

1. *A point of view:* Merely giving away money to others with good intentions and a view of social progress is no longer enough. Traditional philanthropists are trained to consider themselves essentially "facilitative,"

(continued)

---

8 Although this discussion focuses on American philanthropists, we should note that the features discussed are in evidence globally, which is not surprising, as national boundaries mean less in the context of Web-based communications and an increasing emphasis on knowledge transfer around solutions.

making change through others, and in line with the views and actions of others, and therefore in pursuit of that own point of view (POV). This is changing. Passionate beliefs and a personal POV as a centerpiece of philanthropy leads to a different and more engaged philosophical and economic approach.

The new philanthropist has a personal POV and hence has a unique "voice": a POV acts as both a way to screen out opportunities that don't align with a stated vision and as a magnetic force to inspire or attract those that do.

2. *Sector and source-agnostic on ideas and initiatives:* There are multiple angles of entry to engage with complex social problems, and solutions are often found by those seeking commercial applications, without a primary focus on social benefit. Similarly, the public sector is an alternative source of ideas and programs from which private philanthropy can learn.

The desire (and ability) to engage and enlist talent and ideas across sectors is a hallmark of the new philanthropist, who speaks the "languages" of different domains.

3. *A greater interest in influence, not size:* The new philanthropist has emerged from the last few philanthropic decades, characterized by a "biggest is best" attitude, with a contrarian's view that bigger is not necessarily better. When an institution or an individual is onto something important, the mantra of big money philanthropy has historically been: "take it to scale or let it go."

By contrast, the new philanthropist says, "make it matter whether big or small."

4. *Value in distributing knowledge:* As both investors in and consumers of social programs, products, and services, philanthropists have a unique perspective over broad fields of thought and activity. They can see patterns that others cannot.

The new philanthropist understands that harvesting and distributing knowledge (insights and information) from those patterns is as much their responsibility as dispersing a certain percentage of the income earned on their financial corpus.

(continued)

The new philanthropist knows that money alone is not the only tool for social change, and not a particularly powerful one in many circumstances.

Knowledge about what works (and what doesn't) *is* valuable in every context and circumstance. Therefore, *knowledge transfer*—making sure that when someone has figured something out, others learn about it in ways that allow them to act upon it—is critical to the new philanthropist's mission and mandate.

The more we understand new models and approaches to philanthropy and positive social change, the more able we will all be to select and pursue the path best suited to our own interests and abilities.

While it is still too early to predict how the story of American power and prosperity in the twenty-first century will be told by future generations, one thing is certain: there will be a chapter on how we dealt with the social issues of our time, and whether we embraced new approaches to leverage the resources of the few to lift the many.

6. A PRACTICAL FRAMEWORK FOR LEGACY PLANNING

Family enterprises that sustain themselves ultimately believe they have created something valuable together that is worth preserving for another generation, or at least through another planning cycle. Such enterprises all seem to have one characteristic in common: they have decided to invest time and resources in future generations of the family. They view family members as the greatest assets of the family and the development of these assets to be the ultimate goal of the family enterprise.

> Each family needs a unique legacy plan—or multi-generational strategy—to design and execute the actions needed to realize its vision.

This philosophy requires leaders to invest time, money, and thought in planning for the future.

Each family needs a unique legacy plan—or multi-generational strategy—to design and execute the actions needed to realize its vision.

Legacy planning and family strategy involve sourcing and allocating resources, setting priorities, directing and inspiring people, organizing the family, obtaining consensus, and demonstrating through decisive behavior what will be done—and what will not—in the pursuit of a larger vision, goal, mission, or high-level set of objectives.

INVESTING FOR THE FUTURE

To many, the idea of spending money with no immediate return may seem a risk-oriented strategy. It certainly may not appeal to families merely trying to replicate the older generation's lifestyle or to maximize the value of the current generation's trust fund. But those who understand the need for legacy planning are investing assets for long-term family advantage rather than spending them or investing them solely for short-term financial gain. They see it as investing now to reap greater rewards in the future.

These families are sending future leaders to global business schools; are encouraging groups of cousins to travel together to build relationships and look for future investment opportunities; and are establishing a family presence in markets far from home.

Such an investment generates the energy needed to sustain the family enterprise. Asking future generations to be engaged owners and to control their own destinies fosters a new generation of entrepreneurs who have taken the time to reflect on what they want from life, and how they can contribute most to family wealth and legacy in some meaningful way.

However measured, the value of making a successful investment for the future should, from a multi-generational perspective, outweigh any cash costs and even any personal, emotional, or intellectual costs many times over.

Equally, lack of strategy and investment in appropriate initiatives can lead to results far inferior to those available to families whose leaders have thought through, and acted upon, a more solid set of principles, standards and goals.

> "Tactics without strategy is merely the noise before defeat."

A summary of the value of a strategic approach is attributed to military strategist Sun Tzu, author of the classic book *The Art of War*, "while strategy without tactics is a long road to victory, tactics without strategy is merely the noise before defeat."[1]

MANY PLANS MISSING IN ACTION

Research in the family office community shows that, surprisingly, only one in three wealthy families has a strategic plan.

Given the vast amount of wealth at stake, the complexity of the task of passing and enhancing a fortune, and the poor success rates of families trying to achieve results across even one generational bridge, there is obvious room for improvement in both legacy planning and the coordinated actions needed for the preservation of family legacy. Figure 6.1 shows a simple framework[2] that provides a practical guide and checklist for those many valuable legacy plans and family strategies yet to be written.

---

1 Attributed to Sun Tzu.
2 Daniell, *Strategy for the Wealthy Family*, 14.

Figure 6.1: The Legacy Plan: An Integrated Framework for Wealth and Responsibility

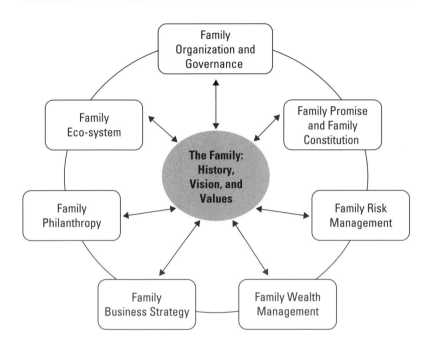

In considering a multi-generational strategy, all of these elements need to be considered separately and together in an appropriately long-term model for family contemplation and action. While the constituent elements of a multi-generational plan remain the same, the content varies enormously from one family to another and from one period to another.

LEADERSHIP IS KEY TO LEGACY PLANNING

Since there is no "off-the-shelf" plan that can be easily imported from other successful wealthy families, each family needs to design and implement its own practical approach to legacy planning. That approach should address family organization and leadership, the Family Promise and Constitution, risk management, wealth preservation and management, family businesses, philanthropy, and the supporting eco-system.

An inclusive approach to legacy planning that focuses on proper training and targeted education of its individual members is a wise, and perhaps even necessary, investment for a successful family legacy.

Good strategy is as much about preparation, leadership, communication, and implementation as it is about detailed planning and allocation of resources and responsibilities.

PROCESS AND CONTENT

As in so many areas of leadership of a wealthy family, ultimate success depends upon getting both process and content right at an early stage.

The process of setting and maintaining focus on a multi-generational plan requires much early planning and collaboration across the family. Frameworks, timing, roles, responsibilities, and the form of the final outcome should ideally be set out as the initial exercise (or updating of the exercise) begins.

> Ultimate success depends upon getting both process and content right at an early stage.

One version of that initial stage-setting and preplanning approach is set out in the following box.

Appreciation and Action

- Develop an appreciation among family members for the value of legacy and/or strategic legacy planning.
- Identify the factors that make legacy planning essential.
- Ensure that family leaders support the planning process.
- Communicate with the larger family about the need for legacy planning.
- Gain consensus among family members to proceed with the plan.
- Select a committee of family leaders to spearhead the process.

WHEN TO START?

At any stage in a family's history, family leaders may act upon an opportunity to design and implement a new strategy, or renew or revise an existing strategy. However, there are three common trigger points that have, historically, caused many families to undertake such an initiative for the first time.

The first is related to a major wealth-creating or liquidity event, such as the sale of a family business. With global industries consolidating and new financial players completing ever more and larger acquisitions, the number and scale of transactions of this type are increasing with every passing generation.

A second trigger for many families is a generational transition. This could be a leadership succession from a concentrated first or second generation to a larger set of inheritors with a more diverse set of skills or interests in a following generation.

The third common trigger is the result of a number of factors moving together at the same time, creating a kind of internal "tipping point" where the confluence of events (i.e. a major liquidity event, changes in the family or family leadership, the desire to create a philanthropic foundation, etc.) coalesce to bring about the need for a comprehensive strategic review and legacy planning exercise.

PLANNING ACROSS GENERATIONS

It is ironic that, in a business world where strategic cycles are getting shorter and shorter, family strategy needs to be extended well beyond the time horizon of most individuals' thinking. Legacy planning, by its nature, needs to contemplate plans and actions that stretch out across many lifetimes. It is impossible to master a multi-generational challenge armed only with a short-term plan of action or limited set of immediate initiatives.

> It is impossible to master a multi-generational challenge armed only with a short-term plan of action or limited set of immediate initiatives.

An effective legacy plan requires a forward view across three or more generations, with each generation addressing its own issues while, at the same time, anticipating those of its children and grandchildren. Only in this way can families make the most lasting and valuable contribution to their own family and financial legacies.

To gain proper perspective in legacy planning, whether addressing formal structures, long-term visions, or educational standards, it is helpful to think about the grandchildren, whether alive and grown up or yet to be born. The most far-sighted leaders even claim that any good legacy plan needs to think through the next unborn generation (at least) to ensure that principles of fairness and a sustainable family model are defined without reference to the situation of any one individual or family structure; this results in "seventh-generation thinking," "100-year planning," and other long-term approaches.

> A legacy strategy may not come to fruition, and its benefits felt, until many years after its architects have passed away.

This is indeed a selfless exercise. Like a tree that only reaches its full height long after its planter is gone, a legacy strategy may not come to fruition, and its benefits felt, until many years after its architects have passed away.

IMPACT OF RECENT EVENTS ON LEGACY PLANNING

Good legacy plans, while constant in their pursuit of a long-term vision, need to address many different issues resulting from both cyclical and secular trends (secular trends being those long-term patterns unaffected by the immediate economic cycle).

Following the most recent economic crisis, deep-seated problems have emerged that may require leaders to consider a more negative environment for their upcoming plans than experienced in previous decades. Across each component of a legacy plan, there are immediate changes, challenges, and risks that cannot be ignored if legacy plans are to be realistic and successful.

THE FAMILY

It is no secret that the traditional family structure and its set of accompanying values are under threat. Divorce rates that exceed 40 percent in some countries, remarriages that lead to children of varying ages and parentage growing up in different households, children born outside marriage, same-sex marriages, adoptions, and a whole host of new family structures have forced families to think about their definition of family membership.

At the same time, globalization means that many wealthy families are split across the world and now often mix nationalities, languages, religions, residences, domiciles, family models, and different sets of national and familial values.

The inherent dynamism of these worldly families brings very practical opportunities, while also presenting challenges in terms of tax, legal, cultural, and legacy considerations. More importantly, these trends can make it harder for family leaders to maintain a strong common family identity.

The Individual Family Member In an age of individuality and a networked world, different approaches need to be adopted to engage, develop, and focus the efforts of a new generation.

While a substantial amount of thought and effort is devoted to thinking about the family as a collective unit, any forward plan needs to reflect the fact that a family is also a collection of individuals whose beliefs, attitudes, behaviors, strengths, weaknesses, and personal decisions will shape the family's future—and make or break its legacy.

Family strategies that are flexible and adaptive, and fully contemplate and cater to individual members' differences, as well as building on their commonality, are inherently more stable and far more likely to succeed than those that attempt to impose a similar life pattern on all of the inevitably diverse family members.

FAMILY ORGANIZATION AND GOVERNANCE

Whether the family is large or small, and whether the wealth is new or old, a critical element in developing a coherent forward strategy is an organized approach to the family, its internal structures and processes, and its leadership model. Designing and obtaining buy-in to the best possible structure and approach to leadership and family decision making is an essential challenge to master as families grow, fragment, and migrate.

Establishing a solid governance structure and clear rules of the game is essential to the development of an enduring legacy. The family itself, its operating business(es), wealth, risk management, and philanthropic activities, its system of employees and advisors, and the individual members of the greater family all benefit from a cohesive and organized approach to internal structures, roles, governance, and leadership.

The issue of leadership is embedded deeply in each of the elements of long-term legacy planning, and its importance is felt in all aspects of family life. Having qualified leaders at each level of the family structure and a documented process for decision making, helps the family to make better decisions together and avoid unnecessary conflict.

Organizing a Large Family

Successful leaders of large multi-generational families:

- Organize a decision-making process and structure that supports the vision.
- Use, as necessary, a governance specialist to review current governance structure.
- Review governance models implemented by other family groups for relevance.
- Identify elements of authority that are appropriate for each level of governance.
- Build an operating structure that clarifies the domains of decision making.
- Construct bylaws that encompass all the elements of governance.
- Develop a mechanism for exiting the family system when not in agreement.

Figure 6.2 sets out the organizational structure of a wealthy family, with no operating business. This approach includes a Family Assembly consisting of all family members, a Family Council of selected members, and other bodies established to represent specific sub groups in the family and to serve specific purposes for the family. If there were an operating business, a Family Business Board would likely be added within the structure.

For a more complete model of a larger and more complex family, see Figure 7.2 in Chapter 7.

Figure 6.2: Family Organization Structure

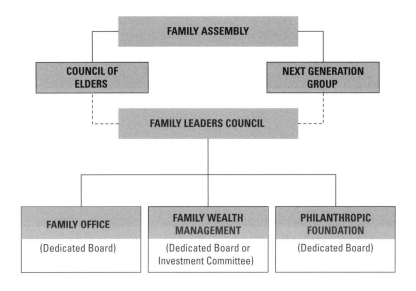

FAMILY PROMISE AND CONSTITUTION

The Family Promise and Constitution (as discussed in Chapter 3) are critical components of the legacy plan that document the shared beliefs, values, attitudes, and principles that guide the family members in their relationships with one another, their staff, advisors, and the outside world.

A well-crafted legacy plan is true to the Family Promise and ultimately sets out the pathway to the family's collective vision for the future.

FAMILY RISK MANAGEMENT

Each family, and each generation of leadership, faces many risks and challenges to its legacy.

Scarred by the financial costs of the recession, many leaders are looking to embed a greater sensitivity to risk in their early warning systems, and to add greater capability and expertise to deal with risks before they ripen into catastrophe.

Anticipating risks, which can crop up in any one of the supporting aspects of a multi-generational plan, is one of the core tasks of leaders and the leadership team. This requires both an effective process to identify and monitor the full set of risks, as well as the ability to implement specific investments and initiatives to address the highest priority risks to family wealth and wellbeing.

Needless to say, these same sources of risk can often bring opportunity as well. Intelligent leaders understand this, and their process considers the upside as well as the downside of changes within the family and in the outside world.

FAMILY WEALTH MANAGEMENT

The post-recession changes and challenges in the area of family wealth management are clear for all to see. Unprecedented changes in capital market and property values, the possibility of collapse of virtually all asset classes simultaneously, the difficulties of the global banking system, the withdrawal of credit, volatile markets, the price changes in oil, gold, and other commodities, the erosion of reliable income-producing investments, and the relentless rise of a multi-polar world paint, a very dynamic picture indeed.

The coming decades will likely be characterized by a continuing shift of the world's economic weight to the East, a rising tax burden in the West, and a decline of U.S. leadership reflected in the continued globalization of business, the need to compete with bigger businesses from the emerging markets, and the possibility of pressure on the U.S. dollar as the sole international reserve currency.

All of these factors point toward a more global (and probably more Asia-focused) future, along with a need to access global investment opportunities to protect and grow family wealth in real terms.

Less clear are the phases, cycles, and specific opportunities appropriate for any one family to consider in the pursuit of its own wealth objectives. These decisions and actions need to be taken over time in a manner calculated to make the best of the investment landscape, while avoiding the risks that will inevitably emerge along the way.

Protecting existing wealth will also be more challenging than ever before for the post-World War II generations of a family. Everything from estate planning, scenario planning, tax management, investment disciplines, spending and distribution patterns, family values, and other elements of a forward-thinking approach to risk management needs to be considered in developing a renewed approach to wealth preservation.

Strategies will require greater creativity, a global focus where possible, and new vehicles and tactics in a world where cash-strapped governments and populist politicians target the rich to pay for the costs of the crisis and for the many initiatives, associated costs, and deficits arising long before the crisis unfolded.

Finding robust and creative solutions to meet a family's wealth preservation objectives will be a constant challenge in the new world order. However, at the same time, new opportunities are emerging for wealth and tax management in the form of welcoming international and U.S. state jurisdictions, creative ownership entities, and new investment vehicles.

In order to take advantage of these opportunities in a world where governments face increasing needs for funds and declining sources of revenue, future generations face a lifetime of tax challenges. To preserve wealth in a carefully structured system, pure formal compliance with structuring is no longer enough. Approaches driven solely by fiscal intent may not be strong enough to stand up to more critical and demanding scrutiny. Purpose, form, and substance now need to be fully present and aligned to support tax and estate planning objectives.

> Approaches driven solely by fiscal intent may not be strong enough to stand up to more critical and demanding scrutiny.

Even long-accepted structures are under pressure as fiscal authorities move from pursuing tax evasion (illegal tax activities such as nondisclosure of accounts as required by law) to demonizing and pursuing tax avoidance (heretofore legal approaches to tax management such as the use of trusts, dual contracts, and offshore administrative activities and entities).

Forward-thinking leaders need to stay ahead of the wave and have robust solutions in place before the next wave of problems arises.

FAMILY BUSINESS STRATEGY

Events of the past few years magnify the significance of any family business that provides income and capital needed to support the lifestyle of family members. The performance pressures and liquidity squeeze made it impossible for many private businesses to finance the dividend stream that shareholders had been accustomed to receiving.

There are now more strategic, management, and performance challenges inherent in any family business as limited credit and onerous credit terms have made it increasingly difficult for privately owned firms to live up to past expectations for growth, profitability, value, and yield.

A family business, which can generate much of a family's income and constitute the bulk of its assets, may require offsetting portfolio management actions. These may include, but are not limited to, diversification, exposure reduction, hedging single-stock concentration risk, financial risk-management techniques (puts, calls, collars, etc.), and other approaches to managing the full implications of such a valuable, but concentrated, asset.

For the longer term, these same families need to prepare their children to manage in a world that will be more complex and globally competitive. Asia and the emerging markets are rising, and with them new leaders of family businesses with global aspirations, strong work ethics, low-cost centers of operations, and a scale domestic market base. Family business leaders from all countries need to ensure that their children are ready to compete with the best of a global business world, whether that elite competition comes from Asia, the Americas, Europe, the Middle East, or other emerging markets.

FAMILY PHILANTHROPY

Many wealthy families share some of their accumulated wealth by supporting charitable organizations or philanthropic causes. Some may even create their own philanthropic foundations and related organizational entities as described in Chapter 5.

As a result of the recession of 2008, many rich families have less financial wealth and income than before, yet the need for charitable support is increasing. This inevitably places pressure on philanthropists and their families to address the appropriate level of philanthropic engagement, and perhaps invest more time and effort in determining where and how their contributions can have the greatest impact.

THE FAMILY "ECO-SYSTEM"

No strategy in any one of the elements in the framework can be pursued successfully, short- or long-term, without the support of the external resources surrounding a family. That interconnected eco-system, consisting of individuals, institutions, and communities surrounding, supporting, and connected to the family, plays an important role in shaping the values and character of the family, and in preserving and enhancing its fortune over time (see Chapter 13 for more detail).

The implications of the recession are that many families are requiring a higher level of performance from their family office and other advisors to meet the more challenging, and even onerous, demands of family organization, enterprise management, investment strategy, tax planning, and family services.

Not all of the old advisors will be up to these new challenges; families, now more than ever, need to review the commitment, capabilities, and performance of the family staff, the family office, and family advisors on a regular basis—and make tough decisions if individuals or firms fall short in meeting the needs of a more complex and demanding environment.

At the same time, another source of support, insight, and joint activity in the eco-system is the increasing reliance of families on networks of other families with similar wealth and stature. Families are networking with like-minded peer families to share experiences and, in many cases, co-invest and share insights on the education of next generation family members.

INTERDEPENDENT ELEMENTS

The first reason to consider all elements of the legacy plan on an integrated basis is that they are all inextricably intertwined. Trust structures influence estate plans and wealth management. Philanthropic objectives influence wealth management and family infrastructure. The family eco-system plays a major role in all aspects of legacy planning and execution.

A second reason is that the interaction of the elements often creates an even better outcome in any one area than would an isolated approach. By considering each element on a stand-alone basis, family leaders and strategists create a series of focused strategies targeted at the achievement of specific objectives in each area. By integrating these individual strategies into a coherent whole, they contribute to overall legacy results which are far greater than the sum of the individual parts.

The third reason to proceed on a coordinated basis is that all elements aim to achieve the same overarching goal; alignment of activities is far more likely to lead to the achievement of the desired outcome. Throughout the process, it should be remembered that the ultimate goal of a legacy plan is to pursue a defined vision and implement the actions that will lead to the greatest possible harmony, happiness, and prosperity for the family across many succeeding generations.

By setting out a practical framework for coherent action, visions can be realized, legacies can be made more lasting, leadership can be made more effective, leaders can have more control, and investing in legacy can be made far more efficient.

INVESTING IN LEGACY PLANNING

Thinking about the future and planning as best possible for a successful and enduring legacy are among the most valuable investments in time and money a family can make. The benefits of such visible actions are both practical and symbolic.

As younger members of the family observe and participate in the exercise of designing and implementing a legacy plan, that experience sends a signal about the importance of the collective family, underscores the benefits of a shared approach to the future, and highlights the benefits and challenges of communal activity.

The common effort of legacy planning in the present orients all family members toward their common future and actually increases the odds, through the commitment, exercise and process of strategy, of that common future being more fulfilling and enriching for all concerned.

Questions for Leaders of Legacy

1. Do you have an agreed framework and process for multi-generational planning for your family?
2. Do you have a clear and agreed legacy plan for your family? Are you implementing that strategy successfully?
3. Do all members of the family understand and support that strategy?
4. Do you have a family organization appropriate to your family's size and complexity, as well as supporting resources well suited to accomplish your legacy objectives?
5. What are your high-priority investments in future legacy? Are they enough to accomplish your more ambitious goals?

Getting It Right—The Evergreen* Family

While there are, sadly, more examples of struggle and legacy decline over time than brilliant successes, there are select individuals who have led their families well, over time and across all aspects of the multi-generational framework.

Along with prominent American examples such as the Rockefellers and other baronial families of the Industrial Revolution, one internationally prominent family has addressed all of the elements of the framework with substantial success across four generations. They know who they are, what they stand for, and what they hope to achieve together. In selected areas their positions are well articulated:

Governance: The family has a clear definition of membership and a written Family Constitution that defines the roles, expectations, and responsibilities of all family members.

Philosophy: The family has a clearly segmented set of assets: one large portfolio is held in stewardship for future generations (language they have used for nearly a century) and managed for long-term return, while much smaller (but still substantial) asset portfolios are inherited for private investment or personal use as family members see fit.

Family Promise: Family vision, values, and principles are clearly spelled out and shared across the family. The supporting documents and commitments between family members support the family purpose and identity. While accommodating different life choices and individual capabilities, the low profile and high standards of the family provide a common approach to their many public and private interactions.

Family enterprise: The family runs an established business, while ensuring separate expert management of a large liquid portfolio of investments, along with property holdings and other balancing interests in their own country and across the world. When necessary, they have not been afraid to sell or acquire businesses and assets to optimize their portfolio.

Family eco-system: The family enterprise has an advisory board of distinguished members from the financial world, along with expert teams in the family office and family businesses.

Education: Family members are expected to obtain the best formal education possible and to gain experience outside the family businesses before moving into any family role with substantial responsibility.

Family unity: The family regularly takes all members of all generations on an extended summer holiday together, providing a platform of shared activity and experience to unite the family within and across generations. An active involvement in their church and family sessions supporting their religious beliefs provides a firm foundation for a common world view, as well as a common view of their future shared legacy.

PART II

FAMILY LEADERSHIP AND SUCCESSION

7. LEADERSHIP CHALLENGES IN THE FAMILY ENTERPRISE

Designated leaders of a wealthy family are responsible for overseeing and maintaining the complex family enterprise, broadly defined as the human, social, financial, and philanthropic activities of the family.

The purpose of this enterprise is to preserve the family's unity, legacy, and wealth, financial and nonfinancial alike. Understanding the broader enterprise that family leaders are asked to oversee is a critical first step in understanding the leadership roles that they are asked to play.

DEFINITION OF THE FOUR PILLARS OF THE FAMILY ENTERPRISE

In its best form, the family enterprise reinforces the values of the family and formalizes the framework for the family to grow and prosper as a perpetual entity. The family as an enterprise typically has at least four main pillars of support:

- **Family legacy**—where the family comes from and where they are heading together.
- **Business legacy**—the cornerstone of the family enterprise that generates the family wealth.
- **Financial legacy**—the financial security and management of assets outside the business.
- **Philanthropic legacy**—the lasting contribution the family makes by giving back in a meaningful manner.

This broad definition of the family enterprise encompasses these four common pillars that define much of, and support all of, the activities of the family and its legacy. Each of these pillars, while remaining important to most families, will evolve over time.

A core operating business typically launches the family as an enterprise through the efforts of exceptional entrepreneurs who become successful and respected business leaders in the local community. As time passes and the business grows, issues may surface around leadership and continuity of the business and future leadership of the family.

EVOLUTION OF THE LEADERSHIP CHALLENGE

As the family, the business, and wealth grow together, the family needs to formalize a governance process to address critical issues of leadership and succession of the business, and leadership of the family outside of the business.

If wealth has been created and distributed to shareholders, the owners now have additional financial challenges related to investing the proceeds of the business safely and in a tax-efficient manner. Business success also typically fosters a desire on the part of business owners to give back philanthropically to the communities they have served through the years, and formal structures such as family foundations or donor-advised funds may be created to administer the family's giving programs and share the family's good fortune with others.

One simple model that identifies the components of the family enterprise is shown in Figure 7.1.

The two outside pillars, the business and the financial legacies, provide the financial strength that supports the activities of the two other pillars of the enterprise, where the family legacy and the philanthropic legacy of the family are found. More family members are personally involved in efforts related to the two inside pillars, and more structure and professional management is characteristic of the two outside pillars.

Figure 7.1: The Four Pillars of the Family Enterprise

COMPLEXITIES OF THE BUSINESS-OWNING FAMILY

While the family still owns one or more operating companies, it is essential for a clear infrastructure to be created to manage the competing priorities in the family enterprise.

Family Business and Systems Interact

"A family that owns a business . . . is at the intersection of several complex systems and serves a multitude of masters, purposes, and constituencies . . . in order to thrive, the family must develop a clear infrastructure to manage the interrelationships of people, business, and investment."

Dennis T. Jaffe and S.H. Lane[1]

For some families, ownership of an operating business gives them a sense of place and purpose. The activities of running a business, and identification of all family members with that business, create sufficient cohesion for the family and confidence in the stability that comes from owning and controlling an operating company.

There are many specific challenges that arise in owning, managing, and preserving a family business. These challenges are magnified through periods of business transition, leadership successions, and the professionalization of management. In addition to these management challenges, strategic and governance issues also arise in differing circumstances, which require thorough discussion and a careful balancing of many factors. The situations that can present substantial issues include the options to acquire and integrate a business, to sell all or part of a business, work in joint ventures with partner companies and families, grow internationally, finance expansion, compensate employees, and manage family members in and not in the family business.

---

1 Dennis T. Jaffe and S. H. Lane, "Sustaining a Family Dynasty: Key Issues Facing Complex Multi-generational Business- and Investment-Owning Families," *Family Business Review* 17, No. 1 (2004), 81–98.

An Enduring Business Legacy

Founded in 1807, during the presidency of Thomas Jefferson, the Wiley publishing business is still going strong in its seventh generation of family leadership.

Qualifying as a "publicly listed private business," Wiley is a global leader in the media world, with an illustrious history of publishing authors from Nathaniel Hawthorne in the nineteenth century to George Soros in the twenty-first.

Peter Wiley, current chairman of the group, attributes the family's business success to six guiding principles:

- Commitment to the mission of creating a special company.
- Family commitment and engagement.
- Treating people with dignity and respect.
- Taking a long view.
- Being flexible, adaptive, and entrepreneurial in pursuing "creative opportunism."
- Thinking and acting globally.

While not claiming to have a universal formula for success, the Wileys' two centuries of family business leadership show that the right approach at each generation can build toward the creation and maintenance of a family's enduring business legacy.

These issues all require elaboration in a manner that exceeds the scope of this book. While fully accepting the importance of these issues to a family's business future, the focus here is more the integrated approach to family enterprise management and not the details of family business ownership, governance, strategy, and management. These issues are now, through the many books and courses on family business, usually well understood by most business-owning families.

What is less understood by most financially successful families is how to organize the aspects of the family enterprise *outside* of the operating business, and how to integrate that organized effort into a single family approach to the family enterprise.

One comprehensive organizational model that identifies the operating structures for the four traditional parts of the family enterprise is set out in Figure 7.2.

Figure 7.2: Operating Structure for Four Pillars of the Family Enterprise

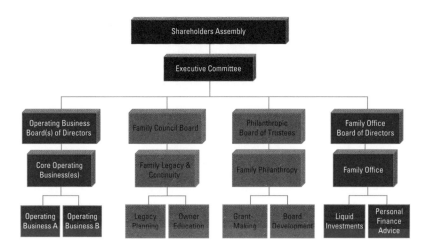

All owners of the family enterprise, who may or may not own shares of the family operating company or companies, are represented in the Shareholders Assembly (top of the chart). A leadership group, often called the Family Council or Executive Committee, is typically formed to expedite the decision-making process regarding matters that affect any aspect of the family enterprise. Below that overarching governing body sit the four different dimensions of the family enterprise—operating businesses, family legacy matters, philanthropic initiatives, and financial and investment activities that are undertaken by members of the family enterprise.

AFTER THE SALE OF THE BUSINESS

One of the major differences between a business-owning family and an investing family is the shift from highly concentrated operating risk to highly diversified capital markets and financial risk. Risk concentration must give way to risk management, which becomes one of the core responsibilities of the enterprise.

Families that no longer own an operating business are often still engaged in a formal family enterprise if they have chosen to stay together in the management of their financial and philanthropic affairs. Non-business-owning families are still viewed as enterprise families if they operate together, and are sometimes called "financial families" to designate the purpose of their enterprise. Some families practice "serial business ownership," where, following the sale of the family business, they purchase another major business together.

Leaders of family enterprises who are not grounded by an operating business often describe the difficulties of keeping family members engaged in an enterprise that oversees intangible assets, including family values and history, pooled investment opportunities, wealth transfer strategies, and collaborative philanthropic endeavors.

It is much easier to get owners engaged and connected to a tangible operating business, especially if the family name is over the door, than to intangible assets that exist to provide financial security and personal enrichment. The first involves a team effort and a visible business product, while the second is about pooling resources and efforts for greater purchasing power or philanthropic impact.

Not the Same

As one family leader said several years after their family business was sold, "It's just not as interesting to sit around and talk about what it takes to stay wealthy rather than to grow the business. We want to stay connected as a family, but it is much harder to do so after the business is gone."

The challenge for the leaders of the family enterprise in its post-sale generations is to create a sense of mutual purpose and family unity in managing the areas that remain: the family legacy, its financial wealth, and philanthropic activities.

Many families who sell their operating companies have a desire to preserve the family history and their enjoyment of each other in some structure, often by formalizing a family office or a foundation bearing the family name. Whichever of these entities becomes the lead endeavor for the family, the family needs to create a place where the family is brought together, and "family matters" are discussed in a formal setting. Such matters might involve the public reputation of the family, their roles in the local community, their interest in politics or public service, and, most importantly, the education of the younger generations about individual purpose, family history, and shared legacy.

One other, more active, opportunity for financial families is to turn their financial activities into the creation of a "second family business," perhaps in the form of a merchant bank, a multi-family office (MFO) with their fellow family members as the first clients, or a private trust company for managing the family wealth of one's own family and others.

One interesting characteristic of these identity-reinforcing MFOs and private trust companies is that the name of the family that created the founding wealth is seldom mentioned in the entity's name. Unlike charitable foundations, most of these types of organizations use names unrelated to any one family or business enterprise, ensuring discretion for its founding clients and the chance for a new business start for its owners and staff.

EMOTIONAL OWNERSHIP

Leadership of a family enterprise after the sale of a core business brings with it extra hurdles to overcome in creating family identity, unity, loyalty, and emotional ownership of financial assets.

One concept that has proven useful in understanding the psychology of family members, particularly younger members of the family enterprise, is the concept of "Emotional Ownership." This term conveys the sense of identification and connection that family members feel for the family business, the collective family wealth, and their evolving legacy.

EVOLVING STRATEGIES AND LEADERSHIP ROLES

However the family evolves, the challenges of family organization, family philanthropy, and multi-generational wealth preservation and enhancement need to be addressed in every generation.

With each successive stage in their evolution, most families become more complex: there are more variables and personalities in play, and there is less certainty about family leadership strength, skill, and capability in a more complicated paradigm. The overall family dynamic, and the risks and opportunities defined by prevailing economic, financial, and legal environments, may be both more important, even if dramatically less predictable, than before.

As a result, strategies also become less concrete and definitive, and more general in content. They are more focused on family capabilities, visions, directions, values, and principles. Leadership roles also become more complex, family dynamics become more central to the family identity, and family leaders may need to create, rather than steer, a sense of emotional ownership and family identity.

Keeping Ownership Alive

The Elm* family has benefited from the leadership of a perceptive family office CEO with the family for 29 years, who understood that his most important responsibility was planning for a smooth transfer of leadership from one generation to the next. The CEO and family leaders believed firmly in educating and preparing the children of the family for leadership by fostering a sense of independence, learned through experience.

In the 1970s, the second generation sold the family business and launched an investment-focused financial office. More than 20 years later, the fourth generation (in their 20s at the time) started an investment fund, where they were responsible for developing strategy, selecting managers, establishing benchmarks for measuring success, and voting on whether or not to make distributions from the partnership. The group also selected its own leaders of the fund and rotated leadership. Those who served as leaders ended up as better participants as a result of their time in the leadership role. The family office CEO served as monitor, coach and referee, but really encouraged them to "figure it out" as a group.

The fourth generation learned many important lessons about themselves and about the challenges of family leadership. Not everyone participates, not everyone agrees on the best process and not everyone honors his or her commitments.

In their family culture, those who show up regularly and take action are awarded leadership roles, and those who sit back and watch the process are not awarded decision-making votes.

This approach has worked. As the fourth generation enters their 30s, they are more attuned to the complexities of shared ownership and much more respectful of their current family leaders.

OPTING OUT OF THE FAMILY ENTERPRISE

Not all family members want to be bound to their fellow family members in the family enterprise, with or without a family business.

The desire to go one's own way, to pursue different investment opportunities, and to work with one's own team of advisors and colleagues leads some family members to want to exit the family enterprise.

As one retiring Chairman of the family council of a prominent seventh-generation family conveyed to his successor during their handover process:

> "Leaving the door open for members to depart is the best way to keep the family together."

Most families have a predetermined formula, codified in their bylaws and other legal and family documents, that specifies how individual members may exit the family enterprise. The formulas used to calculate ownership values are varied, but the most common rules of disengagement say that the exiting party must leave on terms that do not financially damage the other members of the family.

Some families may employ free-market *laissez faire* systems to set an exit price, and others provide specific formulas for the sale, transfer, or encumbrance of the shares of a family business or interests in family wealth vehicles. Pricing varies from full market value paid out immediately, to long drawn-out payment terms made up of a small percentage of the annual free cash flow of the family enterprise, often subject to a cap on payments to any one person if more than one family member is seeking an exit at the same time.

> The most common rules of disengagement say that the exiting party must leave on terms that do not financially damage the other members of the family.

While some members choose to opt out, others may be forced out if they are seen to be a risk to the family legacy and wealth. These situations are uncommon but vexing. Some family Constitutions require a supermajority vote for exclusion, others a mere majority, or even a delegation of the issue to a subgroup of the larger family.

Having a pre-established clause and approach that allows an exit from all or part of a family enterprise may be a pressure valve that releases the energy from potential future conflicts.

Setting up the process for maintaining the family enterprise and enticing family members to become more involved may be one of the largest and most challenging parts of a legacy strategy.

Questions for Leaders of Legacy

1. Do you have a common view about the importance of the family enterprise across the family?
2. Do you have a strategy to foster a sense of family identity and legacy beyond the family business?
3. In the absence of a defining business, is there a clear set of operating roles and opportunities for interaction to keep the family together?
4. Do you have documented exit strategies for family members wishing to leave the enterprise?
5. How can you cultivate a sense of emotional ownership of your family enterprise?

Reflections on Family Sustainability and Leadership

Fredda Herz Brown is Founder of Relative Solutions, a founding board member of the Family Firm Institute, and the author of numerous articles and the highly acclaimed book Reweaving the Family Tapestry.[2] *The following excerpt is taken from Fredda's comments made at the Family Office Exchange Twentieth Anniversary Forum in 2009.*

There are many important issues that leaders of modern families of wealth need to address to create family enterprises that are sustainable in all senses of the word.

Perhaps because of the turbulence of recent years, families and their leaders are seeking ways to ensure that their family assets are capable of withstanding the strains and stresses of difficult times.

The questions of family sustainability and leadership warrant careful consideration by all families of wealth, and I would like to offer a few observations.

Definition of family sustainability

Sustainability, by definition, requires that we can meet the needs of the present without compromising the ability of the future generations to meet their needs. I think that this definition, usually applied to environmental policies, can also be directly applied to the multi-generational family.

In order to become sustainable, we need to look at the difference between needs and wants, and facilitate the acquisition of this knowledge by our children. We also need to look at what is required from us as parents for our families to be sustainable—how much time we need to spend with our children teaching them about values and preferences, and helping them distinguish between needs and wants.

It is important to let our children follow a path of discovery themselves, letting them make mistakes and have a variety of experiences to foster the development of capability.

But the issue of sustainability goes beyond just parenting.

(continued)

---

2 Fredda Herz Brown, *Reweaving the Family Tapestry* (Charleston, SC: BookSurge Publishing, 2006).

Considering the economic and the emotional

One of the important distinctions about working with wealthy families is to recognize that their decision to join with other family members for economic reasons has both risks and opportunities, and adds a level of complexity to their family relationships. This decision has an impact on the families' emotional lives, as well as their shared economic destiny.

Balancing the need for separation with the need for emotional connection and family identification over time is essential for an economic family joined for multiple generations. Failure to pay attention to this balance may leave family members with a sense of isolation and feeling that they have no voice and no way to exit. Such a mixture can lead to negative consequences for all involved.

Personal engagement and active ownership

A final view of sustainability in the context of a family of wealth has to do with the notion of being active about ownership. I have stopped using the term "stewardship" because I believe stewardship implies passivity. It implies that, like a Patek Philippe watch, you just hold it for the next generation.

Passive ownership does not create the kind of engagement which most individuals would describe as appealing or sustainable. Holding something may not give someone a full sense of responsibility and accountability for what happens to the objects he or she is holding. As a client said to me: "I feel like I don't have ownership of anything. I'm just wearing the cloak, and my job will be to pass it on to the next generation; to make sure it goes pretty well. But I don't know that I felt the ownership of it, and have really dealt with the full meaning of it in my life."

Developing a sense of responsibility and accountability to self and others is essential for sustainability, and also for leadership. Without that sense there is little genuine commitment. One of the things that both families of wealth and their advisors seem to struggle with is how to define the qualities of a next generation owner, shareholder, or family member and then how to develop those qualities.

Family office and family identity

One of the reasons single family offices have been so successful is that they offer families who no longer own a business the opportunity to create a new form of economic group, personal identity, and stature. Moving from a business background into a family office offers them a continuing emotional identity. In some ways it provides another platform from which to act together.

(continued)

At the same time, each generation has to be afforded the opportunity to reconsider whether they want to act together, and if so, in what ways. Having an office that supports their development as a family by providing a "place" and a foundation, without doing the work for them, is an important piece of family identity.

Leadership from within

When considering the demands placed on leadership to address the issues of identity, ownership, and sustainability, I think about it not as the exercise of leadership "from behind," but from within the family.

Leadership from within implies leadership that reflects the authenticity of the person and his or her ability to lead the family from "within" it—to assist family members in developing and living by the values and vision they have developed.

Leaders who are able to create a sustainable pattern for their families need to have self awareness, a true understanding of how they operate, an ability to respect boundaries between self and others, and also be creative and authentic to themselves and their families.

Summary

These important questions about the benefits of togetherness versus separateness, the complexity of making emotional and economic decisions when both are interconnected, and the ways to prepare children properly to be competent and active owners of wealth warrant careful consideration by all families of wealth.

Family leaders who understand and manage these issues will not only aid the development of their families, but can add to the collective wisdom in the fields of both sustainability and leadership.

8. PROVEN APPROACHES
TO FAMILY LEADERSHIP

For all families creating wealth for the first time, the land of great wealth is like a new world. There is no precedent or model within their experience to manage such wealth, or address the associated issues of a wealthy family and its financial fortune; there is also no existing model for leaders to apply for the conscious preservation and transfer of this new legacy and wealth across generations.

The answers to simple questions may be elusive for many who lack experience being members of a family with distinct financial advantages and a unique heritage:

- What does it take to define a positive and enduring legacy?
- What does it take to lead a family across generations?
- What can an individual do personally to contribute to the family's future?

For those members of families familiar with multi-generational wealth, there is a different set of leadership challenges to keep the legacy and family wealth alive. The challenges for them are to maintain disciplines, ensure motivation, and keep alive an entrepreneurial spirit in an increasingly large and disparate population of heirs who are likely to spread across generations and geographies, and to develop differing needs, interests, and priorities.

In attempting to answer these questions, successful wealthy families benefit from a clear model of leadership and from the effective leadership of talented individuals. Without proper leadership skills, families of great fortune may not see the full set of challenges they are facing, and may well not have the insight needed to manage the risks that challenge the family and its legacy.

THE STRUCTURE OF LEADERSHIP

A successful model of family leadership is well structured, focused, sensitive in its dealings with people, and swift and fair in its resolution of problems.

In all cases, a well-conceived approach to the organization and structure of a family and its leadership model is a step toward building, and even enhancing, a family's long-term legacy.

The structure and principles of family leadership create an organized approach to roles and responsibilities for the head of a family; they define how other organizational positions work with each other and with the greater family. A leadership model specifies the rights, responsibilities, and processes of leadership within a family. That model needs to outline the broader approach through which its members can be heard, and within which decisions can be made in a fair and impartial manner.

> A successful model of family leadership also needs to remain flexible.

While providing a defined leadership structure and clear operating principles, a successful model of family leadership also needs to remain flexible. Family leaders must strive for family inclusiveness, practice active listening, and involve all members in the leadership processes of the family.

The Zen world view that one must not become attached to a fixed outcome can be an important guidepost for modern legacy families of all nationalities and spiritual orientations.

PROVIDING STABILITY AND CONTINUITY AMID CHANGE

While leaders are most tested during periodic crises such as the Great Depression, the stresses of a wartime economy, and the sharp economic downturn beginning in 2008, their long-term success or failure is determined by their ability to support the family in periods of both continuity and change.

Wealthy families, for reasons both internal to the family and related to changes in the external environment, are in constant evolution and change. Leadership activities aimed at creating stability and continuity require effort and continuous adaptation at many levels.

In *The Prince*, Giuseppe di Lampedusa shares the patriarch's elegy to a fading way of life and a last generation of elegance and privilege in Sicily when he wrote of Don Fabrizio's world of wealth and stature:

"If we want things to stay as they are, things will have to change."[1]

All family members who operate in a family system learn that change, and adapting to change, are two of the most difficult issues that families face together. Members of the family who fear or resist

> "If we want things to stay as they are, things will have to change."

change create tremendous hindrances for the rest of the family in preparing the family system for future challenges and necessary departure from the status quo.

In bringing about this fine balance of constancy and change, families need to define and craft the philosophical and practical elements of their leadership models. There are many options available, but at the core of a successful leadership structure, seven separate elements of an integrated family leadership framework should be addressed to improve the likelihood of attaining the best possible outcomes for the family.

The Family Leadership Framework

1. Build consensus among owners about the importance of developing and supporting family leaders.

2. Establish the rights, responsibilities, and processes for leadership.

3. Manage the governance process for effective decision making and fair dispute resolution.

4. Develop leadership succession plans (both short- and long-term) and document a clear selection process.

5. Implement a formal strategic planning and/or legacy planning process for the family enterprise.

6. Establish a process for educating owners about the importance of legacy, leadership, and family challenges.

7. Develop a process for measuring the success of the leadership team and performance of the supporting eco-system.

---

1 Giuseppe Tomasi di Lampedusa, *Il Gattopardo (The Leopard)* (New York: Pantheon, 1960), 40.

These seven components are not exclusive to family leaders; all members of the family share in its past and future legacy and have a responsibility to contribute to its leadership.

EVERY FAMILY MEMBER CAN BE A LEADER

One of the opportunities for self-determination by family members is to embrace the concept of shared leadership, rather than just selecting individuals to lead the family autocratically. This concept does not develop naturally in families guided for years by a strong patriarch or matriarch, where leadership belonged to one individual or couple. However, as families grow, they discover the value of shared leadership and the importance of pooling skill sets to strengthen the family.

The concept of leadership teams, functioning as coalitions to manage change, allows groups of owners to take responsibility together and reach agreement on what needs to be done. The family uses the momentum of the larger group's energy to counter any sources of inertia that may be settling in the family.

When the second generation is leading the family, the goal might be the development of a clear decision-making process for the family, and the skills needed for that work might include charitable board experience and a peacekeeper's instincts.

When the third generation gets involved, the goal might be greater owner involvement, and the talents needed might include infectious enthusiasm and the ability to inspire members of the younger generation to contribute their talents.

FORMAL AND INFORMAL LEADERSHIP GROUPS

> In a large and significantly wealthy family, formal and informal forms of leadership operate simultaneously.

In a large and significantly wealthy family, formal and informal forms of leadership operate simultaneously. Both provide opportunities for participation by qualifying family members. Individuals take up positions of formal authority and decision making on behalf of the group, while others contribute to the determination of outcomes without holding a formal position of power within the family.

Examples of the latter can be seen in the exercise of influence through persuasion, personal credibility, coalition creation, or the simple exercise of natural leadership abilities.

A successful model of leadership in a family recognizes and values all approaches, and seeks to accommodate informal groups through understanding and broader engagement.

STRUCTURING DISPUTE RESOLUTION MECHANISMS

No one set of structures and organizing principles, no matter how well thought out, carefully crafted, and assiduously followed by all members of the family, can foresee all potential disputes and act to resolve all differences in advance of the advent of a specific contentious issue or broader crisis.

Just as the nation state has a judicial branch to resolve disputes in a manner consistent with its basic constitution and relevant regulations and laws, a family should have an approach to dispute resolution that resolves issues and disputes in the context of its Family Promise, guiding principles, specific rules, and shared values.

Such a system can reduce the risk of an isolated dispute escalating to threaten the structure, unity, or harmony of the greater family.

Without such a mechanism—which can be as simple as a rule that the elders, both male and female, decide in matters of dispute between children, branches, or generations—small disputes can explode into epic proportion in even the most stable of families when voices do not feel heard.

Most problematic is the conflict between certain members of the family, where other relatives may not be willing, or capable, of finding a common way out of the difficulties. In these cases, professional external advisors can play an important role, and are often the only solution to what can become a family-threatening set of issues.

Resolving family disputes requires both the right process and the right people. Leaders have been proven to be most effective at dispute resolution when they understand the importance of all the issues, spoken and unspoken, and even seek professional advice to address the most important family disputes.

IDENTIFYING LEADERSHIP TALENT

One of the responsibilities of being a leader is to understand his or her strengths and limitations, those of siblings and cousins, and to know what resources are needed to create and support a strong central decision-making team.

It is also essential to have a clear understanding of the skill sets of each owner and an appreciation for how they can contribute to the common goals set forth by the family. For example, it may be the soft-spoken sister who speaks up and names the behavior that is most hurting the family's ability to reach agreement or find viable alternatives. That same sibling might never be asked to lead the family, or even facilitate a family discussion, but her ability to speak the truth may make her a natural mediator in the family who serves as a catalyst for breaking down barriers and as an independent counsel on sensitive matters.

Sometimes in-laws and spouses can spot the real issues that challenge a family better than the bloodline members of the family, but they must proceed with caution lest their well-intentioned contributions end up as poorly received intrusions with considerable negative long-term implications.

A FAIR AND EFFECTIVE LEADERSHIP SELECTION PROCESS

The selection of leaders is one of the most important and sensitive processes for a family.

Successful leaders of large families can best identify the need for future leadership skills through a sophisticated assessment process:

- Assess common family goals and challenges.
- Conduct a skills inventory with the potential leadership group.
- Develop a committee to map skills and identify gaps.
- Add external advisors to the team to fill gaps and complement family skills.
- Develop a training process for future leaders to learn critical leadership skills.

In some situations, discord and resentment over leadership selection can last a lifetime and even across multiple future generations. These destructive views and sentiments can be created by lingering resentments over individual decisions and leadership selection processes within a family that were not seen to be fair.

In order to be fair, a leadership selection process must be attuned to the family's ethos and ethics. The mechanics of selection also need to be developed within that context so that all family members can agree with the process and its fairness, if not the outcome (see Chapter 10 for further discussion).

DOCUMENTED SUCCESSION PLANS (BOTH SHORT- AND LONG-TERM)

Succession planning is a key component of the leadership transition process.

To be successful, the family needs to address leadership succession in a formal manner early on, determining the likely successors to current leadership positions and preparing them as needed. Although the final selection process needs to anoint those who best fit the specific requirements, prior identification of likely successors allows better preparation and a smoother entry into the position if long-term plans and expectations work out.

In one Indian family, for example, future family leaders are evaluated on the playground and identified as having leadership potential as early as six years of age. In another European family, leaders assert that they can identify, with a high degree of accuracy, who will be the next set of family leaders by the age of eight.

Often, however, long-term plans run awry. People selected to be future leaders fail at their prior jobs, or the nature of the leadership model changes. Family situations change: people die, lose interest, get married, and move far away from the center of family activities. The process of finding a long-term successor for each key position needs to be under constant review and maintained with a constant spirit of readiness for potential change.

In addition to long-term plans, there should also be a list of names to replace key family members, their staff, and advisors on short notice. Resignation, early retirement, illness, or death can force a family to take swift action to replace a lost team member, even on a temporary basis. Having had the chance to think through the alternatives in advance allows a family to be well prepared for any unexpected disaster or other change that may require swift and decisive action.

RESPONSIBILITIES OF THE LEADERSHIP JOB

When family members consider taking a leadership role in the family enterprise for the first time, there is often a lack of clarity about the actual tasks involved in the job. Since the job seems somewhat political ("keeping everyone happy"), somewhat nebulous ("developing a common vision of the future"), and very time consuming, most family members are apprehensive about the responsibilities of leadership. If the family has not yet developed a culture of teamwork among leaders, it can also seem like a very lonely job that involves pushing unwilling parties in directions they would rather not go.

The question often asked by candidates for leadership is, what is it you need me to do as a potential leader of the enterprise?

In an effort to answer that question in a comprehensive manner, a summary of seven of the key responsibilities of a family legacy leader, with an expanded explanation of the content of each headline area of responsibility, is provided below. Each has been discussed in more detail in other chapters of the book and a summary is shared here as a job description, of sorts.

Responsibilities for consideration include:

1. **Develop an appreciation among family members for the concept of the family enterprise, family leadership, and legacy planning.**
   - Identify the main "pillars" of the family enterprise.
   - Gain support from family leaders for the enterprise concept.
   - Communicate with the wider family about the need for enterprise leadership and legacy planning.
   - Gain consensus among family members to develop a formal legacy plan.
   - Select a committee of family leaders to spearhead the process.

2. **Recognize and reflect on shared legacy and values in the family.**

   • Map historical patterns and guiding principles in each "pillar" of the enterprise.

   • Identify core values and core competencies as a family and in each area of the enterprise.

   • Discuss the amount of togetherness that feels appropriate across the enterprise.

   • Choose patterns of behavior to carry forward and those to leave behind.

3. **Identify challenges of shared ownership and shared risks.**

   • Understand current ownership structures that affect the enterprise.

   • Discuss ownership goals and opportunities for collaboration across branches.

   • Identify common risks that most challenge family branches or generations.

   • Discuss implications of common risks and changes that may be required.

   • Develop strategies and committees to mitigate high-priority risks.

4. **Develop a shared vision for the future and a set of common goals.**

   • Identify areas of affinity and common interest across the family groups.

   • Identify common goals and common structures (often by generation or by branch).

   • Prioritize the family's common goals (using a group process).

   • Gain agreement on the shared goals for the future of the family enterprise.

5. **Identify leadership skills needed and a team of qualified leaders.**

   • Conduct a skills inventory with the potential leadership group.

   • Develop a committee to map skills and identify gaps.

- Add external advisors to the team to fill gaps and complement family skills.
- Develop a training process for future leaders to learn critical leadership skills.

6. **Organize a decision-making process and governance structures that support the vision.**
   - Understand current operating structures and governance process.
   - Review governance models implemented by other family groups for relevance.
   - Identify elements of authority that are appropriate for each level of governance.
   - Build new operating structures that specify the domains of decision making.
   - Create a proper governance process to support the structures.
   - Construct bylaws that encompass all of the elements of governance.
   - Develop a mechanism for exiting the family system.

7. **Develop a process for identifying and measuring success for the family enterprise.**
   - Ask family members how they want to measure the success of the enterprise on an ongoing basis.
   - Study examples of how other family groups measure their success.
   - Develop a set of metrics that are measurable and meaningful to the family.
   - Revise the metrics after testing their value and relevance over time and revisit them annually.

After reviewing this daunting list of responsibilities, many candidates might not feel fully qualified for such an imposing job, and no candidate could be expected to tackle all elements of the checklist at the same time.

However, if a team of capable family leaders prioritizes these objectives, subdivides the assignments, and tackles them systematically over a period of years, the family will have a system for assessing and selecting leaders that would serve the family well through the generations.

A good leader, well supported and thoughtful in the definition of job content, and realistic about the goals, timing, and measures of success, can work through many of these issues successfully, albeit only over an extended time frame and with the support of all the family and its surrounding eco-system.

RESULTS CONFIRM THE MODEL OF FAMILY LEADERSHIP

The legitimacy of leadership is based upon agreement, trust, and integrity, but is validated by results that would not be attained under a different model of family organization and leadership. Excellence in outcome and a continuing and enthusiastic mandate are the final tests of family leadership and a legacy strategy.

Success may be defined as preservation of capital through effective crisis and risk management, and enhancement of total family capital (as described in Chapter 1) as and when opportunities arise in times both turbulent and stable.

The greatness of any family leader can be seen in the total impact he or she has had, over time and across an entire career as a family leader, on those matters that have the most substantial impact on family legacy, and those component parts of family capital and true family wealth, across many future generations of the family.

Questions for Leaders of Legacy

1. Do you have a clear model of leadership, which includes structure, operating principles, the leadership selection process, and succession plans?
2. What are the strengths and weaknesses demonstrated by your model of family leadership over time?
3. Do you have a clear plan to foster family involvement in the leadership process?
4. Are your future leadership plans, including short- and long-term succession plans, and candidates up to the challenges that your family's future leaders will face?
5. Does your family understand and appreciate the responsibilities of the leadership job for the family enterprise?

Perspectives from Successful Third- and Fourth-Generation Family Leaders

Although stories of great success are not common, there are a number of extraordinary family leaders who have contributed part of their personal lives to the stewardship of a larger family enterprise, and achieved substantial success in their efforts.

Coming from disparate backgrounds and achieving their successes in different situations, each leader cited below found himself or herself with different attitudes, observations, and insights over time. Their words and deeds can stand as examples of the spirit of leadership in the real world:

Charles B. Grace Jr. is a third-generation family leader, whose wealth originated from the Bethlehem Steel Company. The family has had a family office for over 50 years, and Charles led Ashbridge, the Grace family office, for 32 years. During this time he established one of the earliest multi-family offices and successfully merged it with another MFO in 2010. In short, Charles played a role in the creation of a modern family office and the development of the MFO model that is a force today in the wealth management industry. Charles has always said,

"One of the keys to managing family wealth successfully is broad family participation, with family members playing a role in a chosen capacity. At the same time, independent directors are important to good governance, and they helped me in immeasurable ways when making decisions and balancing the interests of five branches of my family."

Harold B. Smith is a third-generation member of the Harold C. Smith family, whose predecessors founded the Northern Trust Company in 1889. Harold still serves on the Board of Directors. He is also chairman of the Executive Committee of Illinois Tool Works and was president of the company from 1972–81, prior to serving as chairman since 1982.

More important than his business accomplishments has been his tireless stewardship of the family for 40 years. Harold is known for his insight regarding family matters and his unique way of looking at challenges and opportunities presented to the family. Through the years, Harold has earned the respect of his cousins for his thoughtfulness and collaboration with other family leaders, forming a true "cousins' consortium" for leadership. When Harold saw the need for leadership succession, he got the fourth generation involved early in the discussion regarding how leaders would be selected and trained. In his words:

(continued)

"The bridge from the third to fourth generation is a critical juncture for our family. We want to build a collaborative effort to involve all branches of the family who are interested and committed to the future of the family."

A **fourth-generation leader** from one of America's leading banking families has played a key leadership role in her family despite suffering great personal loss at an early age (losing both parents, a sibling, and a valued trustee). She has not lost her ability to keep a balanced view or to trust and rely on others. She has retained an entrepreneurial spirit and a calculated risk taker's mentality throughout her life. Although she oversees a number of complex legal structures and properties, she still yearns for greater simplicity in her financial affairs.

She is now planning to set up workable structures that allow her children to make thoughtful, independent decisions for themselves as individuals, so they are masters of their own legacy. She wants certain responsibilities to be delegated to the family office, with

"a management team that plays defense, so I don't have to worry about managing the risks, but can focus my energies on the development of the next generation."

Dirk Jungé is a fourth-generation descendant of John Pitcairn, the Scottish-born co-founder of Pittsburg Plate Glass (now PPG Industries) in Pennsylvania. Dirk has earned the trust of his family and the respect of the private wealth industry by being realistic about goals and humble about accomplishments. As chairman and CEO of Pitcairn, Dirk has never shied away from the risks associated with strategic change in moving his family and its business forward. In 1985, Dirk successfully lobbied his uncles to create one of the first family advisory councils to provide a cutting-edge approach to develop family leadership for Pitcairn's board. Then in 1987, Dirk recognized the potential for using the well-developed infrastructure of the Pitcairn family office to serve other multi-generational families and transformed the Pitcairn single family office to a multifamily office.

There is an old saying that Dirk likes to repeat, which is a fundamental belief that underlies the Pitcairn business model and speaks volumes to Dirk's ability to anticipate as well as adapt to change:

"If you don't create change, change will create you."

Louis F. Hill is a fourth-generation descendant of James J. Hill, founder of the Great Northern Railroad. The family's financial capital was generated

(continued)

through this original railroad, followed by further successful family enterprises in timber, oil and gas production, and mining. Louis committed more than 20 years to promoting family goals, being of significant service to others, and advancing the philanthropic legacy of the Hill Family.

He has been quoted as observing that preserving family legacy is a lot like the timber business:

> "You always have to plant new seedlings among the mature trees, harvest the timber at critical times, and plan the roadways for exiting the forest early in the process."

Alex Scott is a fourth-generation member of the Scott family from Kendal in the United Kingdom. Alex led the sale of two family businesses, Provincial Insurance and Exeter Bank, in 1994, and founded an MFO in 1996. His was the first family-owned MFO to register its family investment funds with the Financial Services Authority (FSA), and he spent years making sure the family investment process was both transparent and accessible to all family members.

Alex has been a tireless speaker on the value of an MFO model, which allows members of his own family to benefit from the combined purchasing power and the insights of other wealthy families who are clients of the office.

> "This path has provided many benefits: delivering an appropriate, contemporary and competitive solution for my family's investment needs upon the sale of our business; providing an outlet for my own entrepreneurial energies; creating a new operating business in a fiercely competitive market; evolving our business practice in response to competitive pressures; and for my family, relieving them of the need to expend valuable time on the minutiae of wealth management oversight."

One leader in a well-established and successful family summed up his feelings and personal thoughts, no doubt shared by many other leaders in similar positions, as he took on a leadership job for the first time:

> "I look in the mirror each morning and say to myself 'Please God, don't let things get messed up on my watch.'"

These perspectives convey the focus on "family first" that is a hallmark of strong family leaders.

In addition to their contributions to the development of their families and their demonstrated role as custodians of steadfast family values, these different leaders all reflect, at a personal level, the very natural humanity and humility necessary to cope with the responsibilities—and pressures—that come with a leadership position in a large family.

9. LEADERSHIP SKILLS FOR THE TWENTY-FIRST CENTURY

In addition to creating a lasting structure of leadership within the family and rising to the challenges of management in times of both stability and crisis, individual leaders must look inward and ensure that their own approaches prepare them well for their responsibilities as a twenty-first-century family leader. In challenging times, family leadership demands flexibility, inclusiveness, and a willingness to adapt to the inevitable changes the future brings.

WHAT MAKES A GOOD LEADER?

Leading a family enterprise is a calling that demands a unique collection of quantitative and qualitative skills, which varies depending on the nature of the family, the specific time and context, and the family's goals and challenges. However, despite the particularity of a family's needs, the following list of proven leadership characteristics identifies some of the timeless qualities that distinguish many more successful family leaders from their peers:

- Having no vested interest in the outcomes—caring about a collective solution.
- Serving as a guardian—wanting what is best for the family.
- Being articulate about why a shared vision matters to the family.
- Building consensus among constituents (managing the fine difference between agreement and consensus).
- Being clear about where the family is in the process of reaching consensus.
- Identifying the benefit for each owner ("What's in it for me?").
- Recognizing differences and making them an asset of the group.
- Naming the problems and helping to find solutions.
- Finding an artful way to identify and train successors.
- Working realistically with the different levels of emotional maturity.

MASTERING BASIC QUANTITATIVE SKILLS

Family leaders need to have a working knowledge of information systems, investment policy, tax and estate planning, accounting, regulation, trusts, corporations, and alternatives in asset structuring, and other technical disciplines relevant to the preservation and growth of family wealth in both its narrow and broader definitions. Access to experts as needed, and good strategic and organizational skills are also required.

DEMONSTRATING NEEDED QUALITATIVE SKILLS

Mastery of quantitative skills is not enough. The management of people within the family, requiring more qualitative skills, has always been the greatest challenge for family leaders. This challenge was accurately described by one leader, who said that the "soft stuff" is really the "even harder stuff."

Conflicting personalities, emotional history, divergent ages and interests, differing levels of capability and motivation, egos, alliances, affinities, and varying philosophies create an enormous challenge. It is very complex indeed to understand and master the challenges of a group most often defined by common DNA or marriage rather than by common personality, similar ability, shared interest, self-selection, or informed assignment.

Perhaps the greatest challenge for family leaders is to lead this collection of individuals toward a better future than they might have had without the leader's insights and actions. This is no easy task.

The most successful leaders of wealthy families share certain common personal attributes. They have a sense of purpose or commitment to something larger than themselves. Their passions and interests typically go beyond material goods. Having a sense of humor is invaluable in the work of guiding the family; the ability to "play well with others" and genuinely enjoy the creation and use of wealth is both a key skill and a useful personal character attribute.

Strong leaders convey consistently a sense of gratitude for their good fortune and have empathy for others. They respect different opinions and are able to build confidence across the family. They are good communicators who are committed to keeping others informed, and they have the courage and voice to take risks when and where appropriate.

Above all, successful leaders are guided by strong values and a moral compass that ensures that their efforts are focused on doing what is best for the greater family. They are honest and transparent in their dealings with all.

To cite the successful Singaporean entrepreneur and family patriarch Tony Chew Leong Chee, "You don't employ people any more, you need to engage them."

Leaders who ignore that perspective may miss out on an approach that addresses the issue of motivation within the family and its supporting organizations—the necessary human dimension to strategy.

> Above all, successful leaders are guided by strong values and a moral compass that ensures that their efforts are focused on doing what is best for the greater family.

By reaching the hearts as well as the minds and financial interests of family members, and by responding to their desire to contribute to something greater than themselves, an effective leader may be able to release new levels of energy to contribute to a family's current and future prosperity. "A leader is best when people barely know he exists, when his work is done, his aim fulfilled, they will say: 'We did it ourselves.'"[1]

The Character of an Authentic Leader

"Leaders are defined by their values and their character. The values of the authentic leader are shaped by personal beliefs, developed through study, introspection, and consultation with others—and a lifetime of experience. These values define their holder's moral compass. Such leaders know the 'true north' of their compass, the deep sense of the right thing to do."

Bill George[2]

---

1 Attributed to Lao Tzu, sixth-century B.C. Chinese Taoist philosopher.

2 Bill George, *Authentic Leadership: Rediscovering the Secrets to Creating Lasting Value* (San Francisco: Jossey-Bass, 2004), 20.

BUILDING CONSENSUS ACROSS THE FAMILY

One of the biggest challenges for any leader is to build consensus. Leaders must therefore master the art and science of achieving consensus in a wide range of circumstances and on a wide range of issues. A working consensus, rather than perfect agreement, may be a more realistic objective for families with diverse views, creating room for the coexistence of difference and increasing the odds of a family staying together despite a lack of shared perspective in many areas.

Proven Principles in the Creation of Consensus The creation of consensus amid diverse views is a constant balancing act. All views need to be considered, and all voices heard, before a single set of decisions can be made and one mutually acceptable pathway forward agreed. The principles common to many leaders of diverse families successful in building consensus include:

- "Communicate, communicate, communicate" about what is going on.
- Use a Family History Map to identify the patterns of behavior to carry forward and those to leave behind (and even work together on ways to leave them behind).
- Identify the areas of disagreement and discuss them ("We don't seem to want the same things," "We don't feel the same way about risk-taking," etc.).
- Use affinity groups (in a large and multi-generational family) to form committees around topics of common interest.
- Create educational forums to increase awareness and understanding (outside experts are helpful here).
- Identify what challenges the family the most—identify the risks the family is facing and use risk mapping to set appropriate priorities on investment and action.
- Use scenario planning to envision the future and identify the risks in each potential outcome.
- Use outside facilitators who have experience with other families to help isolate and understand the problem areas that most need to be addressed.

DIFFERENCES BETWEEN FAMILY LEADERSHIP AND CORPORATE LEADERSHIP

The uniquely human nature of the family as a unit, based more on a shared history, compact of family trust, and cultural tradition than on purely rational economic behavior, is what sets it apart from the corporate and publicly listed business world.

Decisions and actions are often taken in the family with personal issues and interests at the fore, rather than selecting the outcomes that short-term cost and benefit analyses or pure business logic might dictate. In addition, the nature of the family's system of consent and consensus means that solutions cannot be dictated; the views and interests of family members need to be identified and discussed before a common pathway forward can be defined and pursued.

Many business models are not applicable to the core issues faced by most wealthy families. In most cases, it is the differences found within a family, rather than its more obvious similarities, which may negate the applicability of pure economic rationality and mandate the consideration of a broader set of issues, and the use of a more collaborative process.

In family situations where there is a strong sense of legacy and shared ownership of assets, there is an instinctive loyalty to the family and to the legacy shared by each member of the family. Families who grow up together have a much more homogeneous culture than any corporation can ever create. There is often a deep-seated sense of responsibility on the part of most family members to do what is in the best interests of the larger family, pursuing the "greater good for the group," rather than focusing on maximizing shareholder return or individual glory.

FAMILY DEMOCRACY VERSUS MERITOCRACY

A strong corporate culture is built on a meritocracy, based on proven performance, and supported by business experience gained on the job. In a family enterprise, owners view themselves as peers, regardless of their background, capability, and experience. Ability, experience, and technical qualifications are not always the key factors that enter into

Offshore and Over His Head

Following a stellar career in a large, public company in Europe, a CEO was hired into a smaller, but still extensive, family-owned conglomerate operated by an established Continental family.

The family had made the choice of CEO based upon a nonspecific sense of "need" and "fit," and had done little to define the roles and responsibilities of the CEO, or prepare family members for his pending participation in the various activities and governing bodies of the enterprise.

The decision to hire this particular individual was initially seen to be a positive step for the family. The new CEO was a self-made man with little formal education and an aggressive style. The family thought that this approach would help them bring about needed change in a business that had grown complacent under its long-serving, but apparently too-comfortable, professional managers. The tough-minded CEO was hired to make difficult decisions and implement changes, which might be too emotionally difficult for family members with extensive relationships with their family business managers.

From day one, the CEO got off to a rough start. He made quick decisions where the family, who had not prepared the CEO or themselves for the consequences of dramatic change, would have preferred to have held prior consultation and broad debate. His abrasive style created far more problems than solutions within the various family businesses. Family members soon faced a firestorm of complaints about the new hire from managers of their family businesses and from long-standing employees within the family office.

The CEO, sensing he was struggling to meet expectations, floundered even further by making investment decisions in meetings where family members were not present, or even informed in advance of the need for a decision on a proposal. In an effort to prove himself as a tough and effective boss, he made even more questionable and hasty decisions.

The cultural and stylistic gap between the new leader and the family became more pronounced and, in less than a year, the CEO was gone.

The family began a search for a new CEO, entirely different from the "breath of fresh air" who had so visibly failed to adapt his corporate leadership style to the needs of a business firmly embedded in the family culture. The family breathed a sigh of relief as he left, and turned their attention to an internal candidate who proved fully capable of making the needed changes with far less upset than that generated by his immediate predecessor.

the family leadership selection process. All branches may need to be represented at the governing table, sometimes even taking turns in the leader's seat, based on a family culture of sharing leadership between branches. This kind of system, founded on a distinctly noncorporate set of considerations, is based on a principle of equal inheritance passed down by the founders of wealth.

Wanting all children to share equally in the family's financial success, and all succeeding generations to share equally within their branch, is a common goal for parents in many cultures.

DIFFERENCES IN DECISION MAKING

In some cultures, family and family business decision-making power and control is defined by the ownership of assets. The degree of control is determined by the share of aggregate wealth owned. In other cases, total wealth is used as a proxy for voting rights in the family, so branches that have been more successful investing their money become more powerful over time in family decision making.

The most distinctive difference between corporate and family cultures is the pace of the decision-making process. In democratic family systems, one cannot move forward productively until the majority of the family is in agreement about addressing change. In a fully democratic family enterprise, everyone must be allowed to voice an opinion, and good leaders are careful to make sure that all voices are heard. This can be very time consuming for all parties.

One insightful sixth-generation leader cautioned, "We have to wait for the rest of the family to get on board before we can move forward. In a corporate environment, you take action as soon as you have enough information to make an informed decision, but in a family, you have to give the family the time they need to reach consensus."

> "We have to wait for the rest of the family to get on board before we can move forward."

DEALING WITH CONFLICT

One of the other dramatic differences between family cultures and corporate cultures is the reluctance of most families to create or address conflict.

In some corporate settings, the expression of conflicting views can be viewed as a healthy and effective way to test ideas and find the optimal solution for a specific business challenge. Depending upon the culture of the business, these discussions can be "full and frank," surfacing criticisms, dismissing ideas, and resolving differences between views in a robust and, occasionally, contentious manner.

However, in a family setting, where the group shares emotional ties and relationships built from birth, there is an overriding ethos for "getting along" with relatives. In these situations, the avoidance of conflict becomes a guiding family principle. Disagreeing publicly or vocally with a relative can be viewed as disrespectful, disruptive, and emotionally distressing to other relatives. As a result, disagreements are often not voiced in family meetings, but surface in side conversations, or are dealt with in separate, more private, sessions.

All families have disagreements. If left unattended or addressed improperly, these conflicts can spread and create significant longer-term problems.

Helping family groups to address fundamental differences openly, and to view conflict and disagreement as a natural part of the development of the family as it gets larger, almost always requires outside assistance from a trained specialist in family dynamics, conflict resolution, and mediation. Sibling rivalries or subtle conflict between cousins (or groups of cousins) can be a source of great risk to a family's long-term legacy and wellbeing.

Outside parties can often uncover the sources of disagreement that families have difficulty seeing because they are emotionally involved in "keeping the peace" and can voice some concerns that no family member would be willing to name.

CONSENSUS-BUILDING PROCESS

The characteristics of a good family leader are thus distinctively different, in many ways, from a successful corporate leader. While both require facilitation skills and consensus-building talents, the primary role of the family leader is to make sure all voices are heard, and that governing boards are representative of the many constituent groups that develop in a family.

Strong leaders may be appointed primarily to serve as facilitators of the family process. They ask questions of the group and strive to get family members thinking about alternative outcomes and potential risks to the family system without making them fearful. One of the main functions is to move the debate forward in the family, so the process does not get stalled or sidetracked by less significant issues or individual concerns.

INCLUSIVENESS THROUGH LEADERSHIP TEAMS

Large, multi-generational family groups often develop a leadership team structure to facilitate greater participation from the family at large.

As a family group grows in size, it is natural for smaller groups of constituents to place different levels of importance on different issues or to represent polarized views (e.g. proprietors versus stewards).

Typically, in large and well-organized families, subcommittees or working groups are formed around topics of interest, and every family member is asked to find an area where he or she can make a meaningful contribution to the larger family's goals.

It is essential for the designated leader to recruit others to lead the various constituent groups, so that every family member can find some aspect of the family legacy about which he or she feels connected and passionate. Otherwise, family members will gradually drift away from the group, which, over time, will erode the bonds of a common family legacy.

OBTAINING HONEST FEEDBACK

One of the challenges in the development of family leaders is finding the opportunity to gain self-awareness and get the training they need to guide the family process.

Because owners are viewed as equals in most families, and there is equal opportunity for participation by all owners in the family governance process, many family members believe that they have the skills needed to lead the family. In many cases, these same members are not adequately aware of their own strengths and weaknesses, nor have they had the management experience, externally or within the family enterprise, that allows them to see themselves accurately or develop an effective process to guide others.

Ironically, in many families in which members take up leadership positions without requisite experience or training, feedback systems and development opportunities are substantially less developed than in the private sector. Few families have comprehensive and honest feedback systems that can help leaders to identify and address weaknesses in capability or style.

> It is a rare family that has an effective system of performance review and development of its leaders.

Because of lack of experience, an aversion to conflict, the desire to avoid the emotionally difficult experience of a "bad review," and sensitivity to the preservation of family harmony and individual relationships, it is a rare family that has an effective system of performance review and development of its leaders.

Review and participation by outside experts and peers can thus be invaluable in strengthening a family's leadership team, and hence its legacy but are, sadly, more often missing than present in families.

DEFINING AND MEASURING SUCCESS

Family leadership is a great privilege that carries with it great responsibility. It is also a complex task, where a clear definition of success may be difficult to ascertain. In a well-run corporation, all managers operate with a common set of objectives, clearly defined and communicated, and are measured against a predetermined set of performance criteria that define group and individual success.

In a family culture, there is no single set of guidelines. The definition of success can be less clear, or even varied across branches and generations of the family. Examples of family success metrics may include the ability to keep the family together, preserve purchasing power, control risk-taking, or make a meaningful philanthropic impact.

Reaching agreement on the most important metrics and deciding how much family time to invest in reaching these goals is a critical step forward in the family process. Families who do this best have formal discussions about "investing in future generations" and clearly articulate a vision of where they want to be in 50 to 100 years as a family enterprise, and what leadership skills are needed to get them there.

From managing the family's long-term legacy plan to finding creative ways to minimize conflict and mentor future leaders, the family leader must draw on a vast array of quantitative and qualitative skills to guide the family forward and create his or her own legacy.

Successful leaders put the goals of the family before their own, recognize their own limitations, and apply the strengths of the collective family for the good of all. A system to define, measure, and celebrate success can be a valuable component in an overall family leadership model.

Questions for Leaders of Legacy

1. What has made the leaders in your own family successful or unsuccessful?
2. What process does your family use to reach consensus and resolve conflict?
3. What skills will help you master challenges and earn the necessary support of the greater family?
4. Does your leadership style, and that of other family leaders, reflect the best practices of successful family leaders?
5. What will define the success of your family's leaders, and how will that success be measured?

Leadership Skills for the Twenty-First Century

Marty Linsky is a founder and principal of Cambridge Leadership Associates and has been a member of the faculty at the Harvard Kennedy School for over a quarter of a century. His most recent book, coauthored with Ronald Heifetz and Alexander Grashow, is The Practice of Adaptive Leadership.[3]

Is the current turmoil simply a bump in the road or a sea change?

If a bump in the road, we can all hunker down and wait until it is over.

If a sea change, then we have to think about how we are going to be different in the world going forward to continue to be effective in pursuing our deepest purposes in the face of a new reality.

To me, the data are pretty compelling that this is a sea of change:

We are in the midst of **economic uncertainty** unlike any we have seen since the Great Depression.

Environmental challenges threaten sustainability for millions of people and perhaps for the livable planet.

The **technological revolution** has flattened the Earth and turned us former typists and telephoners into technophiles and technophobes, social networkers, and IMers.

The **generational divides** are more palpable than they have been since the 1960s. The baby boomers are retiring, or were until the stock markets crashed, and the millenials bring a different set of values and norms to the workplace and to the family creating conflict, miscommunication, and huge succession issues.

The era of **U.S. hegemony is ending.** Americans who became accustomed to power and privilege are now waiting in the long "Other" line when crossing international borders.

And the world of nations is facing a **new kind of international threat**, from loosely connected factions undefined by national boundaries or twentieth-century modes of warfare.

If we are in a sea change, the new normal will be characterized by three qualities: future uncertainty, inadequate information, and constant change.

How will we have to modify our leadership?

There are six skills that will be essential going forward, partially replacing those with which we are more familiar and comfortable: Adaptation, Experimentation, Collaboration, Orchestration, Imagination, and Self-Preservation.

(continued)

---

3 Marty Linksy, Ronald Heifetz and Alexander Grashow, *The Practice of Adaptive Leadership* (Boston: Harvard Business Press, 2009).

For each of us, the challenge will be to give up some of what we know how to do and do well and learn something new.

1. **Adapt, not just execute.** For decades, organizations have focused on executing well. But in the new normal, the skill of adaptation will be equally important. Adaptation requires making hard decisions about which of the things that you value are essential and which are expendable in order to make progress.

2. **Run experiments, don't just solve problems.** In a world of uncertainty and interconnectedness, problems are not discrete and do not get "solved." Every initiative has unintended consequences. Today's "solution" is just a temporary resting place. We will now need to bring an experimental mindset to problem solving. Thinking that way allows you to run multiple initiatives at the same time to see what works, to monitor closely, make mid-course corrections, and to treat lack of success as a learning opportunity rather than a failure.

3. **Practice interdependence, not just self-reliance.** In a flat world, practicing interdependence, internally and externally, will be an imperative. Internally, that means that the future will have to be invented by people at all levels of the organization, not just by those at the top. And externally, it means that alliances will be the norm, especially unusual ones with former adversaries and factions who previously seemed unconnected to your work.

4. **Orchestrate conflict, not just resolve it.** In a time of uncertainty and rapid change, conflict will typically represent underlying unresolved value issues. Increasingly, it will be the role of bosses and parents to surface those issues ("Let's talk about what kind of an organization, what kind of a family we want to be…"), rather than to resolve them. In a conflict of values, once the senior authority takes a stand, then he or she becomes the issue.

5. **Look for next practices, not just best practices.** In a period of deep uncertainty, the challenge will be to invent the future, rather than have it invented for you. Best practices are always useful, but when you are going where no one has ever been before, what has worked in the past is of limited utility.

6. **Finally, take care of yourself, rather than sacrifice your body for the cause.** Uncertainty breeds anxiety and stress. People who depend on you need you to be at the top of your game. Under these circumstances, taking care of yourself is an imperative, not a self-indulgence. Getting enough sleep, taking regular exercise, and eating right are the easy parts. More difficult sometimes, and certainly more sensitive to talk about, is the importance of getting the love and affection in appropriate places that you need to feel like a whole, and valued, person.

10. PASSING THE TORCH

By all accounts, the wealth passing from one generation to another in coming years will be unprecedented in scale, as will the leadership challenges that accompany these transitions.

Navigating that successful transfer of wealth will be an unfamiliar challenge for many families, who have little or no precedent to guide them on the transfer of financial wealth, business leadership, or family responsibilities.

Some portion of this wealth will be passing into the hands of a third generation, often the critical generation in determining a family's long-term wealth stature, because they are usually the first generation not to have grown up under the direct influence of the founders. This generation also faces the reality of the pattern of riches to rags in three generations.

Wealthy families have good reason to be concerned about the challenge of wealth and family leadership transitions. Research conducted by Roy Williams and Vic Preisser[1] shows that nearly three-quarters of wealth transfers fail to meet the wealth owner's initial objectives.

The reasons for this are many, but the vast majority of problems arise from the family itself—the "soft" issues that are tested at critical transitions—and the preparation of heirs. Only 15 percent of failures are attributed to poor estate and tax planning, or incompetent investment advice. Sixty percent are the result of family disputes and breakdowns. The remaining 25 percent are attributed to a lack of preparation of heirs for the responsibilities of their inheritance.

TRANSFER OF LEADERSHIP AND WEALTH OWNERSHIP
A DUAL CHALLENGE

Although there are separate challenges related to the transfer of ownership of wealth (which affects all heirs in different ways) and the succession in leadership of a family (which affects a smaller set of family members), the two may come together, which raises complex issues to consider and to resolve.

---

1 Roy Williams and Vic Preisser, *Preparing Heirs: Five Steps to a Successful Transition of Family Wealth and Values* (Bandon, OR: Robert D. Reed Publishers, 2003).

> It is essential to have a 20-year plan for an organized transition and a 20-second plan for change over in the case of an unexpected event.

A discussion of some of the issues inherent in preparing family members for inheritance is set out in Chapter 4. The issues dealing with family leadership succession are raised in Chapter 8 but discussed in detail in this chapter alone.

LEADERSHIP SUCCESSION: A CONTINUOUS PROCESS

The high rate of failure in successful wealth transfer reflects the difficulty of succession. Transitions create turbulence, and change always brings with it risk and consequences that may not have been foreseen.

Successful leadership transitions are continuous in nature. Many multi-generational legacy families say that they prepare for significant transitions for decades. They never stop thinking about, planning for, and executing leadership successions. The most forward-thinking families have a current plan for both long-term (planned) succession and contingent (short-term) succession.

A successful leadership succession process addresses all of the relevant issues: economic, fiscal, and human. Key advisors, influencers, spouses, and colleagues should be included and prepared for this important transition long before it arrives.

As one family member put it, it is essential to have a 20-year plan for an organized transition and a 20-second plan for change over in the case of an unexpected event. These plans need to be kept current and updated regularly if needed. Death, resignation, scandal, illness, and accident can all remove an existing or even future family leader.

Preparation of the individuals taking up leadership positions starts even earlier. Ideally, education, training, and communication on family business and philanthropic matters are part of the fabric of the lives of future family leaders from an early age.

When families are not dealing with a crisis transition, they are wise to implement a leadership succession process that involves eight important steps. These steps, when carefully followed, can reduce the risk of an undesirable outcome and enhance the likelihood of a seamless transfer of power.

Thoughtful Planning: One Family's Legacy

The Olives,* a U.S. family that created a modestly successful family business in the 1930s, had the good fortune to send their son to Columbia Business School. When he graduated with an MBA and returned to the family business in the 1950s, his father put him in charge of the company's pension fund. The bright young man delegated the management of the pension fund to his roommate from Columbia, a young investor named Warren Buffett, and over the next two decades, the retirement funds steadily outgrew the profits from the declining business.

When the leadership transferred to the second generation after the sale of the business, the daughter's husband became the next leader for the family. What was unique about the second patriarch in this family was his thoughtfulness about the family's history and their future together. He wanted all of his children to be well prepared and well cared for, and he made the children feel responsible for making that happen for themselves. Their weekly Sunday dinners together were an essential part of their legacy.

The family had a thoughtful discussion about creating a private family office to manage the family's growing investments, and almost a decade went by productively before a tragic accident took the lives of many of the adult members of the family in an airplane crash on a family vacation, leaving two of the five children and their spouses to face an unimagined and uncertain future.

The survivors were thrust into leadership roles in a time of crisis, caring for their own five children as well as their nieces and nephews. Few parents ever anticipate that their children will be faced with such tragedy, thrust upon them so suddenly, and without the strong parental guidance they had depended upon for years.

Planning for specific events such as these is impossible, yet this family's preparation for crisis management, immediate succession, and continuity in extreme circumstances, was able to both lessen the emotional trauma and preserve family cohesion, even in a time of unimaginable loss.

SUCCESSFUL SUCCESSION: THE PROCESS

In putting together a succession plan, following these successive steps can lead a family through a process fraught with complexity: emotional, cultural, and organizational. By implementing the following steps in a steady, careful, and timely manner, leaders can ensure that their own succession plans have the greatest chance of success:

1. **Review the overall legacy plan and specific succession needs.** The first step involves a thorough review of the family legacy plan to ensure that the original thinking about vision, values, goals, and the consolidated aspirations of the family is still reflective of the current family situation and future plans.

2. **Define the future leadership model and identify critical succession issues.**

   Before diving into the succession plan, it is important to review and confirm the family's leadership structure.

   Each succession contains risk, but also carries with it a unique opportunity to broaden the number of family members involved in family leadership, eliminate structural problems and conflicts from the past, make changes to the eco-system, and consider other possible improvements for the family enterprise.

3. **Identify the skills and attributes needed for future leadership.**

   Having a detailed inventory of the skills and attributes required for success in leadership positions is of great benefit for the candidate or candidates, as well as for the greater family.

4. **Define and implement a fair and effective selection process for leaders.**

   For families with a policy of primogeniture, there is no issue as to whom the next family leader shall be. But in other situations, the approach and answer are less clear cut. First- and second-generation families may use an informal process, and may rely more on family discussions on who has the interest and aptitude for leadership than any comprehensive list of criteria or formal process.

   In large, multi-generational families, the selection process is often much broader, and is carefully designed and participative to ensure that it is fair to all parties involved. The process may include working with current leaders to map out the steps and set a timetable for the selection process, forming a committee to spearhead the selection process (selecting the members of this group carefully), or developing a formal application process and having current leaders campaign to attract talented candidates.

It is critical to document the selection criteria for each position and to have a confidential process for candidates to communicate their interest or, in a large family, submit applications by a specified date. It is also valuable for candidates to complete a skills assessment inventory to identify their strengths and "fit" with the rest of the leadership team or governing body.

The governing body should interview candidates in a timely fashion and work to reach consensus on the most qualified candidates for committee consideration or family vote.

5. **Educate future leaders in advance of their service.**

Significant wealth often prevents young owners from experiencing the trials and tribulations that can make a leader successful. This is why many business-owning families require their children to obtain work experience elsewhere in "the real world" before joining the family business.

Leadership training requires opportunities for development in the form of challenges rather than privilege.

Staying the Course

One prominent retail family in Europe insists that all future leaders have at least 10 years of work experience outside the family company. During a recent crisis in company finances, the most likely leader of the next generation offered to cut short his non-family business experience to work on a needed restructuring and refinancing of the family business.

Family elders turned him down.

They told him that they could manage this crisis without his assistance, but wanted to make sure that he was properly prepared for the next one.

---

6. **Develop a system for leadership performance reviews.**

For many reasons, some families avoid the costs, emotional upheaval, and discipline of a formal review process for family leaders and members of leadership teams. This is not good for either the family enterprise or the individuals concerned.

To build an enterprise as well-managed and meritocratic as possible, all members of the leadership team should receive feedback on a regular basis, and design and implement personal development plans to execute the potentially beneficial changes highlighted in the review.

7. **Prepare for and execute a clean transfer of leadership.**

One of the hardest things for a family leader to do, and one of the most important aspects of leadership succession, is to let go.

In royal traditions, succession takes place only at death. The cry "The King is dead, long live the King" has resounded across the ages as marking the transfer of power from one royal generation to another.

In modern wealthy families, transitions may not be so clear. Semiretirement, returning during crises, overruling the decisions of a younger generation, or even just showing up "to see how things are going," and other lingering signs of an inability to let go may muddle handovers, generate resentment, and create confusion about who is truly in control in the minds of those taking over as well as for the rest of the family. If at all possible, there is great value in a clear and clean handover, with all actions by the old team supporting the new leadership order.

8. **Post-succession, support the new leader and begin preparing for the next succession.**

A thoughtful succession plan may include specific objectives and activities with annual checkpoints thereafter for a number of years, leading up to the next leadership succession. Resources and reviews are integrated into the plan—a valuable investment in time and thought for an enduring legacy—to ensure that there is the highest chance of success and the lowest chance of failure possible.

In a family serious about preservation of multi-generational wealth and legacy, leaders begin to think about the next succession early in their own leadership era, in some cases as an explicit part of the first day's work.

Waiting in the Wings

Two wealthy and established families, resident in the same city, faced very different succession issues, with neither experiencing a positive result, but both providing valuable lessons to others.

The Sycamore* family had an intergenerational problem. The second generation still held all of the voting shares in the family business and controlled a world-famous art collection. The third generation, impatient for its inheritance and a turn at family leadership, was chafing under its lack of engagement.

What made this situation particularly unique was that the elder members of the third generation were in their mid- to late 60s, and the family patriarch and brothers were all alive and active in their early 90s.

Although there was constant conversation about retirement, there was no sign of change in the family policy of holding shares and exercising voting rights until death or disability. This forced "younger" members of the family to pursue their own entrepreneurial activities as wealth creators in their own right as best they could, operating with the knowledge that their own activities could be cut short by a need to serve the greater economic interests of the family once they eventually inherited.

Lesson learned: Be clear about retirement dates and succession plans, as procrastination and uncertainty can have a negative impact on individual careers, family unity, and trust between generations.

Across town, the Frangipanis,* another multibillion dollar family that shared many cultural and religious traditions with the Sycamores, opted to hand over shares to their "next generation"—the fourth-generation family members in their 30s and 40s. Although shares in economic participation were transferred while the older generation was still alive, the control over business decisions was not.

The result was chaos, conflict, and a series of situations in which the older generation intervened to change decisions made by their children. The situation became heated, and family relations very publicly broke down. Eventually, a forced sale of a famous family business was engineered at a difficult time for the family as the only solution.

Lesson learned: Make a clean break. Allow following generations to make their own decisions, and occasionally their own mistakes, in pursuit of their own legacy objectives. If not really willing to let go, do not hand over the reins to the next generation.

Still living side by side, these two families' fortunes reflect how difficult it can be to organize a succession of ownership and leadership, no matter which path is taken.

PASSING THE TORCH—WHEN THE TALENT IS NOT THERE

Obviously, not all family leadership successions go as planned.

In some cases, there are disputes and problems surrounding the choice of a leader. In other cases, there is no real leadership talent capable of fulfilling the job requirements, even if willing candidates present themselves for consideration.

Acknowledging that a family does not have anyone in a generation capable of leading the family successfully is not an easy conclusion to draw. However, it may be necessary to reach this conclusion and act accordingly to protect both fortune and legacy.

Once it is determined that there are no viable candidates, a number of options need to be considered and decisions made. Each carries with it different costs, risks, and impact on individual roles and family legacy. These options may include:

- Skipping a generation and selecting a leader from the next generation.

- Selling a family business to reduce job complexity while retaining wealth.

- Building a model of joint leadership, sharing power for decisions between the selected family representative or representatives and an outside executive or team of professionals.

- Bringing in an outside chairman or CEO as co-leader to shepherd the family through to the next generation.

- Selecting a group of family leaders, perhaps from representative generations or branches, to act as an Office of the Chairman under the guidance of a single outsider or family member.

- Selecting from the pool of in-laws or other related groups of candidates.

- Dividing leadership roles, if individual members are capable, in each of the key areas of the enterprise—business matters, family matters, philanthropy, and financial management.

Some of these options can be, and have been, successfully pursued in combination or in succession.

Skipping Generations

Although generation skipping in a wealthy family is usually related to asset ownership to manage inheritance taxes or estate duties, the same technique may be employed to avoid the results of unsuccessful family leadership.

One family from the southern hemisphere, lacking any candidate for leadership of the family enterprise in the third generation, selected a very young member from the fourth generation to succeed his grandfather as company chairman of a large manufacturing business. Although only in his 20s, the young man proved that he possessed exceptionally good business judgment, was commercially astute, and had a depth of wisdom about life and people beyond his years.

To everyone's surprise, his highly successful grandfather was soon deferring to his grandson, who, within a few years, had put the family business on firmer footing and looked set to build a second great fortune on the foundations of a 100-year-old commercial enterprise.

The unusual, and somewhat controversial, choice to skip a generation in selecting a leader for the family's biggest asset was eventually applauded by all members of the increasingly wealthy family.

PASSING THE TORCH—WHEN THE INTEREST IS NOT THERE

An even greater challenge arises when there is sufficient capability, but insufficient interest on the part of potential family leaders.

Indifference or resistance to a leadership role can come from issues related to location, career interest, nuclear family issues, lack of confidence, fear of conflict, or even aversion to a life focused, at least in part, on the management and investment of substantial financial wealth.

The only way to resolve this problem is to gain an understanding of the reasons for resistance and work to overcome them if possible and if desired. Potential options for consideration include: finding a way to engage and motivate capable leaders to take on the jobs envisioned; addressing the leadership structure (e.g. shorter terms, joint responsibilities, separate responsibilities); or providing specific personal accommodations for leaders to adapt to conflicting demands (e.g. travel limitations for those with a young family).

DELEGATING LEADERSHIP TO OUTSIDERS

Although not the norm, there are examples of outsiders coming in to bridge the gap between generations where a family solution, even if desired, is not available.

In one U.S. family, a highly accomplished executive was brought in to shepherd the family through a fractious third generation. In another family, an external chairperson was hired to provide leadership and cast deciding votes, equalizing representation between the family branches (some of whom did not have adequate representation) with an overall mandate to uphold the "best interests of the family" at all times.

Preparing for a successful transition of family leadership is complex and never ending. Documenting a fair and consistent leadership selection process, continually evaluating the enterprise structures and operations, providing the next generation with opportunities to gather the experience they will need to lead the family, and ensuring that a clear handover takes place are all wise, and necessary, investments in the future of any family.

Questions for Leaders of Legacy

1. How has your family identified and prepared past leaders, and what lessons were learned in the process?
2. Do you have a 20-year and a 20-second succession plan?
3. Do you have a fair and effective leadership selection process for future leaders?
4. Who in the next generation is prepared to lead your family enterprise, and who is best suited to play other leadership roles?
5. What more can you do to ensure a smooth transition of wealth, power, and leadership when the time comes?

Leadership Succession: Are We In Good Hands?

Ivan Lansberg, Ph.D., is a founding partner of Lansberg, Gersick & Associates, LLC and the author of Succeeding Generations: Realizing the Dream of Families in Business *and numerous articles on leadership. His article "The Tests of a Prince"[2] provides more detail on the issues he addresses below:*

The transition of family leadership from one generation to the next is never a smooth road. Family members are often confused about their roles and apprehensive about where a new leader might take them. It's no surprise then that many families avoid facing the challenge of transition until it is inevitable.

Every stakeholder in the family enterprise wants to know how their lives will be affected by the new leader's ability to cut it. Anyone in a position of leadership will be tested. They cannot hold their position unless they can answer the stakeholders' questions.

To determine whether or not to grant authority to leaders, stakeholders subject them to a series of trials or iterative tests. This testing falls into three basic categories: institutional, situational, and instrumental.

Institutional testing is based on the credentials the leader brings to his or her position. Where did the person go to school? How did he or she do there? What kind of positions did he or she hold outside the family? The more institutional testing that has taken place before the person arrives in the leadership role, the easier the process will be for the leader.

Good leaders embrace institutional testing in the following ways:

- They view tests as opportunities to prove their mettle early.
- They proactively engage in shaping institutional tests to play on their strengths. They prepare themselves. They strengthen their resumes. They take on tough-but-doable assignments that fit their skills.
- They pay attention to followers' concerns and manage the attribution process. They behave in ways counter to nepotistic stereotypes. They act with humility, pay dues, seek good education and tough assignments. They welcome institutional accountability such as executive assessments.

(continued)

---

2 Ivan Lansberg, "The Tests of a Prince," *Harvard Business Review*, September 2007, 92–101; Lansberg, *Succeeding Generations: Realizing the Dream of Families in Business* (Boston: Harvard Business School Press, 1999).

Situational or circumstantial tests measure a leader's response to something that occurs during the course of leadership. For instance, many would say that the terrorist attack on September 11, 2001, was the ultimate situational test for former U.S. president, George W. Bush, and that his response cemented his authority. In a family enterprise, a leader might be tested when a branch of the family wants to cash out, a family member doesn't pay dues, or market downturns jeopardize a family fortune. The keys to successfully passing situational tests include:

- Keeping the followers' eyes on the context, rather than on the leader.
- Choosing experienced advisors with complementary skills and leveraging their wisdom.
- Reframing "tests" as a collective challenge.
- Being available to the group in a non-hierarchical way.
- Taking the blame but sharing the glory.

Instrumental tests are tests that leaders put on themselves. The leader stands before the stakeholders and says he or she will meet certain objectives. The stakeholders then evaluate the leader based on his or her performance. The leader puts instrumental tests in place by:

- Picking announced goals carefully and making sure they are challenging but deliverable.
- Knowing when to seek information and involvement from followers to increase performance.
- Calling attention to circumstantial factors in order to "hedge" results.

New leaders are often surprised by iterative testing and shy away from it. They take it personally. However, effective leaders embrace iterative testing and manage the process. An essential component of leadership is appreciating tests as an opportunity to convey what you have to offer.

It is important to understand the distinction between power and authority. Power is a person's capacity to influence someone else. Often, family members have power because of their last name. But true authority is earned by leaders and granted by the followers in the organization. A terrorist has a lot of power, but no authority. Followers grant authority to someone who gets them to believe they are a good leader.

William Shakespeare's *Henry V* illustrates how new leaders are challenged. The young heir to the throne is tested by traitors inside his own camp. Later he inspires his troops by showing that he understands their situation. And at the end of the play, his soldiers follow him into battle, although he has given them the opportunity to leave.

(continued)

Renaissance political philosopher Nicolo Machiavelli wisely observed, "Leaders who come to power easily have a hard time holding it." These leaders face the toughest tests. The converse is also true. Leaders who are tested before they come to power are already known by their constituents and will have a much easier time holding true authority. A leader anointed by virtue of only a last name can expect to have more trouble leading than one who has already paid some dues in the organization.

How the leader responds to these situations is a wonderful way to find out whether the leader can deliver on his or her promise.

11. CROSSING GENERATIONAL BRIDGES

For many complex reasons, it is difficult for family members to predict how the dynamics in the family will shift when the elder generation relinquishes control and a new generation emerges from under the guidance and control of the old.

There is a unique set of challenges that faces each generation of the family as it comes into power, but there is a striking consistency, even across different cultures, when family members from the same generation talk about what challenges them the most.

The manner in which families address these common challenges is different in each culture, and the strategies that work in one family might not be successful in other families, even in the same culture. But it is helpful to understand the shared sources of challenge, predictable patterns of behavior, and the common set of issues that seem to be present for each generation.

With more than one inheritor in each generation, the objectives and primary risks are shown in very summary form, in Table 11.1.

Some founders are exceptional in their thoughtful planning for future generations, organizing financial structures to support each of their children and to provide options and opportunities for collaboration without binding the children together legally or financially. Children are allowed to develop their own definition of shared assets, their own views about the future and what they want to do together as siblings, ranging from family dinners to family foundations to family offices.

Their degree of family cohesion and their desire for family collaboration determines the smoothness of future generational transitions.

FIRST-GENERATION CHALLENGES

Many creators of great wealth are often brilliant individuals whose vision and drive on the factory floor, in the laboratory, or in the boardroom does not make them necessarily perceptive about, or even interested in, their own family's dynamics.

Table 11.1: Generational Differences

Family Roles	Motivators	Greatest Challenges
First generation *Originates the dream* *Creates a vision*	• Entrepreneurship • Individuality • Control • Risk-taking	• Letting go of operational control • Passing leadership to the next generation • Letting children struggle • Designing a philanthropic mission • Creating a legacy • Educating the next generation
Second generation *Initiates the dynasty* *Develops a frame-* *work for family* *governance*	• Equality • Simplicity • Independence • Risk avoidance • Conflict avoidance • Fear of failure	• Living in the shadow of a successful entrepreneur • Finding a proper role or being an active owner • Sharing ownership and/or control with siblings • Developing a philanthropic vision with siblings • Inheriting or living with financial complexity • Simplifying operating structures • Parenting privileged children
Third generation *Refines* *representative* *governance* *Accommodates* *diversity among* *cousins*	• Ownership control • Diversity • Flexibility • Consensus • Family legacy	• Living up to the family legacy • Collaborating with cousins over distances • Developing a new vision for staying together • Balancing nuclear family and legacy family • Finding meaning in a privileged life • Developing seventh-generation thinking

Most busy business owners do not think enough about the legacy they are leaving for their own children and grandchildren, or about the potential philanthropic legacy they might develop with their grandchildren.

They are often more focused on building a business legacy than a family legacy, and that message is often clear to the children who do not get the attention they need from one or both parents.

The founder's generation often has trouble letting go of operating control and offering real leadership opportunities to the next generation. They worry about the passive nature of the second generation and their potentially polarized views on risk-taking.

The founders want their children to share equally in the good fortune of the family and, as a result, they expect the children to get along harmoniously and to share equally in the financial rewards.

Siblings, who may have had trouble sharing toys and time together as children, are asked as adults to share ownership of assets, to share control of decisions, and to look out for each other's interests. Having grown up with very different aspirations and abilities, it is often difficult for them to develop a common view of what is in the best interest of the family.

Many family offices are formed to provide the equality and equilibrium that parents want for their children and to manage the financial realities of shared wealth.

Unexpected Outcome

The thoughtful patriarch of the Spruce* family liked to control the outcome of things. He had done so successfully in his 40 years in private equity ventures, and spent another 20 years running his own family office for the benefit of his wife and two daughters. Family members met with him every quarter to hear about what was going on with their investments, but they really had no voice in making investment decisions and no ability to access the money that was held in their names.

In his 70s, this founder was smart enough to ask, at last, his daughters how they felt about their financial future. Their initial response was that they did not want to be in charge of a family office, and they preferred to have professional advisors to make decisions. When the transition process began, however, they surprised themselves.

After all the years of watching their commanding father drive the process, more of his thinking had seeped into their psyche than they realized.

They had a tough time delegating the decision-making to others after all, and had to find a wealth advisor who would listen to their views and opinions. Through all those years of sitting at the table, the training had rubbed off on them, and they were more comfortable asking tough questions than they ever expected.

It wasn't the legacy they expected, but one of which their father would have been the most proud.

SECOND-GENERATION CHALLENGES

The challenges for the second generation most often arise from living in the shadow of successful and busy business founders, managers, and owners.

Each of the siblings struggles to find a proper role in the family and the community (successor, entrepreneur, mediator, community leader, spouse, parent, aunt, uncle, etc.). They may have to learn how to share ownership and control with siblings or to share leadership of a family fortune they did not create, and that they may neither own nor control.

The siblings' generation often says, "None of this feels like my money," even though they may have inherited complex financial structures set up for tax planning reasons to optimize their own after-tax wealth. They also wrestle with their own challenges of parenting privileged children, especially when grandparents want to see their grandchildren avoid the struggles they had to face.

When the founders' generation passes on, siblings often have one of two very different reactions—feelings of trepidation about finally being in charge, or eagerness to take over responsibility for their own affairs. For many sibling groups, there is also a desire to change the ground rules on how decisions are made, either granting more independence to individuals, or incorporating more collaboration and injecting new voices into the process.

After some sparring and debate, an agreed decision-making process usually evolves, typically involving some form of democratic process where each sibling or each household has a vote, and every vote counts equally.

Sibling challenges are magnified when their personal goals are not aligned with those of the other siblings, or the siblings are not able to talk comfortably about their different views. It is the exception, rather than the rule, that second-generation owners are comfortable sharing their influence and their assets with each other, so it is not unusual for the dialogue about the future together to be a difficult conversation.

In families that make it successfully through the sibling stage of development, the differences are not ignored, but remain at the center of the family discussion until a workable solution is formed. Siblings who stay together learn the importance of discussing thoughtfully their shared goals as owners, as distinguished from their personal goals, and respecting the differences between the two.

Many wealth inheritors feel bound by the family legacy to support the founder's vision, since they did not create the wealth themselves and were lucky enough to be born into a family with business successes that generated exceptional financial resources. James Hughes cautions owners not to spend their lives living the founder's dream,[1] since this encases the younger owners in someone else's reality, and produces feelings of entrapment and potential conflict among family members.

The Essential Question

A representative of the Spanish Arbora* family spoke eloquently to a group of his peers about the most important meeting he has each year with his employers, three brothers who own a business together. In this forum, only one topic is on the agenda—an intense discussion about whether there are still compelling reasons to stay in business together.

The advisor believes that this annual session solidifies in their minds (and hearts) the important reasons they are choosing to continue to share ownership and control of family assets.

Second-generation owners, who may not have mentors or role models training them about business matters, do not often gain the experience they need to manage a labyrinth of complex legal structures. Their lack of training often results in their taking a more passive approach to ownership.

It is common to hear them say, "I am not equipped to manage these complex structures and don't want my life to be consumed by these endless financial details."

Some perceptive owners in the second generation realize that their lack of experience handicaps them severely in business dealings, and they tend to simplify the tasks or unravel the complexities created by their parents, and move on with their lives.

---

1 James Hughes Jr., *Family Wealth—Keeping it in the Family: How Family Members and Their Advisors Preserve Human, Intellectual and Financial Assets for Generations* (New York: Bloomberg Press, 2004).

THIRD-GENERATION CHALLENGES

One of the most difficult transitions is the handover from second-generation siblings to the third-generation cousins' group. Members of the third generation, typically five to 15 cousins spanning an age gap of 10 to 20 years, often struggle to build their own definition of the family legacy. They have to collaborate with cousins across much greater distances, to launch their own successful careers, and to balance their new nuclear family with the larger legacy family.

They often struggle to find meaning in the midst of a privileged life and to select the path that best suits their own interests, not the views of the rest of the family. Some family members, preferring to remain anonymous, feel the need to leave the town they grew up in if it is linked too closely to a family business or family history.

Because cousins do not grow up in the same household together and do not share close ties or feel the effects of intense sibling rivalries, their dynamics for working together as a team may be very different from that of their parents' generation.

If the sibling group in the second generation was not close, the cousins may have an easier time than their aunts and uncles did identifying common goals and working productively together. They can often appreciate the family history and forget the childhood grievances that some siblings never overcome.

If the siblings were polarized in their views about what was best for the family, the cousins may inherit these differences, resulting in a generation of distrust and the carrying of branch biases into their own dealings with each other.

It is essential for cousins to establish a communication process early in their relationship together that allows each person to be heard. Differences need to be discussed and respected to ensure that the differences become assets of the family rather than long-term liabilities.

"Everyone needs to buy in to the notion that we are better together than apart."
Third-generation family member

Cousins, who learn from their parents how to distinguish between individual goals and group goals, and to respect the value of both, are better able to build a solid foundation for future generations.

FOURTH-GENERATION CHALLENGES

Members of the fourth-generation group often suffer from what is called "the law of large numbers" of cousins. If the family enterprise is still intact at the fourth generation (which is quite rare), there are probably 30 to 45 cousins in that generation. Family gatherings have more than 100 participants when spouses and children are included, and decision-making can take a very long time indeed if the family adheres to a fully democratic model.

Fourth-generation owners are defined by their differences in attitudes and situations—different levels of wealth by branch, different views about being wealthy, varying views on being stewards versus proprietors of wealth, risk-taking attitudes, engagement, views on how leaders should be picked, and how decisions should be made.

It is usually up to the fourth-generation cousins group to make important decisions about continuing to stay together; the cousins must determine whether there is still common benefit from staying together, since none of them knew the founders of the legacy and much will have changed since the patriarchs died.

Often they are committed to using the purchasing power of the combined family assets or to working together on an inherited philanthropic legacy. They may see the need to foster entrepreneurship and risk-taking skills in their own children because they can see the day when the size of the family will outgrow the size of the wealth, and the financial safety net that has protected the family for generations will be gone.

For fourth-generation cousins who have children of their own, they need to identify what is important enough in the larger family to preserve for their own children. The challenge they face is whether there is enough agreement across such a diverse base of family members to hold them together as a family enterprise beyond social ties and family stories.

A common question that fourth-generation cousins often discuss together is: "What do we want to be here for our children when they are the age we are now, and how can we afford to provide for them as we were provided for by our parents' generation?"

By the time the fourth generation comes into leadership, the family legacy has been in existence for more than 100 years. This group of cousins is typically the first generation to consider whether they want the family to stay together for another 100 years, and what it might take for the legacy to survive across four more generations. Families who reflect thoughtfully on this question begin to have conversations about developing an entre-preneurial spirit that can sustain the family culture and legacy into the future.

GENERATIONAL BRIDGES

In addition to generational differences, it is important for finan-cial families to recognize their stage in the family's evolution or, put another way, to identify the generational bridge upon which they are traveling. Each generation is a participant in an overlapping set of generational bridges that span the history of the family and provide continuity for the family over time.

For example, the first generation founders often think about "the future of the family" in terms of their children and grand-children. The second generation inherits from strong founders, and then builds a bridge that spans from the second generation to their grandchildren in the fourth generation—a span of at least 100 years (looking back at their parents and forward to their grandchildren).

For each generation, as time passes, their place on the bridge changes; initially at the foot of the bridge as an adolescent, moving to the middle of the bridge in midlife during the leadership phase, and then to the end of the bridge as active engagement in the family enterprise comes to a close. Being able to "see" the section of bridge that each generation stands on and understand one's own current and future place on the bridge, is the key to understanding the tran-sitions and tasks that await.

Siblings' or cousins' ability to share ownership and stay "family" in spite of disagreements is essential for the future of any family enter-prise. Their ability to find a way to make decisions together, through trial and error, is critical for the passing of legacy and wealth from the first to the third generation.

Most importantly for the family, the second-generation siblings serve as the first role models for group decision making in the family. The third-generation cous-ins are watching eagerly from the sidelines for clues to their own roles in the family enterprise system and the financial busi-nesses they may inherit.

> The second-generation siblings serve as the first role models for group decision making in the family.

At some point in their development, the members of each generation become aware that they are the bridge that links the family legacy to all future generations.

In the first- to third-generational stage, the second generation is learning about sharing leadership and control among siblings, and worrying about how to raise responsible children who do not have an attitude of entitlement. As the founders step back or pass away, the second generation's role is to start another span of the bridge—the second- to fourth-generational stage, in which their job is to get the third generation ready to guide the legacy and provide the leadership for the fourth generation.

> Members of each generation become aware that they are the bridge that links the family legacy to all future generations.

When families struggle to work through a leadership transition, it is often because family members are not asking the same questions, even if they are standing on the same span of a generational bridge. For example, one group of cousins may be asking, "What's in this for me?", while another group of cousins from the same generation may be focusing on "How will this impact my grandchildren?"

These cousins are not focusing on the same issues, and are not likely to see eye to eye about the critical risks facing the family, or share a vision for the family's future together.

The third-to-fifth generational stage is perhaps the most challenging of all phases because the family must transition from a small family of 15–20 people to a family community with more than 200 participants (including spouses).

This evolution from the dining table to the conference center is an extraordinary transformation, requiring great wisdom and foresight about where the family is headed, and how to keep the clan together around important areas of shared interest.

INEVITABLE CONFLICTS

In multi-generational families, conflict often arises when the siblings or cousins cannot reach agreement about their priorities and do not share a view for the future.

If there is shared ownership of property, the difficult questions to consider before disputes arise are, "What are we going to do when

Preparing the Next Generation to Cross the Bridge

In a successful European family that recently sold their brand-name operating business, the fourth-generation owners do not plan to start another venture but have put their energies behind opening a family-branded MFO to manage their own assets, as well as those of other families.

The fourth generation sees that a dramatic shift has occurred in their family's culture of centralized control of assets, and they are starting a new span of the family bridge which will represent the fourth- to sixth-generation stage of their history.

One of the investments they have made in the business involves a program to educate young owners of the family, so that they understand business opportunities and risks well enough to make good financial decisions for themselves as fifth-generation owners. The family legacy at this stage for the family has much more to do with preserving an impressive family history than with preserving financial capital, so the focus for the training program is on venture investing and supporting young entrepreneurs (the millennial generation) in the family who can create the family's next wave of wealth.

At the very least, the fourth generation argues, they will have given all of the cousins a springboard for their careers by helping them with skills assessment and job placement activities.

we don't agree on what is best for the family's shared interests? How are we going to resolve our differences of opinion?"

According to Kenneth Kaye, author of *The Dynamics of Family Business*, this may be the time when intervention and guidance by an expert advisor is most desirable.[2]

One of the roles of a conflict resolution advisor is to help family members in this situation to set aside the immediate issues and go to the root of the problem. In many cases, an advisor can help family members define the scope of their trust in one another because this is often the source of conflict.

---

2 Kenneth Kaye, *The Dynamics of Family Business: Building Trust and Resolving Conflict* (Bloomington, IN: iUniverse, 2005).

Family members need to ask themselves, "What responsibilities and obligations am I entrusting to the leaders of the family?" and "What is expected of me in return?"

Family members may feel distrustful of each other because their expectations lack definition. It is not unusual for an individual to find another family member or family leader untrustworthy because of a prior experience with that person. However, the real issue may not be about the person, but about the scope of the trust placed in that person and the

> Family members may feel distrustful of each other because their expectations lack definition.

resulting outcome. Negative judgments may be based on unclear expectations of family behavior in a defined situation. Lack of trust is a symptom or result of some prior failure of one or both parties to provide what was expected by the other, not necessarily an ethical or performance shortfall.

To resolve these situations, it may be helpful to involve an objective third party (mediator or therapist) to get to the heart of what was expected, but not provided, from each party's perspective.

TRUST AS A KEY ELEMENT OF AN ENDURING LEGACY

Distrust is not a "dysfunction" in the family enterprise. For individuals, it is the way they protect themselves from real dangers, and a sign of learning from experiences good and bad. For families, trust and distrust operate both productively and in a destructive manner if historic issues are not fully understood and managed.

Because trust is inherently uncertain, the healthy family will continually assess and adjust the trust extended by every individual to every other member of the family.

> "Trust is always uncertain: the fact that one trusts another does not mean he is sure the other will perform. It means he will take the risk of that performance, monitor it, and adjust future trust based on the outcome."
>
> Kenneth Kaye[3]

---

3 Kenneth Kaye, "Trust in the Family Enterprise," 2010 www.kaye.com/fambz/Trust2.pdf.

People in every culture in the world have a strong drive to acquire trusting and trusted relationships. Understanding and communicating one's expectations for others in the family may help to foster a greater sense of trust, itself a key attribute in a family legacy based upon bonding, shared effort, and working together over time for a better future.

There is no doubt that trusting family relationships make crossing the generational bridges easier for all. However, each generation faces its own unique challenges.

Whether it is the second generation's need to define its own vision or the fifth generation's decision to stay connected, having an understanding of these challenges and a recognition of their place on the bridge allows each to lay a better foundation for those who follow.

Questions for Leaders of Legacy

1. How well has your family addressed past generational transfers of wealth and leadership?
2. What lessons can be learned from your and other families' transitions, and how can you apply them to your own situation?
3. Does your generation (and your family leaders) share a common vision of the transitions and challenges ahead?
4. What can you do now to minimize the challenges faced by the next generation?
5. What more can you do to address future challenges and foster a sustaining legacy of trust among family members?

The Important Role of the Matriarch

No work about family leadership would be complete without some commentary on the role of women in general and the matriarch in particular.

In traditional families, at the center of a successful enterprise, or supporting a busy business owner, there is often a powerful female force that holds the family together. While the business owners are focused on building a successful business, the matriarch frequently is the source of the emotional foundation of a legacy that endures for the family.

The personality profiles of these imposing matriarchs are varied among families, but the important role they play in shaping the family is always significant. The matriarch passes on values, beliefs, and attitudes that shape the next two generations in the family, and often serves as the "glue" that holds the growing clan together. She establishes the manners, the morals, and the sense of fair play that define the relationships between siblings, and often serves as the peacemaker and peacekeeper regarding disputes in the family.

There are also many examples in the twentieth century of surviving spouses who took over complex family businesses when their husbands passed away suddenly, often serving as an interim leader for the family until a son or daughter could gain enough experience to take over. This has proven true around the world and over time, with the Krupps in Germany, the Schuellers in France, the Tans in Singapore, and the Bustani family in Lebanon who have all benefited from strong and capable female leadership. In the United States, Katherine Graham wrote in her autobiography about the challenges of being thrust into this role as owner of the *Washington Post*.[4]

Death of the matriarch

Upon the death of a strong matriarch, a great void is felt in the family, and there is uncertainty about who will fill the role previously held by the nurturing or controlling mother figure. Often the sisters in the second generation choose to share that role, instinctively understanding that no one of them would ever be accepted as a full replacement for the matriarch in the family.

There is often posturing and power shifting when the matriarch is gone, with many of the siblings wanting to recast their role in the family system

(continued)

---

4 Katharine Graham, *Personal History* (New York: Vintage, 1998).

and wanting to realign their interests as priorities in the family inevitably shift during this stage. When the matriarch is no longer there to sit at her place at the dining table with the children to keep peace and settle disputes, it is often time for a more formal governance process to fill the role of the peacekeeper with an orderly and equitable decision-making process.

Uncommon women

Most of the great matriarchs were not described as such during their lifetimes, and they often present themselves to the outside world as gracious and unassuming women. But they provide a subtle stability to support the official leaders and have an ability to bring out the best in the rest of the family.

One legendary grandmother in Texas was exceptional in her efforts to formalize the process of staying together as a family, perhaps because she and her siblings had not been able to accomplish that goal in their own time.

She brought the whole family together every year to celebrate the family history, to learn about the family businesses, and to enjoy each other as people. This woman had lost brothers and a sister, had buried husbands and children in her lifetime, and yet she still found enjoyment in the building of future leaders. She took time to meet monthly with her children and grandchildren to teach them about giving back to the community and rewards they could enjoy from their philanthropic activities.

A well-known family in an industrial business also spoke about the important role of the matriarch in their family's history. Their matriarch was described as "gracious but tenacious" by all who knew her. She would bring everyone in the family together for Sunday dinners and holidays at the family estate, and she would lead the storytelling about the family's history. Her job was to orchestrate the family photographs on the lawn, and she made a point of being inclusive and welcoming toward all the spouses as the family grew.

At her death, there was clear agreement among her descendents that no single individual could fill her shoes, so the siblings thoughtfully split up the duties of chief hostess, chief historian, and chief story teller.

Their consideration and caring in trying to replicate the different sources of the matriarch's contributions stand as a great testament to her contribution to the lives of her descendants, and will make a contribution to the family legacy which extends forward across many generations.

PART III

THE MANAGEMENT OF RISK AND CHANGE

12. MANAGING RISKS TO WEALTH AND WELLBEING

Wealth owners always have a greater appreciation for the impact risk can have on their lives after a major crisis, disaster, or loss of wealth. Owners may have been exposed recently to financial outcomes they never expected, and are paying much more attention to the unintended consequences of the plans they put in place. Owners who pass wealth successfully to future generations are paying attention to the process they must develop to manage opportunities and mitigate risks.

Unlike a wealthy individual who can make independent decisions, wealthy families often own assets collectively, adding more complexity to the ownership and more time to the decision-making process. Their future is a shared future, and any risks that threaten their ability to interact and communicate effectively with one another can affect the future of all of their relatives.

WHAT KEEPS YOU UP AT NIGHT?

Risk, as a concept, varies enormously between families. Even the definition of risk is unique to each family member and shaped by each family's history. For some owners the ultimate risk is the loss of family reputation, while for others it may be the loss of capital or the loss of financial security.

> "The first step in the risk management process is to acknowledge the reality of risk. Denial is a common tactic that substitutes deliberate ignorance for thoughtful planning."
>
> Charles Tremper [1]

Taking time to reach a common understanding of where the family is vulnerable, and what risks need to be addressed, is important for every family and each family leader. Yet even before setting out to define and manage risk, families must agree on its importance and place in their collective lives.

---

1 Charles Tremper, "Securing the Future: Managing Threats and Opportunities Through Effective Risk Planning," Family Office Exchange White Paper, 2009, 9.

Once the family starts a conversation about risk-taking, critical questions will surface that have no easy answers. What are the levels of risk that are tolerable across the family? What will the family do about the risks that are not tolerable? How does the family reconcile differences of opinion about appropriate levels of risk-taking?

Figure 12.1 is a simple framework which identifies some of the areas of risk faced by most family enterprises.[2]

Figure 12.1: Shared Family Risks

Business Ownership and Control

- Family control
- Family leadership of business
- Family dynamics
- Alignment of interests
- Business strategy
- Business governance
- Business operations

Wealth Preservation and Enhancement

- Investment goals and objectives
- Asset diversification
- Manager selection
- Investment performance
- Public equity concentration
- Private equity control
- Private equity distressed situations

Shared Risk

Financial Reporting and Compliance

- Legal exposure
- Fiduciary roles and responsibilities
- Wealth transfer protection
- Physical asset protection
- Financial leverage
- Financial oversight
- Financial reporting/compliance
- Family office oversight

Family Unity and Governance

- Family legacy
- Philanthropic legacy
- Family governance and decision making
- Family relationships
- Family reputation and public image
- Personal security and privacy
- Personal health and wellness
- Personal ownership responsibilities

Business Ownership and Control For families who still own and operate a family business, retaining that control and ensuring the continued success of the family business is usually the paramount risk. Issues related to succession planning, capital financing, dividend funding, and effective management of the business are critical and can consume a great deal of the owners' time and energy.

Wealth Preservation and Enhancement The inherent challenge of wealth preservation is the understanding that the number of wealth

---

2 Family Office Exchange, "Recasting the Central Role of the Family Office as Risk Manager," Family Office Exchange White Paper 2006, 5.

owners typically grows faster than the buying power of the assets. In many families, the number of owners grows exponentially, while wealth grows arithmetically. Preserving and enhancing financial wealth to keep pace with the growth of a large and growing family requires long-term forward planning (three generations can now span almost 100 years), effective investment management, thoughtful fiscal planning, and the determination of appropriate distribution policies and disciplines.

Sustaining the purchasing power of the family across generations requires the full commitment of the family and careful execution of an integrated, long-term plan.

Financial Reporting and Compliance Financial security means different things to different people. At a minimum, the goal is typically to ensure that family members can continue to pursue their current lifestyles while preserving the financial wellbeing of future generations. This is only sustainable when calculated risk-taking and diligent risk management are combined with an integrated planning process that incorporates wealth transfer and tax planning, accurate reporting and control, conservative distribution policies, long-term investment planning, and, typically, philanthropic strategies as well.

Family Unity and Governance Family unity and continuity are the result of preserving the uniqueness and positive aspects of the family—its shared history and values, its leadership strengths, and vision for the future. Success requires consistent investment in the governance and organization of the family. It also requires agreed strategies, the education of all wealth owners, and development of a predictable decision-making process. All of these elements are essential to ensure that the family's legacy is preserved.

KNOWN VERSUS UNKNOWN RISKS

The family's ability to address known risks and to prepare for unknown risks (the "unknown unknowns") may strengthen the financial outcomes for the family enterprise more than any other strategy they undertake. Wealth owners make a great leap forward when they recognize that they cannot predict or control what is going to happen in all cases, and that a process that prepares the family to address the uncertainty in the future will serve them best. Table 12.1 categorizes some of the elements of uncertainty facing a family, and shows that some are easier to quantify than others.[3]

Addressing both known and unknown risks in an honest discussion is an important step for the family. Most families are not comfortable with the unknown risks and costs that may result from risk-taking, or with the unintended consequences that their actions may cause.

Table 12.1: Elements of Uncertainty

Risks that are easier to quantify	Risks that are harder to quantify
Family lifecycles	Family dynamics
Business success or failure	Entrepreneurial instincts in family
Spending patterns among owners	members
Tax policies	Interaction of asset classes over time
Market returns	Systemic risk in financial markets and
Inflation	global infrastructure
	Major shifts in government policy

IDENTIFICATION OF RISKS AND OPPORTUNITIES

Just as the true definition of family wealth extends beyond purely financial issues to areas of individual wellbeing, the risks against which a family needs to be protected include those threatening more than just the financial assets of the family.

In 2007 and 2009, FOX surveyed ultra-wealthy families to identify key risks and priorities. Table 12.2 shows the two very different set of results of these surveys.

Table 12.2: Key Risks and Priorities in 2007 and 2009

2007 Priorities and Risks	2009 Priorities and Risks
• Family legacy	• Economy and financial markets
• Family governance and decision making	• Family relationships
• Family relationships	• Financial constraints

---

3 Family Office Exchange, "Securing the Future: Managing Threats and Opportunities Through Effective Risk Planning," Family Office Exchange White Paper, 2009, 13.

This change in priorities demonstrates the fluid nature of risk management, the potential for an external event to shift priorities, and the importance of a disciplined approach at all times. Any one of these risks is enough to destroy family wealth or family unity, with worst-case scenarios taking down both at the same time.

Research clearly shows that families cannot preserve wealth beyond three generations without a systematic process for evaluating and embracing reasonable levels of risk-taking. Calculated risk-taking is an important part of the family enterprise that needs to be embedded in the culture of the family, rather than avoided at all costs. This topic is addressed further in Chapter 16.

Effective risk-taking is the key ingredient that distinguishes families that embrace rather than avoid opportunities to grow and enrich their enterprise.

Embracing Risk

"Why are we so afraid of risk and uncertainty?

Consider that the greatest discoveries of the past five centuries have been stimulated by the willingness of explorers, inventors, politicians and scientists to take chances of great loss in return for even greater potential gain. That, to my mind, is the essence of the human spirit, this quest for the new and unknown. Yes, we are faced by uncertainty whenever we make a decision. The decision itself creates uncertainty as to outcomes. But some of that uncertainty can be measured, thus becoming 'risk,' and through this measurement we position ourselves to make better decisions, pushing human boundaries outward.

The current problem is the prevailing definition of 'risk,' a definition that is creeping into the vernacular. Safety, public policy, and insurance professionals continue to see 'risk' primarily as negative—something to be avoided, reduced, or shifted.

Risk always involves a potential reward, whether real or imagined, tangible or intangible. That's why we make decisions involving risk, our personal measure of the uncertainty. To deny the reward element is to distort any subsequent decision. This, to my mind, is why we must break the icon that 'risk is bad.'

Taking risk is the defining element in human existence. We should relish, not avoid it; balance, not eliminate it."

H. Felix Kloman[4]

THE IMPORTANCE OF RISK PLANNING

Effective risk-planning techniques shape the financial future for every family enterprise. When risk planning is part of the fabric of the family, there is a constant monitoring and management of upside and downside risk.

"It's not about knowing what to do; it's about getting family members to agree to take action—that is the bigger challenge."

Lex Zaharoff, Investment Strategist[5]

Perceptive families recognize the value of risk sensitivity and ideally develop a formal risk management structure as part of their planning process. Just like an emergency medical response team, the system automatically kicks into operation when a crisis occurs. That same system also functions as an anticipatory mechanism for reducing risks before they ripen into catastrophe.

Just as emergency response teams have formal procedures that allow them to make decisions under stress and move forward in the face of rising risk, strategically-minded families need to develop similar systems and establish their own response teams.

These teams outline how decisions are made and establish a chain of command that determines who will make which decisions in a crisis and how these decisions will be made. This allows the team to address the chaos and avoid the confusion that can otherwise take over in times of turmoil.

The decision-making process needs to be well-constructed in approach and dependable in operation. These pre-thought systems can increase the likelihood that critical decisions made *in extremis* are more likely to enhance legacies rather than end them.

---

4 H. Felix Kloman, *Mumpsimus Revisited: Essays on Risk Management* (Bloomington, IN: Xlibris Corporation, 2005), 41–59.

5 Lex Zaharoff, comment made at FOX Thought Leaders Round Table, Chicago, June 2009.

RISK AND OPPORTUNITY

Risk and opportunity often can be found in the same events at the same time, albeit from very different perspectives. Successful leadership requires both to be viewed and managed together, raising issues of investment, action, and potential outcomes. The two Chinese characters that make up the concept of crisis are instructive—one (*wei*) indicating risk or danger and the other (*ji*) indicating opportunity.

It is not just in the ideographic symbols of Chinese language that the two are brought together. Lord Rothschild's famous exhortation to "buy property when there is blood in the streets, even when it is your own" reflects the very real value of seeking out opportunity when risk is high, prices are low, and others are fearful.

RISK PLANNING COMMITTEE

Large families may commit both their time and financial resources to create a formal risk management process, possibly led by a risk planning committee in a larger family, that guides their decision-making process. To provide real long-term value, this cannot be a reactionary exercise that surfaces only during a crisis, but must be in place and functioning in times both good and bad.

Family members, family office managers, and experienced external advisors can all be a part of the risk planning committee. Documenting expectations, roles, and responsibilities for each involved party and establishing periodic reviews (at least annually) of the process are all critical components for success.

PROCESS FOR MANAGING CHANGE

Once a path to managing risks has been identified, the next steps involve allocating responsibilities to implement the action plans and following up to ensure that the responsive actions have had the desired effect. Without accountability and a timeline to meet, even the best of strategies may be reduced in value through lack of implementation or incomplete follow-through.

Stakeholders Evaluate Key Risks

A third- and fourth-generation family who sold their business 30 years ago has a family office that supports their commitment to staying together as a family. The family holds a Family Assembly meeting every summer to discuss the development of family and financial capital for the next year.

A Family Council provides leadership for the Family Assembly, and a Board of Directors oversees the family office.

In preparation for a recent annual Family Assembly meeting, the leaders of the family decided to gather the family's views regarding what would challenge the family most in the next decade. The six-person Family Council developed a list of 28 key challenges that seemed relevant for the family. A survey was developed and sent to all of the stakeholders, asking them to prioritize the top 10 risks from the list of 28. The committee members called family members to encourage them to complete the survey, and 72 percent of the family participated (see Figure 12.2).

Figure 12.2:   Top Ten Risks Identified Based on a Survey of Family Members (ranked highest to lowest in priority)

% Responded

	% Responded
Selection of qualified board members	20
Engaged family members	15
Clear communication among family members	14
A clear decision-making process	12
An appropriate governance structure	11
Interpersonal family relationships/conflicts	9
Development of representative family governance	7
Transition of family leadership	7
Respect for personal differences/learning styles	6
Support for family leaders	5

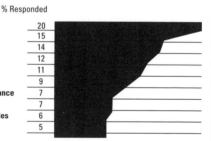

At the summer Assembly meeting, the results of the survey were shared with the entire family. The top five risks were discussed further in breakout groups, with each stakeholder selecting which topics he or she wanted to address. Each of the five groups developed an action plan for addressing the challenge, identifying ways the family risk could be mitigated by the stakeholders if they would get involved. Action plans were presented to the entire Assembly, and committees were formed to address three of the areas.

Considerable progress was made toward getting more family members engaged, one of the key challenges in every family, by getting more members involved in diagnosing their problems. Additional progress was made throughout the year with various committees working to implement action plans.

Figure 12.3 illustrates the risk management process in action.[6]

Figure 12.3:   Risk Management in Action

Identify Risks and Priorities

Risk: Fourth- and fifth-generation family members were not prepared to lead the family or make informed decisions about the future of the family business.

Source: The third generation of the Beech* family was intimately familiar with the family business; however, they did not pass on the same involvement to their children and grandchildren. Once members of this generation passed away the business was left in the hands of younger family members who were disengaged from both the family business and enterprise.

Opportunity: The family had the chance to bring in outside leadership to enhance the business and also help develop new family leadership.

Assess Risk Appetite Among Owners

Before moving forward, the Beech family needed to evaluate their desire to depart from the existing strategy and make real changes to the family business and enterprise. The Beech family elected to grant significant decision-making authority to a single fourth-generation family member and gave him a mandate to make major operational changes in order to turn around the business.

Evaluate and Mitigate Risks

The following key risks were preventing the business from moving forward:
- Lack of next-generation involvement in the business
- Lack of knowledge about the business within the family
- Too many family members on the Board who lacked proper experience

Manage Opportunities

After identifying their critical risks, the family took the following steps:
- Established a Family Council to separate family leadership and family issues from those related to the business
- Created a leadership development program to train high-potential leaders from younger generations
- Brought in outside board members who were instrumental in making critical business decisions

Measure Impact

Family members strongly believe that, after a period of adjustment, their leadership development efforts have had a positive effect on the family and the business. As evidence of this fact, the newest CEO of the company is a family member who went through the leadership development program. In addition, family members who were once solely focused on the risks of change now have a more balanced view of "risk" that includes the threat of stagnation or inaction. Younger generations, especially, are more comfortable with risk-taking in both the business and the family enterprise.

Identify New Risks and Opportunities

Through the company board and the Family Council, the family has new, formal channels for oversight of both the family and the business.

---

6 Family Office Exchange, "Securing the Future: Managing Threats and Opportunities Through Effective Risk Planning," Family Office Exchange White Paper, 2009, 29.

FAMILY LEADER AS RISK MANAGER

There is perhaps no better response to the full array of risks to family wealth and wellbeing than strong leadership based on a clear understanding of what is most at risk for the family. By anticipating future risks, setting priorities, and putting the structures and processes in place to deal with crises yet to emerge, strong leaders will be better prepared to react quickly to reduce the likelihood of a manageable risk turning into an unmitigated disaster.

Both the content and process of risk management have been the subject of recent scrutiny and increasing family control. Building approaches that monitor a broader set of risks, and responding more quickly to warning signals and alarm bells, have become priorities for most families with multi-generational wealth.

Many families and family offices, based on the heightened awareness of risk exposures that resulted from the economic crisis of 2008, have restructured their approaches to risk management. How the family identifies and responds to risk and how the family delegates responsibility to manage risks (and spends family money to do so) can influence family financial and legacy outcomes for many generations.

Successful leaders identify challenges of shared ownership and shared risk:

- Understand current ownership structures and their impact.
- Discuss ownership goals and opportunities for collaboration across branches.
- Identify common risks that most challenge family branches or generations.
- Discuss implications of common risks and changes that may be required.
- Develop programs and committees to mitigate high-priority risks.

Getting members to acknowledge that a broad set of risks needs to be managed, and to decide to spend money to mitigate risks, are two of the biggest hurdles that families face. Ensuring that the family's advisors understand and respond appropriately to the family's definition of risk is a key task for the family leader.

ENGAGEMENT OR ALIENATION?

Active family engagement in risk management and an orientation for framing priorities and taking action are critical to develop in wealth inheritors who do not typically take direct responsibility for managing family risks. Wealth inheritors are often inclined to ask others to take the initiative when it comes to managing their financial risks. Most parents teach their children to trust the professional advisors regarding this complex and critical process because they lack the

Common Understanding of Risk

A story from the history of a Canadian family highlights the need for a common definition and interpretation of acceptable risk.

When a tree was damaged on one family member's property during a construction project, the family office staff brought in an arborist to evaluate the tree's condition. The family did not hear anything more about the damaged tree and assumed that the staff had addressed the risks created by it.

A year later, the family patriarch brought an advisor to the property to determine the property insurance needs of the family. When the patriarch pointed out the damaged tree, the advisor recommended that the family bring an arborist in every six months and file a report of his evaluation. The patriarch returned to the family office and asked to see the tree reports that the arborist had initially filed. The reports indicated that the tree was a "critical risk" and should be removed immediately.

When the family member went to the president of the family office with his findings, he was surprised to hear the president had indeed read the reports and had determined that no action was necessary. The president felt the cost of having the tree removed from the family's property outweighed the risk the tree might fall. The patriarch countered, "What risk do you think my family should be willing to take of this tree falling and killing someone on our property?" The president responded that the patriarch was overreacting.

This experience reinforced for the family the important role of the family office as a defensive strategist and risk manager. The family wanted their family office staff to be proactive and protective, managing every possible scenario where the family might be at risk. In this case, the family office's view of acceptable levels of risk was at odds with the family's views. This case highlights the importance of talking about risk and risk tolerances, within the family and with the family's advisors, to ensure that the advisors understand the family's view of risk and its acceptable limits.

training themselves, and mediation among the children might be required.

Often, wealth owners disengage too much from the process and do not monitor the outcomes or the implications of the plans put into place. That disengagement can prove disastrous for owners who are not paying enough attention to this critical function.

DEVELOPING A ROBUST RISK MANAGEMENT MENTALITY

While there are many contributing factors to the long-term maintenance of wealth, there are several risk-management practices that stand out as critical strategies for success, chiefly:

- The willingness to communicate attitudes and concerns about the future and to reach consensus about key risks within the family and with advisors.
- The ability to scan the environment continuously and concentrate on addressing the most strategic risks.
- The discipline to design internal processes for managing threats and identifying wealth enhancement opportunities.
- The recognition that wealth comes from taking risk and the benefit of fostering a culture of calculated risk-taking in younger generations.

Families that employ these practices are better prepared to manage and embrace change, and understand that risk is not a situation to be avoided or a problem to be solved.

Family Risk Management: A Way To Keep It Simple

Over the years the process of risk management has been encrusted with many overlapping steps, complicating what should be simple. The process has two easily remembered steps: 1) Risk Analysis, and 2) Risk Response.

(continued)

Risk Analysis includes the identification of possible unexpected events, their measurement in terms of likelihood or consequences and public perceptions, and their assessment in terms of an organization's objectives.

Risk Response encompasses the controls adopted to balance risk, measuring and monitoring performance and communication with stakeholders. The discipline answers the questions, "What could happen?" and "What should we do about it?"

Risk management remains a developing discipline, even as it expands to encompass the entire enterprise. It embodies the basic caution that we can never know the future, but we can prepare for it more intelligently.

Critical steps in risk management:

- Board and senior management commitment.
- Broad view of risk encompassing *both* reward and penalty.
- Common framework for the integrated analysis of all risks.
- Single independent leader or coordinator for the process.
- Bottom-up risk assessments, updated regularly.
- Clear and timely data.
- Two-way communication with key stakeholders.
- Creation and maintenance of stakeholder confidence through improving stakeholder "value," creating a healthy internal risk culture.[7]

These families practice effective family risk planning and management by developing a culture that balances the management of threats with the recognition of opportunities. They have conversations about the things that keep them awake at night and talk about possible responses to the issues they can and cannot control. They set priorities on collective risks and develop plans to monitor or mitigate them. They allocate the resources (people, time, money) necessary to manage risk and change over time.

Effective risk (and opportunity) management, a structured approach to family organization and leadership, and careful preparation of the next generation are important steps to help ensure the preservation of wealth and success of the family legacy.

---

7 Kloman, *Mumpsimus Revisited.*

Questions for Leaders of Legacy

1. What roles have risk and risk management played in your family history—both positive and negative?
2. What keeps you and your family up at night?
3. Do you have a list establishing priorities for the greatest risks (not just financial) to the family?
4. Do you have a robust risk management process, and are you satisfied with the proposed actions to mitigate the highest priority risks?
5. Who is responsible for the family's overall risk management process, and does he or she clearly understand what actions are in the best interests of the family?

13. DESIGNING A FAMILY "ECO-SYSTEM" WORTHY OF TRUST

No wealthy family operates in isolation.

A legacy family and its members rely upon a host of advisors, trustees, institutions, industries, friends, and like-minded families that create a vast and ever-changing "eco-system," which both supports and shapes the family's human and financial capital. A well-designed and properly managed eco-system is a powerful partner in the pursuit of the family's long-term legacy goals.

A critical role for the family leader is to optimize the talent and experience of this team of individuals and advisors on behalf of the family. Managing these relationships to ensure that the family's best interests remain well served and fully aligned requires clear and consistent communication about expectations and continual monitoring. Just as the well-designed eco-system is a powerful partner, a poorly designed or misaligned eco-system can be harmful to a family; it may take years to rectify ill-conceived initiatives and outright mistakes made by participants in the system.

UNDERSTANDING THE ECO-SYSTEM

Although the scale and role of an eco-system vary depending on the size, mission, and goals of the family, the common participants in a family-eco-system are illustrated in Figure 13.1.

Each of these parties influences the family's ability to meet its goals and achieve its legacy plan. Asset managers, brokers, bankers, trustees, and risk managers have a fundamental impact on the growth or decline of financial wealth, while lawyers and tax advisors (and trustees again) play key roles in defining how a family structures and protects that wealth.

In a less direct manner, schools, universities, churches, friends, and other families help to shape the lives of and decisions made by family members. Having a strong sense of values and the support of these important networks can have a lasting impact on the family and help many defend against the negative consequences of wealth.

Lead advisors, or the family office if one exists, can play a dual role as part of the eco-system and as the central advisors on the design, selection, management, and alignment of that system.

Figure 13.1: The Family Eco-System

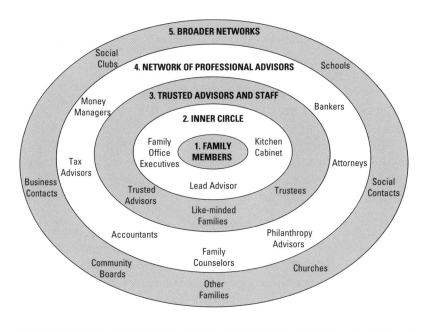

The nature and importance of these relationships continually changes depending on the challenges facing the family at different points in time and their need for external resource support.

COMPONENTS OF THE ECO-SYSTEM

Family leaders must understand all of these varied and ever-changing sources of support and influence surrounding the family and work to direct them in a coordinated effort on behalf of the greater family.

An eco-system is far more than the set of formally appointed advisors. It is made up of a wide collection of advisors (formal and informal), friends, institutions, influences, and influencers, who can have a substantial impact on individual members of a family and the family as a whole.

Failure to manage the entire eco-system can put the family at risk. The fallout from adverse relationships that do not serve the family's best interests can be costly, time consuming, and lasting.

Family Members The family lies at the heart of the eco-system. All members, and leaders in particular, play a central role in the determination of the shape and operation of the overall eco-system.

The Inner Circle Just as every head of state or corporate titan has a "kitchen cabinet" of trusted friends and advisors outside the formal structures of power, most family leaders benefit from the insights and advice of an "Inner Circle" of trusted advisors. Members of the Inner Circle are typically long-term advisors or family friends who understand the family, its business (if there is one), its history, and its culture. Their knowledge of the family's strengths and weaknesses, combined with their "non-family" and perhaps objective perspective, makes them an invaluable resource, especially in times of uncertainty or change.

The Role of the Lead Advisor—Lead advisors are rare indeed and often fit the description of the true Renaissance men of fifteenth-century Italy, who were capable of "mastering and integrating the disciplines of their time."[1] While the historic Renaissance men mastered science, art, and history, modern lead advisors need to master and integrate the disciplines of asset structuring, business strategy, wealth management, family governance and the all-too-human psychological dynamics of the wealthy family.

Increasingly, with so much complexity and change, larger families are formalizing the role of a lead advisor, hired in as a specialist from the outside, or found within their family office chief executive, to provide guidance and advice on integrated strategy and the structure and operations of the family's eco-system. A lead advisor provides expertise, and possibly implementation support, in all areas of a family's legacy plan.

Trusted Advisors and Staff The employees of each of the entities play important but varying roles in the eco-system on behalf of the family. The family's level of reliance on and involvement in the family office, for example, determines its overall importance and influence within the eco-system.

In many cases, the manager of the family office is considered a member of the Inner Circle. For families where the family's philanthropy is its focus, the foundation director may play a similar

---

1 Speech by Orit Gadiesh, Chairman, Bain & Company, World Economic Forum Annual Meeting 2002.

role. In others, an outsider is brought in to give a consolidating view, reinforcing a family policy of separating employees from the family's Inner Circle.

Family Office Manager as Trusted Advisor

The family office of the Pine* family is one of the main links between the family and the business. The leader of the family described their trusted advisor in the following way:

"The reason this works so well is that the person who heads our family office worked in the business and has intimate knowledge of all of its different parts. He has also worked with my husband and I so he knows and understands our values and the way we do things. He has known the children since they were young and has developed a good relationship with each of them.

He was the natural choice to head the office because of his knowledge of both the family and the business, and because of the great trust both generations have in him.

He is a 'Dutch uncle' for our children and plays an important mentoring role for them. He is an ideal person for this role because he is a highly ethical person and comes from a family business himself."

Trustees, Protectors, and Private Trust Companies—Trustees and Protectors (also known as Enforcers in some jurisdictions and structures) are associated with the establishment and functioning of trustee relationships and private trust companies (PTCs) and can therefore play a key role in the financial, trust, and tax affairs of a multigenerational legacy family.

The trustees are the individuals or corporate entities responsible to act in the long-term best interest of the current and future beneficiaries of the trusts they manage. In a PTC model, the company directors may act as trustees, with the family interests represented by Protectors or Enforcers, who have the right at any time to remove and replace directors who are acting in a manner believed to be inconsistent with the family's values and interests.

Although trust structures usually rely on individual or corporate trustees to act to implement the wishes of the settler of the trusts, the rise in the use of private trust companies and the evolution of family offices into private trust companies are trends that move forward the approaches taken by families in the United States for more than a century.

This trend is also becoming topical for some international families, encouraged by the availability of a new custom-tailored offering of a trust with an embedded private trust company available in, for example, Singapore and New Zealand. This allows a family to achieve the many benefits of a trust establishment without handing over permanent and unlimited decision-making power to a third party.

Community of the Like-Minded—In the wake of the latest recession, wealthy families are increasingly seeking out other family peers who are facing similar issues. They gather at industry conferences or join peer networks to share investment ideas, co-investing opportunities, creative strategies for preparing their children to be responsible owners of wealth, and much more.

Network of Professional Advisors In addition to members of the Inner Circle, the network of professional advisors within the eco-system provides the technical knowledge and experience needed to preserve the family's wealth and legacy. These advisors include lawyers, accountants, tax advisors, private bankers, asset managers, risk managers, brokers, and other professional advisors.

Broader Networks Surrounding all prior elements of the eco-system is a broad network of institutions, influencers, and individuals who provide a constant flow of interaction, influence, and impact on the family. Reflecting a global connectivity, this "network of networks" may have a different, and growing role to play in the lives of each family member.

LEADERSHIP OF THE FAMILY ECO-SYSTEM

It is clear that disciplined leadership is needed to identify the elements and manage the strengths and weaknesses of the eco-system. The leadership team establishes criteria for participation, monitors the system, and makes the changes necessary to build and maintain an eco-system that is capable of protecting a family from a crisis, and which proves over time that it is worthy of trust.

A family's eco-system must be developed in support of its long-term vision and legacy plan. All advisors in the system are governed by the family leadership, which is responsible for thorough due diligence before selection, continual oversight, and periodic re-evaluation. Ensuring sufficient checks and balances and appropriate diversification (e.g. avoiding over-reliance on a particular firm or individual) within the system are important considerations.

An integrated and aligned eco-system is greater than the sum of its parts. The challenge for family leaders is to optimize performance in each area while ensuring that the overall impact is consistent with the family's long-term goals. Successful leaders spend substantial time managing relationships within the family, among advisors, and on behalf of the greater family to ensure that all members of the eco-system are informed about their specific goals as well as their impact on the goals of the greater family.

CRITERIA FOR ADVISOR SELECTION

Members of the family's eco-system must be professional, expert, and ethical in word and deed. Having a detailed due diligence process is essential and should include documenting the family's service needs, establishing selection criteria, soliciting recommendations, checking references, reviewing research and marketing materials, conducting interviews and site visits, talking to existing clients, and evaluating alternatives before making the decision to hire an advisor. There are far too many examples of families who do not properly invest in this process and end up, to their great regret, trusting the wrong people.

In addition to ensuring the competence and integrity of its advisors, each family should consider the balance of quantitative and qualitative skills within the eco-system. One family met with their advisors to understand better their collective skills inventory, as well as what was needed to enhance the team. Table 13.1 shows how they catalogued their skills and capabilities.

One of the greatest disappointments in the recent economic crisis was the degree to which interests between advisors and the family were found to be fundamentally misaligned. In many cases, advisor compensation is determined by product sales or the achievement of client profitability targets, encouraging advisors to push products or pursue behavior that does not always work to the benefit of the client.

Although family leaders are not often able to influence directly advisor reward, promotion, or compensation, they can at least reduce the risk of inappropriate pressure being applied if there

Table 13.1:   Leadership Skills and Capabilities

	Quantitative Skills	Qualitative Skills
Family Leader	• Wealth management • Organizational design • Business strategy • Communication • Advisor management	• Vision • Values • Consensus-building • Inspiration • Leadership
Family Mentors	• Governance • Finance and control • Asset protection • Human resources • Philanthropic leadership	• Understanding and empathy • History of storytelling • Active listening • Achieving consensus • Dispute resolution
Family Advisors	• Tax and audit • Legal • Psychology • Investment • Strategy • Integration of the disciplines	• Individual counseling • Planning process • Group dynamics • Education • Scenario planning • Holistic integration and future view

is full transparency regarding advisor compensation and clear documentation of the family's collective goals and preferences.

THE ADVISORS' OWN ECO-SYSTEMS

There is clear evidence from sophisticated family offices that the network of advisors selected for the eco-system (ring 4 in Figure 13.1) is integral to the financial results the family achieves. Experienced family office executives can spend a third of their time managing these outside advisors because they are such critical resources in the eco-system. The executive's ability to get the best outcomes is partially dependent on his or her ability to get these advisors to work together effectively.

It is also important to recognize that the advisors selected to serve the family have their own networks and eco-systems. Advisors in each technical discipline form their own formal and informal networks with other advisors to ensure a steady flow of business referrals. When asking an advisor in the eco-system to recommend another advisor, it is essential to ask the referring party how many of his or her new business referrals each year come from that advisor. If the referral is a "payback" from one advisor to another, the family's best interests may not be served by the relationship.

MANAGEMENT OF THE ECO-SYSTEM

Most advisors want to have their performance assessed. Many families do not have a consistent process to assess the value of their advisors on a regular basis. Ironically, most advisors want to have their performance assessed and to have frank conversations to define where they are falling short, and where they might invest to reinforce the relationship and increase its value.

Annual performance reviews with all advisors, along with regular and objective reporting on performance against benchmarks or established goals, are a critical part of the management of a family eco-system.

Sometimes change is required to keep the system fresh and to keep advisors focused on delivering excellent service. Many families, however, fall prey to inertia or the "10-year rule," whereby knowing and interacting with someone for at least a decade creates a sufficiently substantial base of shared experience and trust that it is difficult to remove them, even with evidence of underperformance. Even if a family does not change the design or membership of its eco-system, thoughtful consideration of each advisor's performance and contribution within the system may yield substantial insights.

A key component of the advisor's annual review should involve an assessment of the value generated by the service provider for the price paid. An important role for family leaders or the family office is to ensure that the eco-system is both effective (obtaining the desired results) and efficient (doing so for the lowest possible cost).

Although eco-system costs vary, both in absolute terms and as a percentage of family assets, family leaders must monitor the structure carefully and continually, ensuring family control, and minimizing the total cost of the system. Operating a system where family office and investment advisor costs alone can average between 1 and 2 percent of assets under advisement (AUA) demands proper oversight and management.

Modern family eco-systems are more complex than may be readily apparent. In a recent survey, an average family unit with a net worth of $500 million had a dedicated staff of seven people in its family office, with an interdisciplinary team of 36 advisors (including money managers). Nearly one-third of a family office CEO's time was spent managing these advisors.[2]

BREACH OF TRUST

Unfortunately, in recent years many families have felt disappointed or betrayed by the eco-system they had in place. Failure to anticipate negative events, misalignment of interests, poor governance, and inadequate risk management systems have all contributed to a fundamental loss of trust in many long-established members of a family's eco-system.

> For any legacy family, their supporting eco-system must be worthy of trust.

For any legacy family, their supporting eco-system must be worthy of trust.

Trust is a conditional state of mind, and is based on emotion, expectations, and experience. Trust between individuals, families, and firms is a rare and valuable bond; it is also inherently fragile and sensitive to any experience that reflects a failure to meet expectations, a lack of trustworthiness, or misalignment of interests and values between the involved parties.

Shortcomings of a Long-Term Relationship

The Redwoods,* a billion-dollar family into its third and fourth generations, had used a much revered family lawyer as its sole trustee for more than a decade.

An avuncular and expert lawyer in his home jurisdiction in more than one area of law, the lawyer had been relied upon by the family to provide advice and guidance on many issues for three decades. He was its preferred legal advisor and trusted family lawyer in its home city, and was eventually nominated to be the sole family trustee upon his retirement from his law practice. For years the relationship remained stable, with no major surprises or problems emerging.

(continued)

---

2 Family Office Exchange Family Office Benchmarking, 2008.

However, when the family members decided to review the performance of all of the advisors in their eco-system after the shock of an economic crisis, using a structured "peer review" approach, they found that their trustee had fallen short on many of the most basic trustee requirements:

- The trustee had not organized an audit of the whole system on an integrated basis for more than a decade.
- The family office had not been registered as an asset management firm as required.
- There were no review systems or succession plans in place for the trustee, key advisors, or senior family office staff.
- There was no risk management system in place.
- Reporting lacked forward cash flow forecasts and scenario plans.
- There was no formal process for drafting and approving a long-term legacy plan or an Investment Policy Statement (IPS).
- Investment decisions were made more on an *ad hoc* and personal relationship basis than through a disciplined and data-driven approach.

After much thought, and with full respect for the role the trustee had played for the family, the number of trustees was increased, the approach professionalized, and, eventually, the lawyer-turned-trustee retired with due thanks and words of appreciation from family leaders.

SUCCESSION PLANNING IN THE ECO-SYSTEM

Family leaders also need to consider long- and short-term succession plans for key advisors within the eco-system.

Members of the eco-system provide continuity and stability for the family, and unexpected turnover can be disruptive for the entire system. Proper succession allows for a smooth transfer of power and may also lead to a better alignment of advisors with generations of a family. Particularly for younger members of the family, having access and exposure to advisors of a similar age and world outlook can be advantageous.

"Who's going to be left for us?"

A "next-generation" heiress in the Acorn* family, one of the more outspoken members of her generation, attended a full meeting of family trustees and key advisors for the first time.

(continued)

> After listening intently, she met shortly after the session with the family patriarch and the family *consigliere* for a quick debrief over a cup of tea. After commenting on the complexity of the trust structure, she plaintively noted that everyone at the meeting was very capable and very experienced, but also very senior in age. "They're all very nice," she said, "but who is going to be left for us?"
>
> Her penetrating question led to her family initiating a review of future advisory needs and commencing a well-structured search to select a trustee successor, investment advisor, and tax lawyers of approximately her age and with whom she believed she and her many active siblings could develop a positive, long-term working relationship.

THE ECONOMY AND THE ECO-SYSTEM

A negative economic environment tests the eco-system and all other aspects of a legacy family. Some elements of family capital and legacy emerge intact and strengthened from the experience. Others show their weaknesses, and require leaders to determine what went wrong and what needs to be done differently going forward.

In this most recent crisis, many leaders learned that their eco-systems, and the individuals and firms within them, were not worthy of their trust.

- Economic interests between advisors and client families were often misaligned. For example, many financial brokers and private bankers were receiving compensation for the sale of financial products that may have been poorly understood or excessively risky in adverse environments.
- "Relationship managers" were all too often revealed to be salespeople for in-house products, regardless of their true risk, relative historic performance, or claims to have an "open architecture" approach.
- Hedge funds sold by once trusted advisors also proved to be a mixed bag, with many long/short funds revealed to be truly only levered beta or long-only funds whose managers had cast off the disciplines and costs of their stated risk management policies in pursuit of personal economic gains. Others imposed gates and unexpected lockups in the midst

of the crisis to tie in family investors beyond the expected and contracted terms.

- In some extreme cases, carefully selected investment advisors and managers simply cut off communication and surrendered their businesses to the storm that had destroyed both performance and client trust in their services.

Overall, many individual investments and family portfolios carried more risk than their families realized and insufficient liquidity to prosper in turbulent market conditions.

NEW WORLD, NEW OPPORTUNITIES

Most family eco-systems have been thoroughly tested in the latest crisis. Risks have been identified, and changes are being implemented. Careful management and monitoring of advisor relationships are becoming the norm, and concerns about transparency and alignment of interests are changing the nature of many advisor relationships.

Armed with these insights, family leaders are better able to design, populate, and manage an eco-system which will stand up to the stresses and strains of future difficulties. By ensuring that the family's eco-system is well structured and well managed, as well as constituted by high-quality individuals and organizations, leaders can create an eco-system truly worthy of trust.

Questions for Leaders of Legacy

1. How well designed, aligned, and managed is your current eco-system?
2. Are the current advisors reflective of where the family has been, or where it wants or needs to go? Are they properly selected and managed by the family?
3. Do all members of the Inner Circle understand and support your Family Promise?
4. How often do you meet with members of the eco-system to review family priorities, advisor and staff performance, and opportunities to improve cost relative to benefit?
5. Are you satisfied with the eco-system's current performance and potential capability relative to both current and future challenges?

A Matter of Trust

Dr. Kenneth Kaye has published dozens of articles and books about resolving the disputes, rifts, and intergenerational tensions that threaten to hobble family enterprises. The books most relevant for this audience are Trust Me: Helping Our Young Adults Financially *and* The Dynamics of Family Business.[3]

Trust is always situational, conditional, and uncertain

We tend to talk about trustworthiness as though it were a general attribute of a person, and we make the same mistake in saying that someone is a trustful or a distrustful person. In reality, every person is trustworthy for some purposes, in some relationships, to some extent, under some conditions. And everyone is willing to trust some people for some purposes, etc. Furthermore, the knowledge we rely on, in ourselves as well as in those we trust, is *learned.* So one's willingness to rely on another person ought to take account of where he or she is on a learning curve.

It's never just a matter of degree of trust, in general. It's trust within some domain. Research findings consistently distinguish between trust in someone's technical competence or knowledge, and trust in his or her honesty and commitments.

In the context of a family enterprise, there are three or four distinct types of trust

The first type is whether they trust the *honesty* of the other individual, and the second is whether they trust the other's *intentions.* The third deals with competence or *judgment,* and a fourth distinction is about *reliability.*

The trust relationship is three dimensional. Trust depends on the *situation:* one trusts a person more in certain areas, less in others. Trust is *conditional:* one trusts the other only so long as certain criteria are met. Even within those contexts and conditions, trust is always *uncertain:* the fact that one trusts another does not mean he or she is sure the other will perform. It means he or she will take a chance on that performance, monitor it, and adjust future trust based on the outcome.

(continued)

---

3 Kenneth Kaye, *Trust Me: Helping Our Young Adults Financially* (Bloomington, IN: iUniverse, 2009).

To trust anyone, therefore, is always to run the risk of disappointment, betrayal, anger, distrust and sooner or later, trusting again—because our life literally depends on relying upon others, imperfectly reliable as they are.

Trust is a process

A's trust in B is always a work in progress, because it is always context-dependent and always being tested. Meanwhile, the same goes on with respect to B's trust in A—which is not necessarily reciprocal. One may be more trustworthy than the other, in any or all areas of their relationship. However, trusting and trustworthiness have an unfortunate correlation—a positive feedback loop. Someone who is less trustworthy has less reason to trust others. And someone who is highly *distrustful of* a particular person has less reason to be *trustworthy for* that other person. (Being trustworthy, after all, is also a risk.) That correlation is inevitable, but unfortunate in a way, because a disappointment on *either* side leads to less trust and less trustworthiness on *both* sides.

Trust is emotional

Trust is a decision process—choosing to rely on another party under a condition of risk—but it is equally an *emotional* state. Although it rarely appears on a list of the emotions, trust manifests itself like all of those, as an awareness. Emotion occupies the body as a whole, lasts anywhere from minutes to days, and we're generally conscious of our emotions (we feel them even when we don't label them). Thus we *feel* trustful or distrustful of a person in a context, and we experience that as a state of being, rather than a momentary perception or reaction.

In short, to trust or not to trust is never simply a matter of deductive reasoning. Nor is it primarily a conflict between two people or groups. It is an inner, emotional conflict between people's need to count on other people's reliability and the fact that they can never be sure of it. They have to put their business, personal safety, even their children's or grandchildren's security, at risk—constantly. Therefore we can't resolve hurt about perceived breaches of trust by appealing to reason. The question of who was right, who wronged whom, or the parties' incompatible stories, is less important than their emotional intelligence about one another. When events suggest that people's risk was greater than they thought, they don't do a mathematical recalculation. A more primitive mechanism intervenes—*emotion* drives their behavior toward distrust.

(continued)

Problems in family trust

Shouldn't family members be able to take one another's trust and trust-worthiness for granted? No. The more interdependent a relationship is, and the more different situations it covers, the more each member has invested—risked—in that relationship. This is all the more reason *not* to take one another for granted.

My observations suggest that both generations in the typical early stage of a family enterprise make errors of too *much* trust (relying on hope rather than experience). A parent hires a son, daughter, or in-law for a position the latter isn't qualified to enter. Or a young person takes a job in the family business expecting to be treated more generously than is prudent, given their value to the company or the personalities involved.

But the process is self-correcting. Conflict prompts the members to reduce trust until problems can work themselves out through the normal process of testing and adjustment.

14. MASTERING NEW CHALLENGES TO FINANCIAL WEALTH

Financial wealth is one of the most important elements of true family wealth.

For many families the ownership, structuring, and management of financial assets absorb the largest allocation of their time and are the greatest focus of their efforts. Especially in the wake of the economic downturn of 2008, many families are paying strict attention to their investment portfolios and looking for heightened security and reduced risk, while still seeking reliable sources of income and capital appreciation.

Managing financial wealth is an important topic that cannot be fully explored in these few pages. As with family business, family wealth management is a vast topic capable of filling many books. Rather than gloss over a complex subject, this chapter focuses only on some of the more recent, high-level realizations about wealth management in the family context, and highlights some of the issues family leaders encounter as they seek to grow and preserve the family's financial assets.

In the wise words of Warren Buffett, there are two key rules for investment, with a negative environment ruthlessly exposing those who wandered too far from his home truth:

Rule Number One: Don't lose any money.
Rule Number Two: Remember Rule Number One.

Bad investment decisions and bad investment advisors can ruin a family, often in a single generation. The loss of financial wealth can have a significant impact on other types of family capital as well, with family harmony and unity placed under stress when loss of capital or income is involved. The costs of financial loss are often felt for generations to come.

Strategic Failure and the Loss of Family Legacy

One of the wealthiest legacy families in U.S. fell from the peak of wealth, power, and influence to a far less exalted position within one generation as a result of a few seemingly intelligent decisions made by one of the most illustrious business names of his generation.

One of his advisors, lamenting the loss of wealth and stature, reminisced about the day the losing strategy was announced:

"In the early summer of 1974 we sat and took notes (that was our job) as the patriarch of one of America's great families addressed his adult relatives. He had summoned the next two generations to explain why he had just instructed the family's trustees to sell all their stocks and to invest only in bonds and cash.

The patriarch reminded his family that he had had the privilege to come of age during America's brief period of greatness, when the country had emerged from a devastating depression to win the Second World War and went on to build an economy that was the envy of the world. But somewhere along this happy road, 'America lost her way' and was suffering a great loss of confidence.

For the family, the patriarch's decision was a tragic error. By 1985, the family was poorer than they had been in 1965 in absolute dollars. In inflation-adjusted terms, the family's buying power had dropped by two-thirds. And since many more family members had been born than had died over those two decades, the per capita wealth of the family was a small fraction of what it had been.

"By the turn of the twenty-first century no one knew its name."

In the 1960s the family was known and admired across the United States and Europe. By the turn of the twenty-first century no one knew its name."[1]

INVESTOR REACTIONS TO THE LATEST (BUT NOT LAST) CRISIS

The initial reaction of wealth owners in 2008 and 2009 to the battering they received has already been the subject of thorough research. A study of 76 families[2] reflected the degree of impact and concern

[1] Greycourt & Co., Inc, "Is It Different This Time?," White Paper 46, 2009.
[2] Family Office Exchange, FOX Investment Survey Results, 2008–09. FOX Member Research, www.familyoffice.com.

that resulted from a crisis few predicted, and for which even fewer were fully prepared. Wealth owners have had emotionally charged reactions to the collapse in asset prices and the values of their holdings. Many felt unable to plan for the future until they had seen the bottom of the market downturn, especially when they knew they could not recreate the wealth once lost. Those who had strategic advisors to help them "stay the course" seemed to be able to weather the storm better than self-directed investors, whose desire to control the situation caused them to abandon their investment policies and to make decisions based on instinct rather than investment analysis.

Owners who pass wealth down successfully are paying more attention to the process they must develop to manage future opportunities and mitigate future risks.

Advisors are having a much more substantive conversation with their clients than in the past decade about proactively sustaining wealth and developing a thoughtful strategy that can withstand unexpected events.

The events of 2008 and beyond have forced many investors to recognize their intolerance for volatility and to clarify their appetite for risk-taking in uncertain economic conditions. One advisor observed:

> Many families had a one in one thousand positive event to generate their wealth, but they cannot imagine a one in one hundred negative event that impacts the wealth.

"Many of the families we work for had a one in one thousand positive event to generate their wealth, but they cannot imagine a one in one hundred negative event that impacts the wealth."[3]

Investors have had two gut-level reactions to uncertainty in the markets over the past year. The skeptics dug in for a long and slow recovery. These investors were traumatized by the uncertainty in the markets and became totally focused on protecting what they had left.

The opportunists believed that there must be great opportunity in the dislocation of the markets, and were actively seeking new ways to invest their liquid assets. These owners either had basic lifestyle needs protected, or they had confidence that they could recreate the wealth if they lost it.

---

3 Comment by Scott Welch, U.S. Family Wealth Advisor made at FOX Thought Leaders Round Table, Chicago, June 2009.

CHANGES IN INVESTOR BEHAVIOR

Most wealthy families will remain long-term investors with long-term goals, but the way in which they invest and manage investment risk is likely to change. The full extent of these changes is as yet unknown, but change is indeed a likely outcome following the pounding many took during the recent economic crisis.

Greater Responsibility for Ownership and Oversight Families increasingly recognize the need to assume greater accountability for their own investment risks and processes.

In practice, many delegate investment and risk management tasks to a family office, MFO, or outside wealth advisor. However, the aftermath of the crisis revealed that many investors were exposed to risks and invested in products that they did not fully understand.

The family investment committee and family leaders have to retain responsibility for understanding the rationale behind investment decisions, how their portfolios generate returns, and how various types of investment vehicles function in different circumstances.

Greater Reliance on Collective Process, Not Individual Behavior The best risk safeguards are those embedded in disciplined processes and structure—not those dependent on intuition or individual human behavior. From a risk perspective, one behavioral shortcoming is simple forgetfulness. As one observer commented, "Vital investing practices, such as avoiding managers with conflicts . . . are important to investors right now, but they will be forgotten after the first bull market."

Consequently, many investors anticipate rising demand for more transparent investment vehicles, investment processes with additional checks and balances, and shifts to advisory firms with conflict-free revenue models. If history is the guide, it is unlikely that families will exhibit permanent behavioral shifts, but rather they may use the downturn as at least a catalyst to design or reinforce systematic safeguards.

Sustainable Long-Term Investment Model Long-term investment success is often characterized by diversification of assets, lack of leverage, low volatility, and investment in undervalued opportunities in geographic and industrial sectors with long-term growth potential.

Many families make the mistake of pursuing the highest possible return too avidly, assuming excessive risk in the process, and are dismayed when a crisis hits and their wealth declines. An approach that seeks to balance solid return with security and quality, avoiding both the highs and lows of more aggressive investment styles, may be far more valuable and better suited to a legacy family in the long run.

Seeking Views from Other Families Individual families are now more than ever seeking opportunities to meet with peer families to compare data on asset managers and direct investments. Increased levels of due diligence on many funds with complex performance characteristics can be a burden on any single family; sharing the costs of analysis and benefiting from the comfort of co-investment can be a welcome step forward for family leaders seeking the best available information.

CRISIS FALLOUT: TAX COSTS AND LEGACY THREAT

One of the consequences of this recession will be the need for future generations to pay for the excesses and failures of their predecessors.

The International Monetary Fund (IMF) estimated that a future tax bill of US$2 trillion globally would have to be met to pay for the full costs of the crisis of 2008–09, with the bulk of increased demand forced on wealthier taxpayers.

Given a confluence of factors, governments are likely to seek substantially more tax revenue from the wealthier end of the economic spectrum. These factors include:

- Declining income from taxes: corporate, capital gains, income, property, and inheritance.

- Increasing demand for revenue: bailout and stimulus, unemployment, health care, government pensions, war, etc.

- Unpopularity of the wealthy class (bankers, brokers, fund managers, etc.) leading to the imposition of more aggressive tax policies on salaries and bonuses.

- Increasing tax rates at the high end and the establishment of special units to investigate wealthy "customers" of revenue departments.

- Pressure on offshore tax havens and tax avoidance (not just evasion) structures.

- Tighter rules on residency, domicile, disclosure, and exceptions.

- Scrutiny of location and the role of trusts, trustees, family office structures, and investment processes.

THE RISING TIDE OF TAXES

In words virtually identical to those issued in the United Kingdom at virtually the same time, U.S. tax authorities signaled their intention to focus on the wealthy as a source of greater revenue collection:

> "The name 'Global High Wealth Industry Group' sounds friendly enough—like a lobbying firm for family offices, or peer group for millionaires who live on mountains. In fact, it is a new SWAT team formed within the U.S. Internal Revenue Service to target the wealthy."
>
> *The Wall Street Journal*[4]

One of the primary purposes of a structured approach to family asset and wealth management is to minimize taxes wherever possible. This objective, adopted in virtually all countries around the world by wealthy families, may involve both onshore and offshore asset structuring.

In the current environment, active tax management requires more time from leaders of wealthy families. They need to consider both traditional and creative options to manage that burden through asset structuring, shifting assets at low values from one vehicle to another, creating "growth trust vehicles" in other jurisdictions, and crafting other legal approaches to manage a growing global tax burden.

OFFSHORE VERSUS ONSHORE

In Table 14.1, a side-by-side comparison of the impact of two different tax regimes, an Organization for Economic Cooperation and Development (OECD) "onshore" example and an "offshore" low-tax jurisdiction, underscores the importance to financial legacies of appropriate tax planning and the long-term impact of high income tax and heavy inheritance tax or estate duties.

To make it easier to calculate and illustrate the relative impact of two different regimes on multi-generational wealth, it is assumed that a very fortunate individual generated US$100 million of income in one year. For the sake of simplicity, all rates applied are at marginal

---

4 Robert Frank, "New IRS Unit Targets Wealthy Tax Dodgers," *Wall Street Journal*, November 5, 2009.

Table 14.1: Comparison of the Impact of Onshore and Offshore Tax Regimes (in constant U.S. dollars)

A. Tax impact on a $100 million estate with wealth generated by income in the first generation (Gen. 1)	Onshore Tax Rate (%)	Onshore Family	Offshore Tax Rate (%)	Offshore Family
Initial income in Gen. 1		$100 million		$100 million
Marginal tax rate and impact	50	($50 million)	0	—
After-tax income for Gen. 1		$50 million		$100 million
Inheritance tax and impact	40	($20 million)	0	—
Estate value post-inheritance taxes for Gen. 2		$30 million		$100 million
Gen 2. per capita inheritance (assuming three children)		$10 million each		$33 million each
Inheritance tax (per capita)	40	($4 million)	0	—
Estate value post-inheritance taxes for Gen. 3 (per branch)		$6 million		$33 million
Gen. 3 per capita inheritance (assuming three children por member of Gen. 2)		$2 million each		$11 million each

rates to avoid the complexities of small adjustments, and all income generated above the rate of inflation and after taxes is deemed to have been fully distributed.

Without proactive estate planning in many OECD jurisdictions, the greater taxes levied in a high-tax jurisdiction can reduce the ultimate inheritance of a third-generation heir by more than 80 percent, from US$11 million down to US$2 million. In addition, after-tax income from the same investments over the lifetime of the two generations for an OECD resident would be half that of his or her offshore counterpart.

Total tax paid on the initial US$100 million for the OECD resident (and domiciliary) would amount to US$82 million over two generations. For the offshore counterpart, in an extremely favorable tax jurisdiction, the total amount of tax paid on the same amount would be zero.

It should be pointed out that this example presumes that no divorces take place, which could reduce an individual's inheritance by 50 percent, and that there are no other intervening negative economic or family events that would reduce capital or impede inheritance. This model assumes no investment growth beyond inflation (3 percent per year), and that the family will distribute any income and capital earned above the rate of inflation.

For non-U.S. citizens, by moving all family office operations and investment-decision making offshore, or at least a substantial portion thereof, a sufficiently offshore status may be acquired to achieve some meaningful, and fully legitimate, tax savings.

For U.S. citizens and citizens of the many other countries with worldwide income tax regimes, options for tax planning may be more limited, and penalties for evasion severe. It is, of course, always important to be fully compliant with all of the laws and regulations related to taxation in all relevant jurisdictions at all times.

In both cases, purpose, form, substance, and the reality of processes and operations need to support any claim for a status that reduces tax obligations of all kinds, and, hopefully, operate in a sufficiently far-sighted and robust manner to avoid future tax obligations as well.

MULTI-GENERATIONAL PERSPECTIVES

Unfortunately, most economic studies and investment theses focus on limited periods of economic and investment performance. Families thinking across multiple generations, however, require a more long-term view. From a multi-generational economic perspective, cycles and crises will come and go with regularity, and important family issues such as taxes, political risk, credit, liquidity, and distribution demands may be consistently more important to owners of private wealth than to institutions.

A long-term perspective is relevant for many wealthy families who have been influenced by, or even participated in, many great events of the past. A review of the actual events of the past reflects the full range of what may yet come for families in the future.

Many families have lost their wealth forever through political upheaval, invasion, religious persecution, revolution, and other cataclysmic external events. From the default of England in 1340 (and even before) to the subprime crisis of 2008, there have been waves of

banking, capital market, and other economic crises unfolding over time, often
growing out of the problems of one
country to engulf many more in their
shared misery. Some can last for years,
with an average credit crisis, such as that
of 2008 and beyond, lasting an average
of five to seven years.

> Each family leader can expect to face at least three major financial crises in his or her generation.

The most recent recession has been
added to a long list of challenges and crises faced by families and
their leaders.

From this perspective, each family leader, who may spend 30
years or more in a family leadership position, can expect to face at
least three major financial crises in his or her generation. While the
exact timing and nature of the next crises are far from clear, their
appearance and potential impact should be taken into account when
thinking through family policies regarding risk management, wealth
preservation, and the investment process.

FINANCIAL RISK AND FAMILY RETURNS

In *Against the Gods*,[5] Peter Bernstein speaks eloquently about the
laws of nature that cause family wealth to follow a natural regression
to the mean over time, generating "average" results for the family
because they use conservative investment policies that avoid concentrated investment risk.

> "The essence of risk management lies in maximizing the areas
> where we have some control over the outcome, while mini-
> mizing the areas where we have absolutely no control over the
> outcomes."
>
> Peter Bernstein

It is extremely difficult for investor returns to outpace the exponen-
tial growth of the family over generations without extreme levels of

---

5 Peter Bernstein, *Against the Gods: The Remarkable Story of Risk* (New York: John
Wiley & Sons, Inc., 1998).

risk, called the Malthusian effect. However, it is possible to maintain purchasing power if the investment quality, risk, volatility, management, costs, and spending patterns are carefully controlled.

AN ENDURING APPROACH TO FAMILY WEALTH MANAGEMENT

Many families, from 1990 onward, were acting more like market speculators than as conservative family wealth preservers. The Harvard, Yale, and Stanford "endowment model" employed by respected endowment fund managers at these institutions became as widely admired in the family financial world as their colleges and graduate faculties were in the academic universe. Families, ignoring the different inflows of funds, investment sophistication, and top-end fund access, adopted the principles of Modern Portfolio Theory and rushed to emulate the Ivy League endowments' heavy allocation to illiquid alternative asset classes.

The timeframe for investments moved outward and the appetite for risk (or at least for target return) increased as markets rose in the late 1990s and in the first decade of the new millennium. The result was that a great number of families increased their exposure to alternative assets, which also carried with them higher risk, lower liquidity, and, under extreme circumstances, far less exit opportunity and income-generation potential than envisioned.

In response to the events of recent years, many family leaders are revisiting their wealth management goals, dusting off their IPSs, and evaluating their overall investment processes. Those who have weathered the economic storms for multiple generations understand the importance of a purpose-driven approach to the investment process. They understand the complexity involved in managing exceptional wealth for posterity while providing for the current income needs of a diverse and taxable client base, and have aligned the proper team of professionals to assist them with all aspects of the investment process.

A diversified and purpose-driven approach to asset allocation and risk management seems to help families deal with the two extremes of the risk-taking spectrum. Figure 14.1 presents a summary of a simple purpose-driven asset allocation framework.

For the risk-oriented family member, having one layer of the pyramid devoted to "sleep well" assets allows the risk-taker to invest in risky assets in a pre-specified amount, but gives a financial bedrock to fall back on if risk-taking proves unsuccessful.

Figure 14.1: Purpose-Driven Investment Framework

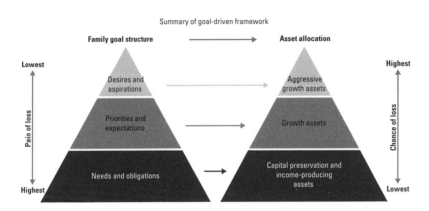

Source: Eton Advisors, L.P.

For the risk-averse family members, having the bottom layer of the pyramid devoted to stable value- and income-producing assets may free them up mentally and emotionally to take more risk in the growth-oriented and more aggressive layers of the pyramid.

A well-conceived investment process should include excellent strategy, thorough due diligence, and informed decision making. The result should be an investment process that is phased, analytical, systematically skeptical, and, importantly, subject to the disciplines of documentation and follow-up reviews.

Questions for Leaders of Legacy

1. How well has your family managed its financial wealth in the past relative to benchmarks and peers? How was its performance during the latest (but not last) crisis?
2. Are your advisors' financial interests fully transparent and aligned with your own?
3. Do you have a structured investment process staffed by high quality employees and advisors?
4. Have you calculated the full tax burden on your financial legacy expected over the next two generations?
5. Are you fully prepared for the risks and opportunities of the coming years—and for the next crisis?

A Theory of Wealthy Family Behavior

W. Jackson Parham Jr. is a former college finance professor with more than 20 years of experience in the private wealth industry. He is co-founder of Eton Advisors.

Psychologist Abraham Maslow (1908–70) introduced his now-famous concept of a "hierarchy of needs" in a 1943 paper entitled *A Theory of Human Motivation*.[6] In Maslow's hierarchy, human behavior is " . . . a channel through which many basic needs may be simultaneously expressed or satisfied." These needs "arrange themselves in hierarchies of pre-potency," that is, " . . . the appearance of one need usually rests on the prior satisfaction of another, more pre-potent need."

Maslow's hierarchy is typically depicted as a pyramid, wherein the most basic needs are shown at the base and higher-level needs are shown in ascending order.

Need for Self-Actualization
Desire for self-fulfillment

Esteem Needs
Desire for a positive, firmly based evaluation of self and others

Love Needs
Desire for affectionate relations with others, group belonging

Safety Needs
Desire for security regarding present and future needs

Physiological Needs
Basic instinctive physical needs; requirements for survival

In such a hierarchy, the Love Needs and Esteem Needs will be pushed into the background until the Physiological Needs and Safety Needs are met.

(continued)

6 A. H. Maslow, "A Theory of Human Motivation," *Psychological Review* 50, 370–96.

When basic needs go unmet, a person may become pre occupied or even obsessed with their attainment, such that higher-level needs go not only unmet, but even unacknowledged.

Maslow's hierarchy has numerous applications to family wealth management, from explaining why and how wealth is created by entrepreneurs, to how wealth is used to support nonfinancial goals, or how we ought to allocate portfolios among asset classes so as to match family goals or behavioral attributes.[7] Moreover, Maslow's framework may help explain the motivations underlying the "buying behaviors" of wealthy families, such as how families shop for wealth advisory services and why they select certain provider firms over others, why some families choose to invest in speculative financial products while others avoid such investments, and why some families struggle to confront issues that are key to their long-term wealth preservation.

Consider several examples:

- In 2006, the son of a family patriarch eschews municipal bonds in favor of allocating 20 percent of his portfolio to collateralized debt obligations (CDOs). He asserts that no sophisticated investor would settle for 4-percent municipal yields when 13-percent yields were available in CDOs.
- The wealth of a fifth-generation family is held in a complex, tax-advantaged legal structure. Unfortunately, family members cannot agree upon what annual income distribution should be made from the portfolio to beneficiaries. Lacking the ability to adopt an acceptable distribution policy, the family chooses to dissolve the tax-advantaged legal structure, resulting in an immediate tax equal to more than 40 percent of the portfolio's value.
- An entrepreneur sells his company to a strategic buyer and uses the sale proceeds to diversify his personal portfolio. Soon thereafter, he invests a significant portion of his liquid net worth in a startup company that eventually goes bankrupt. After the bankruptcy, he invests a significant portion of his remaining assets into a third venture, which is quite successful.

In each of these cases, Maslow's lower-level Physiological Needs and Safety Needs do not fully explain family behaviors. Love, Esteem, and Self-Actualization Needs also served as significant motivators. In each instance, multiple layers of Needs influenced decisions and actions.

In the case of the son who overallocated his portfolio to CDOs, the desire for Esteem—either in his own self-image or in the eyes of his

(continued)

---

7 See Figure 14.1, Summary of Goal-Driven Framework, page 205.

father—dominated his Safety Needs and encouraged him to take ill-compensated risks. For the fifth-generation family who dissolved their tax-advantaged structure, the family's inability to subjugate individual goals in favor of corporate goals (Esteem Needs) left some family members feeling disenfranchised (Love Needs), which resulted in a decision that reduced significantly the family's net worth (Safety Needs). The serial entrepreneur who continues to reinvest in new ventures is focused less on asset growth (Safety Needs) than on exercising his innate desire to create (Self-Actualization), building communities of co-workers and investors (Love Needs), and affirming his resilience as an entrepreneurial leader (Esteem Needs).

No model—no matter how robust or multi-faceted—can fully explain the myriad factors which motivate individual human behavior. The behavior of wealthy families may be even more complex and difficult to analyze. But Abraham Maslow's hierarchy of needs provides us with an excellent starting point for understanding and positively influencing the behavior of wealthy families.

15. STRUCTURING THE FAMILY OFFICE AS MANAGER OF RISK AND CHANGE

The concept of a dedicated, financially oriented family office committed to serving the interests of a single family, or group of families, can be traced back through the centuries.

European families have funded private family banks for generations, and family offices in their modern form began to appear in the mid-nineteenth century to serve the wealth creators of the Industrial Revolution—Rothschilds, Flemings, Rockefellers, J.P. Morgans, and others. The idea has evolved to the point where it is today, a cottage industry with thousands of privately managed family offices around the globe providing wealth management services for multiple generations of wealth owners.

A family office is a unique private family business that is created to protect and preserve the legacy and values of the family and provide tailored personal and wealth management services for individual family members.

It usually makes financial sense for a family with at least US$100 million in assets to consider a dedicated family office if the family has a desire for privacy and control, and is willing to manage a sophisticated financial business.

WHAT DOES A FAMILY OFFICE DO?

While every family office is as unique as the family it serves, most family offices oversee the critical aspects of the wealth management process and serve as an element of continuity for the family group.

While the goals of the family dictate the services provided by the office, most work to preserve the family legacy; provide services to family members in property management, travel and logistics, record keeping and other needed support; coordinate critical aspects of the wealth planning process (financial, tax, investment); and keep track of the family's financial assets (accounting and reporting).

PRIMARY ROLES OF A FAMILY OFFICE

In fulfilling its general purpose of supporting a family and enhancing its legacy along the dimensions illustrated in Figure 15.1, a family office fulfills a number of more specific roles as well.

Figure 15.1: Family Office Services

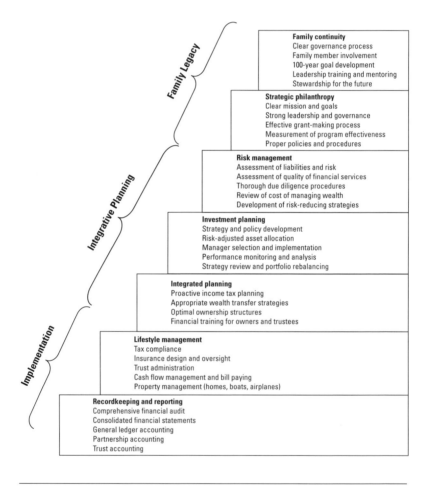

Family Office as Risk Manager Family offices have long juggled the competing goals of wealth creation and wealth preservation. They work continually to manage the expectations and balance the actions of the risk takers and the risk-averse members of the same family. The issue of risk management pervades all aspects of the family office's work, from the investment process to personal security.

The role of the family office as risk manager is part educator, part facilitator, and part compliance officer. The family office staff, who are familiar with all aspects of the financial and family circumstances, are well positioned to help clients make informed decisions.

"For 10 years I thought I was in the investment management business, but now realize I'm in the risk management business."

Ken Mindell, Family Office Executive

The staff are also often the people who are identifying risks and starting important conversations with the family about all of the dimensions of risk a family faces (discussed in Chapter 12). A critical role for the office, especially in light of continually changing tax laws, is to ensure that the family is in compliance with all appropriate regulatory requirements and prepared to take advantage of all planning opportunities.

The "professional team" is involved in risk assessment, risk management, due diligence, and mitigation. Most families value the presence of a dedicated team of experienced professionals who understand the family's goals and who consider systematically the events that put those goals at risk. They use a disciplined approach to risk management and provide assurance to the family that everything possible is being done to protect and preserve the family's assets.

Support for Family Governance The role of the family office in support of an organized family governance process cannot be overemphasized.

The family office manager is typically the sounding board for the owners who must find ways to work together in harmony and with respect for one another. The family office typically works closely with the governing board to: develop the Family Promise (Chapter 3), vision, values, objectives, guiding principles, and educational programs; plan family meetings; and establish regular client communication that fosters family unity and helps preserve the family legacy.

The Importance of a Risk Management Focus

In the Cedar* family, the family members hired a team of experienced investment strategists to launch their new family office. The management team came from a well-respected institution and had a sophisticated game plan for delivering consistent, above-average investment performance. They were used to playing the odds in the financial markets, but not used to managing the risks surrounding someone's personal wealth.

After several years, one of the wealth owners uncovered a series of risk issues that concerned him. When questioned about the procedures, the office staff became annoyed rather than alarmed by the questions. The family member began to realize that his operation was missing a risk mentality and that, for him and his wife, risk management was the *central role* they wanted the family office to provide, above and beyond all others.

As the owner began asking risk assessment questions, he realized that the issues were not on the advisory side of the office, but were related to the office's risk management procedures. This finding raised numerous questions for the owner about the office, including:

- Who has access to confidential information in the office, and what systems are in place to control that access?
- Where are financial documents housed in the office?
- How are critical documents managed and where are originals stored?
- What security checks are completed before hiring a new employee?
- Have all employees been trained to respect privacy and confidential matters?

All of these questions are logical for someone with a risk management mentality. This family learned the hard way that it is possible to outsource the investment strategy, but impossible to outsource comprehensive risk management functions.

Support for Legacy Plans and Financial Strategies The family office is a primary executor of the family's strategic and legacy plans. The work of the family office is directed by the long-term goals of the family identified in their legacy plan. The office staff, with the guidance of family leaders, executes, reviews, and revises the family's plans to ensure that their legacy is preserved for future generations.

The role of the office as an advisor for the larger family allows all family members to benefit from the buying power of the group. The office screens and monitors external advisors to ensure the family's interests are achieved. The family benefits from the team's ability to make investment recommendations, for example, with an understanding of the investment's potential impact on the current tax and estate plans and philanthropic goals.

Integrator of the Financial Process The family office is usually the central repository of all of the financial information about the family, individually and collectively.

No other service provider has access to all of the pieces of a family's legacy—personal histories, values, preferences, financial details, and long-term goals—the way a dedicated family office does.

Clients of the office benefit from the work the family office does as integrator or coordinator of the process. This work involves managing relationships with service providers and regulatory agencies, and delivering services from accounting to bill payment, with careful consideration of their impact on the big picture. This integrated perspective on taxes, estate, and wealth transfer plans, spending patterns, philanthropic aspirations, and other relevant factors optimizes the financial outcomes for the family overall.

> No other service provider has access to all of the pieces of a family's legacy— personal histories, values, preferences, financial details, and long-term goals—the way a dedicated family office does.

Support for Individual Family Members Every family member is a client of the family office in his or her own right. The family office often oversees the financial planning and budgeting process for each family member and his or her spouse, as well as coordinating bill payment, property management, and insurance oversight.

Educator of All Generations The role of the family office as educator varies from office to office. In some cases, the governing body drives the process of owner education and relies on the family office staff for assistance with the execution. In other cases, especially when a family member leads the family office, the family office may drive the effort to educate owners of all generations, taking on the mantle of responsibility for a program of lifelong learning across all branches and generations of the family.

The extent of the family office's involvement in the process depends, as with everything else, on the family's preferences and priorities. Most family offices have some kind of family member training program that is designed to prepare owners for the responsibilities of their wealth. The age at which the process begins varies from family to family but most (72 percent) begin the process when the owner is between 12 and 25 years old.

The office staff often also serve as trusted advisors or mentors for younger family members who are learning what it means to be a responsible owner of wealth.

Starting a Family Office

A family leader from the Eiche* family, a second-generation family business owner, was considering whether or not to start a family office to manage his family's financial affairs. After a review of the financial complexities (which were minor), and the liquidity issues (which were complicated), the advisor to the business owner asked him to focus on his spouse and two teenage children who were unaware of the success of the family business.

As his advisor wrote to him:

"Due to the significant estate planning you have already done, you have created a challenging future for your children. When they become adults in a few years, they will each be worth more than US$50 million (and potentially more), and that can be a terrible burden rather than a benefit if they are not properly prepared for the financial responsibility.

A family office should be an important part of your family planning because it is needed to support your children as they come into adulthood, and to give them someone they can trust in early adulthood without worrying about conflicts of interest. The most important reason to start a family office at this time is to provide a financial education for your spouse, and for the younger generation as they become inheritors of wealth in a few short years."

Transition Coordinator A critical role for most family offices is to support the transitions that every family faces as family members evolve through their respective lifecycles. Most family offices are charged with preparing for these inevitable transitions, which may involve members of the senior generations updating wills and preparing properly executed estate plans.

For the younger generation, this may involve identifying and grooming future leaders of the family.

Guardian of Family Values

An experienced billionaire from the Sakura* family and heir to one of his country's great multi-generational fortunes has argued very strongly in favor of an approach to family infrastructure in which "a family office should act primarily as a repository and protector of family values across generations."

From his perspective, building the correct foundation of values in the younger generations is the best response to the risks of financial ruin, family discord, erosion of the family business, or actions likely to bring the family's good name into controversy or disrepute.

While not abdicating the responsibility of family leadership, he sees the enlistment of support from his family office in this cross-generational role as an essential part of his approach to long-term family wealth management.

Repository of Family Values and Family Legacy There are a number of ways in which a family office can support the clarification, communication, and implementation of the family's values across generations. These include:

- Working with the family to draft a statement of vision and values.
- Developing an education program for the next generation.
- Ensuring that family values are addressed at regular meetings of the Family Council or in discussions with senior family members.
- Ensuring that any implications of family values are built into the family investment policy statement.
- Ensuring that an annual review of a family's progress addresses high-priority values and issues related to those values.

TYPES OF FAMILY OFFICES

The emphasis for each family office will vary. For many families, the office is seen as a dedicated investment business. Its purpose is to provide economies of scale for the family by leveraging the information, investment, and buying power of the group. Family members gain access to investment managers and opportunities that they might not be able to attract on their own because of the power of the family brand and the consolidated purchasing power of the family assets.

For others, the office is the master record keeper, where accounting, reporting, and tax compliance documents are prepared and stored. For families with tax-effective structures in multiple offshore jurisdictions, operating with a collection of varied corporate and trust structures, tax affairs may be of the utmost significance.

Still others start a family office for the intangibles. They want control over all aspects of the legacy process, a dedicated staff, and a way to support family members and keep them connected.

Family Continuity and the Family Office

A member of the Buche* family's view on what she values most about her family office confirms the notion that a family office is more than just a financial services provider:

"I'm proud of the family history that our family office represents. After six generations, it is important to me that we stay together. The office serves as a trusted advisor for financial matters and a solid, secure entity that oversees my financial situation. It provides a family connection for financial, philanthropic, and personal matters, with staff who know our personal situation."

TO HAVE OR NOT TO HAVE A FAMILY OFFICE?

Many wealth owners who continue to run a family business view management of the family's financial wealth and personal needs as a byproduct of the business. Business employees are entrusted with the oversight of the family's financial assets, tax reporting, personal service needs, and management of personal cash. For some, this approach works well. However, the family's goals for its business and the goals of the family regarding its wealth are often very different. The focus of a family business is business growth and the outcome is wealth creation, while the focus for family wealth is most often to achieve long-term wealth preservation. This difference in roles ultimately leads most families to separate the family office and its wealth management role from the operating business to allow each to do its best work in support of the family.

WEALTH MANAGEMENT ALTERNATIVES

Starting and staffing a dedicated family office do not always make sense. For those families who want access to family office services, there are several alternatives.

Some families look to a multi-family office (MFO) to provide some of the advantages of a dedicated family office without the overhead and responsibility of building another complex business operation.

An MFO is a wealth management firm that offers integrated, highly customized services to a limited number of clients who typically have a net worth of between US$10 million and US$100 million. Their services are similar to those of a dedicated family office, often with the same investment, trust, estate, and tax planning capabilities.

Family-owned MFOs typically evolve from single family offices. These families quietly "open their doors" to non-family clients as a way to sustain their family's service while spreading fixed costs and maximizing their buying power by having a larger pool of assets to invest.

Other families look to their private bank or primary financial institution for family office services. Some banks have organized dedicated client service groups to provide for the needs of families with significant wealth, where the interaction with the client is meant to be less transaction oriented and more relationship driven.

There are advantages and disadvantages to each approach to managing wealth. A few of the issues to consider are identified in Table 15.1.

Table 15.1: Dedicated Family Office versus Multi-family Office

Dedicated Family Office	Multi-Family Office
Advantages	
• Vision is jointly developed by the family and senior management.	• Broader base of resources is available from a larger organization.
• Organization, by definition, is the most responsive to client needs.	• Technology systems create operating efficiencies.
• Office may pay for itself with risk management alone.	• Institution offers relationship pricing and access to a range of services.
• Provides a platform for interaction with the community of like-minded families.	• Provides seminars and educational programs that can broaden the network of like-minded families.
Challenges	
• Strategic insight can be difficult to obtain with a small staff if not high quality and well networked.	• Broader client base means less customization.
• Diversity of needs grows as family grows.	• Departments can be territorial and risk averse.
• Consensus among family members on priorities can be difficult to achieve.	• Problem solvers may have limited alternatives or limited authority to do what is right for the client.
• May be insular and lack innovation.	• Primary alignment with rewards linked to MFO profitability, not client value.

THE FAMILY OFFICE TRAP

Having a family office may not be the right answer for every family. Reasons that some family leaders decide not to have a family office include views on cost relative to benefit, concerns that a family office will shield the family from gaining necessary personal knowledge and experience, or that the office will not perform as well as alternatives.

How a family office operation compares with institutional alternatives is a major and constant source of inquiry for well-informed families.

One of the unspoken risks of having a dedicated family office is the danger of falling into the "family office trap," where a family accountant, former company secretary, or advisor takes on the responsibility for setting up and running a family office when the family's wealth is in the early stages of development, but stays on long after the job has outgrown his or her capabilities. Unfortunately, some long-standing family office managers hang on tenaciously to increasingly well-paid jobs (as the money grows) and resist accurate benchmarking or realistic reviews (as performance fades).

> One of the unspoken risks of having a dedicated family office is the danger of falling into the "family office trap."

Some of these underperforming family offices can do major harm to families and their wealth if trust systems are not properly set up or maintained, if sophisticated wealth management challenges are misunderstood or, in the worst of cases, if proximity to great family wealth leads to family staff members defrauding a family, or justifying in their own minds the acceptability of taking "finders' fees" or other inappropriate payments to build their own wealth.

It is critical that proper checks and balances are built into every family office's operating procedures.

Journey Without End

One wealthy family leader insisted on retaining his college roommate as the head of his family office for personal reasons, despite a decade of weak performance, an aversion to change, and, at best, patchy adherence to family values. Unfortunately, the costs of keeping this individual in his position were proving increasingly expensive as poor investment performance, weak governance structures and control systems, high costs, and resistance to needed change mounted.

Eventually the reluctant patriarch was told by a respected member of his advisory team the hard, but valid, observation that:

"You can't get to where you want to go if you take your friend on the journey."

Shortly thereafter, changes in the family office were made that created a more limited role for the former head of the office and a better future for the family. However, the family would never be able to fully recover the losses, and lost opportunities, of the past.

The establishment of a family office is a great exercise in trust and delegation. By definition, a family office takes on some of the most sensitive and important legacy functions of the family. In the best case, this act of delegation creates a foundation of support for the family that is efficient, effective, and better aligned with the family's longer-term vision and fundamental values than any independent organization could be.

POST-CRISIS INTERVENTIONS AND ADJUSTMENTS

Although it was financial advisors rather than family offices that appeared most often as villains in the economic dramas of recent years, family offices have also come under renewed scrutiny for their performance, costs, and future role in the wake of the 2008 crisis.

At the same time, many families have found themselves more reliant than ever on their family offices to provide guidance and implementation support to understand the external environment, organize financing, bolster risk management systems (including deeper analysis and due diligence), and monitor investment portfolios.

The Madoff Test

In the wake of the scandals and losses of the recession of 2008, the head of one of the world's largest family offices offered the following sage observation:

"Have a formal process for reviewing service providers and ask yourself, 'Would our process have caught Bernie Madoff?'

MEASURES OF SUCCESS

The performance of the family office or firm providing such services needs to be evaluated each year. Measures of success vary dramatically from family to family based on each family's definition of success. For some, success is measured by quantitative investment performance; for others, it is based on achievement of the office's annual qualitative goals; for most, it is some combination of the two, creating a "balanced scorecard" approach to team management and assessment.

Some accomplishments are easier to quantify than others. For example, goals related to cost savings or investment performance can be easily measured and reported, but how does one place a value on the savings realized or costs avoided because family members receive a first-rate financial education courtesy of the family office? How does the family office track the bad decisions that were avoided?

If the family and family office team have a proper review system in place, the family office's management and governing body have a responsibility, and an opportunity, to document the value provided by the family office each year.

Figure 15.2 presents some examples of successful achievements that families have noted.

Figure 15.2: Sample Family Office Metrics

Wealth Enhancement Programs	Enhanced Asset Programs
• Wealth transferred to future generations without taxation • Real growth in investment return (after taxes, fees, and inflation) • Income tax savings from annual tax planning • Philanthropic goal development and execution • A more effective decision-making process	• Access to formerly unavailable services • Better financial reporting for better decision making • Development of individual financial and career education programs • Proactive communication among family members • Other strategies to strengthen family ties
Cost Control Programs	**Risk Management Programs**

• Savings from pooled purchase of new services
• Reduction in cost of existing services
• Consolidation or enhancement of external resources
• Analysis of make-or-buy decisions for services
• Effective use of technology
• Management of the family office budget
	• Assessment of potential strategic risks or liabilities
	  −Investment concentration risk
	  −Board member liabilities
	  −Personal property and security
	• Due diligence that avoids imprudent risks
	• Actions to mitigate or avoid potential financial disasters

Source: Family Office Exchange Research

Whether provided by a dedicated family office or a qualified wealth advisor, there is no substitute for a comprehensive and integrated approach to family wealth management.

Having a dedicated resource as a partner in the process of pre-serving all of the family's assets (financial, human, philanthropic) and executing the family legacy plan may be a sage investment whose long-term return is an improved likelihood of preserving the family's legacy for generations to come.

Questions for Leaders of Legacy

1. What is the purpose of your family office and how does it fit within your overall family and family eco-system structure?
2. What are the family, investment, reporting, and tax activities that need to be coordinated on behalf of the family?
3. What is your definition of success, and how would you rate the performance of the office relative to those expectations?
4. What are the risks and opportunities your family office should address?
5. Going forward, is there an opportunity to redefine family roles, the family office role, and key players in the eco-system to be more fully aligned with the Family Promise and vision?

16. CREATING AN ENTREPRENEURIAL CULTURE IN THE FAMILY

Along with a clear understanding of their past, families that sustain wealth successfully over multiple generations take proactive measures to identify and build new sources of family capital along the way.

These families understand the value of and strive to create an internal culture that fosters risk-taking and entrepreneurial pursuits. They often invest in a formal training process that teaches family members how to evaluate opportunities and develop business plans for structuring, funding, launching, and maintaining new ventures. A family that does this well creates a culture that balances caution with encouragement, and pushes family members to pursue their passions in a rational manner.

Families that encourage individual members to reach their full potential are also willing to embrace experimentation, uncertainty, and the possibility of failure. Even while acknowledging that new family ventures may fail, and establishing controls for limiting the impact of failure, these families appreciate the lessons that real risk and occasional failures can teach.

The families that are the most successful at developing an entre-preneurial or enterprising culture are those that recognize that their culture is dynamic. The family's history, the legacy of its founder, and the lessons of its founding business can all fade with time, changing the very culture of the family in the process.

Families that wish to preserve an entrepreneurial culture over time actively focus attention on exploration of risk-oriented oppor-tunities within each succeeding generation, and encourage younger owners to experiment with new ventures. They openly discuss their successes and failures, and they learn from the mistakes that were made to improve outcomes for new initiatives.

FOSTERING THE ENTREPRENEURIAL SPIRIT

An appetite for calculated risk-taking is essential for developing new entrepreneurs to sustain the family legacy.

It is the fate of most fourth-to-sixth-generation families to see the wealth dissipate as the family grows, unless the family culture supports wealth creation as well as wealth preservation. If some portion of the diversified asset pool is directed toward entrepreneurial endeavors, experience and insight are required along with investment dollars to ensure that entrepreneurial efforts create results needed to warrant the risk.

About 20 percent of legacy families formalize a private equity venture business to support entrepreneurial endeavors and to provide experience for future owners of larger businesses.[1]

While these new ventures seldom reach the same level of success as the core business that created the wealth for the family, a venture capital or private equity investment team provides a great training ground for future owners. At the very least, future leaders come to appreciate how hard it is to launch and sustain a successful venture of their own. Some will learn that they are not meant to be entrepreneurs—which is a most valuable lesson in its own right.

PROTECTING INSULATED FAMILIES FROM THEMSELVES

One of the greatest risks that wealthy families need to be aware of and respond to is the risk that results from a lack of business experience, a false sense of capabilities, or an underestimation of how hard it is to compete and be successful in the real world.

Extreme wealth often functions as a bubble or shield that protects owners from life's basic lessons that others learn from common, everyday life experiences.

Wealth inheritors grow up with great abundance, and may never have seen family members struggle to be successful. Their protected world does not require them to face personal challenges that teach other children resilience, and they often develop an entitlement attitude and dangerous expectations that their needs will always be met by others.

Children and grandchildren who grow up receiving messages that they are more deserving than others and entitled to privileges they did not earn are sometimes handicapped by the attitudes they develop. Young people in this environment learn that they do not have to work as hard as others to get what they want, and this leads to the "entitlement syndrome" which has been artfully described by Jaffe and Brown.[2]

---

1 Family Office Exchange, Family Office Benchmarking, 2008.
2 Dennis T. Jaffe and Fredda Herz Brown, "From Entitlement to Stewardship: How a Prosperous Family Can Prepare the Next Generation," *The Journal of Wealth Management* 11, Spring 2009, 11–28.

When legacy families grow up with the core values of perseverance, self-sufficiency, and independent thinking, they are less likely to be handicapped by fear of failure. They learn to be resilient and to bounce back into the game when tossed about by unexpected troubles, or even outright failure.

> When legacy families grow up with the core values of perseverance, self-sufficiency, and independent thinking, they are less likely to be handicapped by fear of failure.

When insight, strategic vision, and luck are added to these qualities, the successful family has the potential to replicate, and sometimes even surpass, the dimensions and quality of the legacy created by the founding generation. One of the behavioral patterns that most often leads to perpetuated success is the development of a culture of analyzing opportunities for entrepreneurial ventures where risk can be properly measured and managed by knowledgeable parties.

Creating Something Together—Again

In the Magnolia* family, involving five family branches living in six different countries, the family members view themselves intrinsically as a *family that stays in business together.* The sixth-generation owners sold a major consumer goods company that they had collectively owned for decades. Within months of the sale, they agreed on the purchase of another business together, which they had already selected for acquisition before finalizing the sale of their other company.

The CEO of the family office described the common philosophy they have about "creating something new together at each generation." The part of their legacy that this family enjoys the most is purchasing and energizing business ventures as a group of shared owners.

The ability for this family to stay together over generations results primarily from two factors: their culture that blends social relations and business networks; and the formality of the governance structure that has been in place for many years.

(continued)

The family office CEO describes them as a "very balanced group" despite the normal differences of opinion that are always involved. Family members socialize together, have common interests, and view business as one of these common interests. The social interaction serves as an aggregator of opinions over time, and because they are tied together by common interests outside the business, they do not have all of their energies focused only on one part of the relationship.

In their formal governance structure there are two critical elements that have provided stability for the family. First is the professional process they have adopted for making decisions together. Each branch of the family chooses a single leader to represent their branch's interests, and the members of each branch support the leader they have chosen. Cousins in each branch are free to use whatever method works best for them in selecting the leader, and the leadership terms are staggered across the branches so not all leaders change at the same time.

The second key element is the freedom each owner has to exit the family enterprise if required, and to choose the investment ventures that are most appropriate for their philosophy and circumstances. Most family members co-invest together in publicly traded operating companies with 30 percent of their wealth, and they invest 70 percent of their liquid wealth through pooled investment funds, so the purchasing power of the family is preserved. No one in the family is forced to co-invest against his or her will, because they buy controlling interests in public companies whose shares can be sold, and they use common investment funds whose shares can be sold when individual liquidity is required.

Family members recognize the value of staying together in these investments, but having options to exit allows them to manage their different needs as sixth-generation owners.

SUSTAINING AN EFFECTIVE ENTREPRENEURIAL CULTURE

Insights gathered from a group of wealth owners provide an appreciation of the methods adopted by these owners who have been able to create and sustain an entrepreneurial culture in their families.[3] A group discussion held for 40 owners and inheritors of wealth was chaired by FOX, with all present brainstorming on ideas about risk-taking and entrepreneurship. This session surfaced

---

3 Family Office Exchange, Fall Forum, Chicago, October 20–22, 2009.

the following insights and initiatives that can contribute to the creation and maintenance of a sensible and entrepreneurial risk-taking culture in the family.

Discuss Real Risk-Taking Experiences One of the participants described a recent family meeting where the third-generation patriarch took the time to walk the family through the successes and failures of their 100-year business history. He emphasized the failures, what had gone wrong at each critical juncture, and the lessons that had been learned the hard way by the owners.

The history provided a perfect springboard for a family discussion about how the next generation felt about taking risks with the legacy they had inherited.

Recognize that Upbringing Has an Impact on Entrepreneurial Attitudes In a family enterprise, the adult roles that each owner is suited for can often be foreseen in the sandbox.

Just as spending and saving habits of children surface by the age of three,[4] the instinct to watch out for brothers and sisters is an inherent quality that identifies children who may make good family stewards of wealth, while children who are risk takers in childhood have a greater likelihood of ending up with extreme results—extremely successful or extremely unsuccessful.

Accept Failure as a Possible Outcome Another wealth owner was outspoken about the need for the family to embrace potential failure. He noted that risk-taking is not a constructive experience if the family culture does not tolerate making mistakes and thus misses out on the opportunity to learn from them. This open-minded attitude is difficult for families that are focused on preserving what they have inherited and place a high priority on not making mistakes that may subject them to family ridicule or financial loss.

"I've been given the opportunity to screw up . . . but with guidance. More importantly, I've been given the opportunity to succeed."

Fifth-generation family member

Do Not Neglect the Hard Work Necessary for Success A fourth-generation family leader describes the value that his family has

---

4 Joline Godfrey, *Raising Financially Fit Kids* (New York: Ten Speed Press, 2003).

gained from looking back to identify the circumstances that had created success in his family's century of experience with substantial wealth. He felt that his family was fortunate to have a founder who had a history of failures before his ultimate success.

The founder, despite three business failures, continued to believe in his ultimate success. The family recognized that his success was due, in large part, to his persistence and his positive attitude.

Balance between Process and Action It is important for families to develop a process for analyzing both the projects that are successful and the ones that fail.

Because the founder often relies on instinct to develop and run the business, there is likely to be little documentation of the process used to make important business decisions. It is invaluable for his children, who would not have the years of experience or natural instincts, to have a more detailed roadmap to guide their success.

Recognize the Unique Challenges for the Second Generation It can be difficult for family members to make their own way in a family culture that is dominated by a strong patriarch, and fear of failure may make second-generation family members more risk averse than others in the family.

Second-generation leaders have shared the following advice:

- Recognize that many second-generation family members are afraid to take risks and lose the money that their elders worked so hard to make.

- Accept that next-generation family members may feel overshadowed or controlled by their elders, especially if they work in the family business.

- Understand that second-generation siblings may feel the need to prove something to a dominant, dogmatic entrepreneur, and may therefore take on risks that are greater than warranted.

- Recognize that a person's appetite for risk often changes with age.

SEVEN STRATEGIES FOR CREATING
AN ENTERPRISING CULTURE

A group of 16 industry thought leaders, brought together Chicago in 2009, brainstormed about the challenges facing those who want to create a risk-taking culture inside their wealth-preserving family enterprise.[5]

They embraced the concept of focusing as much on upside opportunities as on downside risk management to enhance the long-term sustainability of the family. It is much easier to engage owners in something creative when they can see constructive results from their own efforts. The process of preserving wealth does not attract entrepreneurial family members or give them reasons to stay engaged. What they could be attracted to is the following list of strategies developed by the group:

1. Encourage the pursuit of a meaningful, productive, and fulfilling life for each owner.
2. Define an entrepreneurial culture for the family.
3. Separate the sleep-well assets from the risk-taking assets (the "stay-rich" from the "get-rich" activities).
4. Put the family business assets in the hands of owners and managers who are informed risk takers.
5. Regenerate family assets every 50 years—"there is no standing still."
6. Define responsible ownership for each generation based on the challenges at hand.
7. Use the family's most creative strategies in mission-driven philanthropic ventures.

This inventory of strategies highlights the value of creating an entrepreneurial culture, one that puts more emphasis on upside than downside potential, and places as much emphasis on opportunity analysis as risk control. These seven principles are described in more detail in Appendix C.

---

5 Family Office Exchange, Thought Leaders Round Table, Chicago, June 2009.

Some early adopters of this philosophy have been freed from personal constraints and family taboos when they develop an entrepreneurial culture as an important part of the family's strategy for sustaining wealth and preserving private enterprise.

The benefits of making this shift in focus for wealth-owning families have only just begun to be explored, but families are certainly strengthened when they recognize innovation and entrepreneurship as important family values.

Questions for Leaders of Legacy

1. Does your family have an entrepreneurial culture?
2. What can you do to help cultivate a balance of entrepreneurial spirit and prudent risk management in the next generation?
3. What opportunities does the next generation have to learn about risk, risk appetite, and risk management together?
4. How do you select and celebrate the responsible risk takers in your family?
5. What is the best approach to blend future legacy objectives and risk management principles in your family?

Ensuring the Family Legacy

Over the past 150 years, the Laird Norton family has successfully reinvested its capital to create substantial wealth many different times.

Today it is a seventh-generation family that has grown to more than 400 cousins. It has always had a very strong sense of family legacy, with formalized structures for family member education, as well as regular, scheduled family gatherings and social events to build strong intra-family relations. These opportunities for working and playing together as a family are so embedded in the family culture that many family members do not even recognize them as being exceptional or unusual.

To accomplish its financial goals, the family, starting with the first generation, separated a large portion of its assets outside the business to be reinvested in other businesses. This allowed it to build liquid assets outside its core company and prevented it from being financially tied to the performance of a single company or industry. To this day, the family continues this practice and controls several major operating companies.

Elements of a positive risk-taking culture

One main reason that the Laird Norton family has had such success in regenerating their wealth is that the family fosters a positive risk-taking culture in every generation. Some of the specific elements that contribute to this culture are listed below:

"Tight–loose framework"

While family members grow up with a strong sense of family unity, legacy, and history, the structure of the family also encourages individuals to prosper and follow their own paths in life.

Generational harvesting

The family has restructured its business holdings at every generation, which the current leaders have called "generational harvesting." The family stays attached to the family enterprise, and not the business enterprise, since it does want to get emotionally attached to any business investment. Because of its history, the family views its tradition of owning companies to be part of the family legacy. The track record for the business ventures over the past 100 years has been varied, with four tremendously successful companies. It has become a part of the family legacy to take risks and create new ventures together.

(continued)

Family summer camp

For the past 13 years the family has held a summer camp for young family members as part of their annual family gathering. This camp provides the opportunity for cousins who are normally dispersed around the world to build strong, positive relationships that will translate well to the boardroom in the future.

Family education programs

On-the-job training is a key element of the Laird Norton family's education programs. If family members so choose, they have opportunities to sit in boardrooms, evaluate potential business acquisitions, and serve on various committees. These are real work experiences and provide far more practical knowledge than simulations or classroom training.

Leadership selection

Older generations intentionally and proactively push the next generation to be successful but not necessarily to serve the family. This results in new family leaders whose true passion is to guide the family, not those who feel they were obligated to serve or pigeonholed into their role from an early age.

Older generations able to give up control gracefully

Past family leaders and members of the older generations are careful to listen to the next generation of leaders and give their advice if asked. However they do not attempt to control the family or tell the next generation what to do. This gives new family leaders the freedom to make their own choices knowing that they have the support of past leaders.

EPILOGUE
FUTURE LEADERSHIP CHALLENGES

Building an entrepreneurial culture in a legacy family can be a way to bring a family back to the origins of its wealth, and a return to the source of its most important values, achievements, and collective memories. It can also be a valuable step in moving a family forward toward the realization of a common vision and the fulfillment of the individual aspirations of its various members.

The continuing pursuit of that vision, which requires demonstrating and inculcating respect for family values and traditions, honoring the Family Promise, guiding the family through periods of both turbulence and calm, and fostering continuity while overseeing necessary change, is the essence of the leadership challenge for the coming century.

In all cases, there is a common imperative to invest well in the highest-priority legacy initiatives and in the development of true family wealth in all its forms.

Despite the apparent similarities in the overall task, there are always great differences that bring to each generation of family leaders unique challenges, crises, risks, and opportunities. The test of family leaders is whether they master the challenges of their own time, and are able to hand over the torch of leadership to a following generation with certainty that those new leaders will be capable of rising to the inevitable challenges of their own tenure in family leadership.

Yet the future leadership challenge is not only to address current issues and prepare to pass on the rights and responsibilities of leadership to the next set of capable family leaders; full achievement of legacy potential demands that future generations be fully considered in decisions made before they are born. This is the essence of "seventh-generation thinking" and the full measure of a family's visionary capability and legacy values.

The opportunity to look back into the patterns of history, see forward across multiple generations, and act now to preserve and enhance the legacy that will be carried forward into many future lives is the complex task, and the extraordinary privilege, of every family leader.

Membership in a legacy family and, even greater, the opportunity to contribute to the leadership of that family for a time, are indeed both a privilege and an honor. Bearing the mantle of leadership in a family of wealth creates an opportunity for exceptional personal growth, substantial contribution to the family and wider community, and enjoyment of a profound sense of an important life well lived.

The opportunity to pursue a higher purpose and contribute to a continuing family legacy are two of the principal reasons that justify the personal sacrifice and collective investments required by all branches and generations of the family. United, fully engaged, and well led, legacy families can create something together that is far greater than anything they could accomplish, or could be, on their own.

The most powerful and positive family legacies are living examples of the value of common purpose and mutual commitment, which are especially valuable in the most challenging times.

Creating a great family fortune is a rare achievement. Turning that financial fortune into an enduring family legacy is an extraordinary accomplishment and the ultimate goal of most family leaders. The nature of those legacies and the unique journey of each family leader are what this book is about.

These are not ordinary times. In a new era already marked by crisis and facing a future of greater uncertainty than in many recent decades, rising to the challenges of family leadership will be increasingly difficult and will require exceptional insight, courage, energy, and engagement.

It is our hope that this book offers to leaders and family members alike a new set of perspectives, a more positive view of the potential for each family, a realistic hope for a better future, and access to some of the practical tools and approaches available to realize that full family potential.

We hope that the content of this book, and the decades of research and experience captured in its pages, may help you to manage the most important risks and seize the greatest opportunities you face as you prepare your own family to realize its best possible future.

We wish you well on your journey.

APPENDICES

A. PROFILE OF
FAMILY OFFICE EXCHANGE

Family Office Exchange (FOX) is the world's leading peer-to-peer network for ultra-wealthy families and their family offices, and is the leading authority related to matters of sustaining wealth.

With more than 20 years of experience, and a staff of 40 people based in Chicago, New York, and London, FOX is a thought leader in the areas of family strategy and governance, family office best practices, and family risk planning.

FOX serves family groups and their advisors in 23 countries, providing trusted insight and best practices for managing family wealth. The network includes 340 ultra-wealthy families, as well as 170 multifamily offices (MFOs) and advisory firms. More than 6,000 individual family members are served by the FOX global community.

Members rely on FOX (www. familyoffice.com) to help them make better, more informed decisions about their family legacy and their wealth management practices and providers. FOX has established a safe, confidential environment of common interest and mutual trust **to enable members to compare experiences and learn from the collective knowledge of other members in the network.**

Resources available to FOX members include proprietary research on wealth management best practices, peer benchmarking, bimonthly webinars on current trends, and an extensive library of articles and white papers, as well as online discussion forums, regional peer roundtables, and a variety of educational forums.

The annual FOX Forum held in Europe in the spring and Chicago in October provides an opportunity for FOX members to gather with peers and thought leaders to discuss global issues and important challenges facing wealthy families. The Forums address many of the issues of greatest concern to wealthy families and their advisors in the areas of legacy and leadership.

Perhaps most valued by members is the collective intelligence of the FOX network. This accumulated wisdom has been methodically captured by the FOX staff, with full respect for confidentiality and discretion, and archived in a secure searchable database for the exclusive use of FOX members. This collective knowledge, built over 20 years, is what truly sets FOX apart.

Sara Hamilton founded FOX in 1989 to provide objective information and advice on family wealth, family leadership, and different pathways available to sustain wealth across generations.

Helping members preserve and enhance their true family wealth by providing education, insights, and peer exchange is the sole focus of FOX. The firm's success is measured by the quality and value of the experience of its many private investors, family offices, multi-family offices, and wealth advisory members.

True to this original vision, FOX strives to address new challenges and to provide insights on current trends and issues regarding investing, philanthropy, and owner education. As an advocate for wealth owners, FOX provides leadership in the private wealth field, helping to shape the industry and develop standards of performance for industry professionals.

In addition to the legacy established by the FOX private network, the Family Office Blueprint™ has served as a model for many leading families, and countless family office executives have relied on FOX for education of their teams and assessment of their practices.

The range of services offered to members is evaluated annually by members and **more than 90 percent of current family members say they would recommend FOX to other family groups.**

Family Legacy and Leadership: Preserving True Family Wealth in Challenging Times is the first book undertaken by Sara Hamilton and FOX, with the mutual effort, shared guidance, and co-authorship of

Fox Membership Services

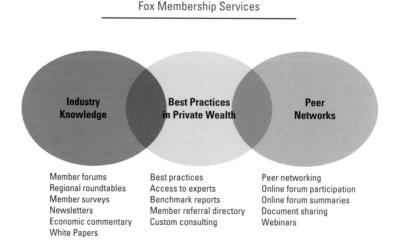

Industry Knowledge	Best Practices in Private Wealth	Peer Networks
Member forums	Best practices	Peer networking
Regional roundtables	Access to experts	Online forum participation
Member surveys	Benchmark reports	Online forum summaries
Newsletters	Member referral directory	Document sharing
Economic commentary	Custom consulting	Webinars
White Papers		

Mark Daniell. Mark is the author of six other books, the creator of his own family office, and an active member in the FOX network. We welcome comments and insights about the book. Send inquiries about FOX to fox@familyoffice.com and insights about this book to comments@familylegacyandleadership.com.

Main Office in Chicago

Email: fox@familyoffice.com
Phone: 312–327–1200
Fax: 312–327–1212
Post: Family Office Exchange
100 S. Wacker Drive
Suite 900
Chicago, IL 60606
United States

London (International) Office

Email: internationalqueries@familyoffice.com
Phone: +44 (0) 207 170 4236
Fax: +44 (0) 207 170 4234
Post: Family Office Exchange
Winchester House, Suite 307
259–69 Old Marylebone Road
London NW1 5RA
United Kingdom

B. OPERATING FRAMEWORKS FOR LEGACY, LEADERSHIP, AND RISK MANAGEMENT

These simple frameworks were developed to help organize the family's thinking about the complex work of sustaining understanding and family legacy, leadership, and risk management. While these outlines are addressed throughout the book, these lists are provided here in one section for easy reference and further consideration.

PART I—THE FAMILY LEGACY FRAMEWORK

1. Develop an appreciation among family members for the value of legacy planning and/or strategic planning.
2. Recognize and reflect on the shared legacy and values in the family.
3. Identify challenges of shared ownership and shared risks.
4. Develop a shared vision for the future and a set of common goals.
5. Identify leadership skills needed and develop a team of qualified leaders.
6. Organize a governance process and operating structures to support the vision.
7. Develop a process for defining and measuring success for the family enterprise.

PART II—THE FAMILY LEADERSHIP FRAMEWORK

1. Build consensus among owners about the importance of developing and supporting family leaders.
2. Establish the rights, responsibilities, and processes for leadership.
3. Manage the governance process for effective decision making and fair dispute resolution.
4. Develop leadership succession plans (both short- and long-term) and document a clear selection process.

5. Implement a formal strategic planning and/or legacy planning process for the family enterprise.
6. Establish a process for educating owners about the importance of legacy, leadership, and family challenges.
7. Develop a process for measuring the success of the leadership team and performance of the supporting eco-system.

PART III—THE CHANGE AND RISK MANAGEMENT FRAMEWORK

1. Develop an understanding of the process of risk assessment and change management.
2. Identify the risks and opportunities facing the family in the context of a changing world.
3. Prioritize the risks and gain consensus among owners about the importance of taking action.
4. Allocate responsibilities for managing risks among responsible parties.
5. Manage the immediate risks challenging the family and assign a specific timetable.
6. Develop mitigation plans for addressing the most important risks.
7. Develop an ongoing process for managing change and measuring the success of the risk management process.

C. STRATEGIES FOR CREATING AN ENTREPRENEURIAL CULTURE

1. Encourage the pursuit of a meaningful, productive, and fulfilling life for each owner.

   a) Identify and discuss the behaviors that define a meaningful life and model those behaviors.

   b) Help each wealth owner define his or her risk-taking appetite using a hierarchy of needs approach.

   c) Let parents raise their own children (without being trapped inside generation-skipping trusts).

2. Define an entrepreneurial culture for the family.

   a) Understand the value of both stewardship and measured risk-taking in the family.

   b) Document the historical risks taken by the family—especially the risks that did not work out.

   c) Encourage entrepreneurs to support risk takers as well as wealth preservers and to let their children make their own mistakes and learn from them.

   d) Use incentive systems to encourage qualified owners to take entrepreneurial risks.

   e) Accept failure as a natural outgrowth of risk-taking.

3. Separate the sleep-well assets from the risk-taking assets (the stay-rich from the get-rich activities).

   a) Partition the investment capital that preserves the family lifestyle (the "sleep-well" funds).

   b) Never assume that the concentrated wealth in the core business is a risk-free venture.

   c) Organize the wealth into hierarchical levels of risk-taking and match to each owner's appetite for risk.

   d) Test the risk tolerances of owners using best- and worst-case scenario planning.

4. Put the family business assets in the hands of owners and managers who are informed risk takers.

   a) Share enough information about the business for owners to evaluate the risks involved.

   b) Clarify the roles of owners, directors, and managers in the future of the business.

   c) Build a base of liquid wealth that allows risk-averse shareholders to sell their shares to other owners.

5. Regenerate family assets every 50 years—"there is no standing still."

   a) Every two generations, have the courage to concentrate investments to regenerate wealth.

   b) Encourage concentrated risk-taking in something the family understands and has thoroughly researched.

   c) Get the education and experience needed before making concentrated bets on new ventures.

   d) Use business schools to weed out the wealth inheritors who will not work hard.

   e) Make family money available for creative, innovative, and entrepreneurial ideas.

   f) Build milestones around each new venture to focus on being successful.

6. Define responsible ownership for each generation based on the challenges at hand.

   a) Build positive self-development plans for each owner.

   b) Make owners hungry for personal success through role modeling experiences.

   c) Mandate that each owner's lifestyle be financed by personal income.

   d) Develop messages to moderate personal consumption.

7. Use the family's most creative strategies in mission-driven philanthropic ventures.

   a) Develop a shared vision for what the family can do together philanthropically to preserve the family legacy.

b) Be a source of regenerative wealth in the family's local community or multiple communities.

c) Commit enough money philanthropically that no owner can rely on inheritance to maintain his or her lifestyle.

d) Make a meaningful impact by measuring outcomes systematically.

D. RECOMMENDED READING LIST

Although there are many excellent works by many authors, who have all, in different ways, contributed to the developing knowledge base on true family wealth, a few may be particularly apt for readers seeking to expand on the topic addressed by this book.

While not meaning to exclude from consideration a far greater list of relevant works, some of which are captured in the following bibliography, a shortlist of works that members of the FOX membership network have cited as of particular value to their own thinking about family legacy and leadership includes:

Bernstein, Peter L. *Against the Gods: The Remarkable Story of Risk.* New York: John Wiley & Sons, Inc., 1998.

Brunel, Jean. *Integrated Wealth Management.* 2nd ed. London: Euromoney Institutional Investor, 2006.

Daniell, Mark Haynes. *Strategy for the Wealth Family: Seven Principles to Assure Riches to Riches Across Generations.* Singapore: John Wiley & Sons (Asia) Pte. Ltd., 2008.

Ellis, Charles D. *Winning the Loser's Game: Timeless Strategies for Successful Investing,* 5th ed. New York: McGraw-Hill, 2009.

Gersick, Kelin E., with Deanne Stone, Katherine Grady, Michele Desjardins and Howard Muson. *Generations of Giving, Leadership and Continuity in Family Foundations.* Lanham, MD: Lexington Books, 2004.

Godfrey, Joline. *Raising Financially Fit Kids.* Berkeley: Ten Speed Press, 2003.

Graham, Benjamin. *The Intelligent Investor: The Definitive Book on Value Investing.* Rev. ed. New York: Collins Business, 2003.

Hausner, Lee and Douglass K. Freeman. *The Legacy Family: The Definitive Guide to Creating a Successful Multi-generational Family.* Houndsmills, Basingstoke, Hampshire: Palgrave Macmillan, 2009.

Hughes Jr., James E. *Family Wealth—Keeping It in the Family: How Family Members and Their Advisors Preserve Human, Intellectual and Financial Assets for Generations.* New York: Bloomberg Press, 2004.

———.*Family: The Compact Among Generations.* New York: Bloomberg Press 2007.

Jaffe, Dennis T. *Stewardship in Your Family Enterprise: Developing Responsible Family Leaders Across Generations.* Omaha: Pioneer, 2009.

Karoff, H. Peter with Jane Maddox. *The World We Want: New Dimensions in Philanthropy and Social Change.* Lanham: AltaMira Press, 2007.

Lansberg, Ivan. *Succeeding Generations: Realizing the Dream of Families in Business.* Boston: Harvard Business School Press, 1999.

Levy, John L. *Inherited Wealth: Opportunities and Dilemmas.* North Charleston: BookSurge Publishing, 2008.

Lucas, Stuart E. *Wealth: Grow It, Protect It, Spend It, and Share It.* Saddle River: Wharton School Publishing, 2006.

Twist, Lynne. *The Soul of Money: Transforming Your Relationship with Money and Life.* New York: W. W. Norton & Company, 2003.

Ward, John L. *Perpetuating the Family Business: 50 Lessons Learned from Long-Lasting, Successful Families in Business.* Houndsmills, Basingstoke, Hampshire: Palgrave Macmillan, 2004.

BIBLIOGRAPHY

"The Moral Dimension of Philanthropy and Social Action." A Concept Paper for a Project of The Karoff Center at TPI, 2009.

Abts III, Henry, W. *The Living Trust: The Failproof Way to Pass Along Your Estate to Your Heirs Without Lawyers, Courts, or the Probate System.* Revised and updated ed. Chicago: Contemporary Books, 2003.

American Bar Association. *Guide to Wills and Estates.* 2nd ed. New York: Random House Reference, 2004.

Amit, Raphael. Single Family Offices: Private Wealth Management in the Family Context. Wharton Global Family Alliance, 2008.

Aronoff, Craig E. and John L. Ward. *Family Business Governance: Maximizing Family and Business Potential.* Marietta: Family Enterprise Publishers, 1996.

————. *Family Business Ownership: How To Be An Effective Shareholder.* Marietta: Family Enterprise Publishing, 2001.

————. *Family Meetings: How to Build a Stronger Family and a Stronger Business.* 2nd ed. Marietta: Family Enterprise Publishers, 2002.

————. *How to Choose and Use Advisors: Getting the Best Professional Family Business Advice.* Marietta: Family Enterprise Publishers, 2004.

Aronoff, Craig E., Joseph H. Astrachan, and John L. Ward. *Developing Family Business Policies: Your Guide to the Future.* Marietta: Family Enterprise Publishers, 1998.

Aronoff, Craig E., Joseph H. Astrachan, Drew S. Mendoza, and John L. Ward. *Making Sibling Teams Work: The Next Generation.* Marietta: Family Enterprise Publishers, 1997.

Aronoff, Craig E., Stephen L. McClure, and John L. Ward. *Family Business Succession: The Final Test of Greatness.* 2nd ed. Marietta: Family Enterprise Publishers, 2003.

Baines, Barry K. *The Ethical Will Writing Guide Workbook.* Cambridge: Josaba Limited, 2001.

Barber, Benjamin. *Consumed: How Markets Corrupt Children, Infantilize Adults, and Swallow Citizens Whole.* New York: W. W. Norton, 2007.

Bartlett, Christopher A. and Ghosal Sumantra. *Transnational Management Text, Cases & Readings in Cross-Border Management.* 2nd ed. New York: The McGraw-Hill Companies Inc, 1995.

Bauman, Zygmunt. *Globalization: The Human Consequences.* Cambridge: Polity Press, 1998.

Beinhocker, Eric D. *The Origin of Wealth: Evolution, Complexity, and the Radical Remaking of Economics.* Boston: Harvard Business School Press, 2006.

Bennis, Warren, ed. *Leaders on Leadership Interviews with Top Executives.* Boston: Harvard Business Review, 2006.

Bernstein, Peter L. *Against the Gods: The Remarkable Story of Risk.* New York: John Wiley & Sons, Inc. 1998.

——. *The Portable MBA in Investments.* New York: John Wiley & Sons, Inc., 1995.

——. *Capital Ideas: The Improbable Origins of Modern Wall Street.* New York: Free Press, 1993.

Bernstein, William. *The Intelligent Asset Allocator: How to Build Your Portfolio to Maximize Returns and Minimize Risk.* New York: McGraw-Hill, 2001.

——. *The Four Pillars of Investing: Lessons for Building a Winning Portfolio.* New York: McGraw-Hill, 2002.

Binney, T. "'The Good Man in Trouble.' (A Sermon delivered on Sunday Morning, November 7, 1852, at the Weigh House Chapel, Fish Street Hill, London)," *Mother's Magazine*, 1853.

——. *Money: A Popular Exposition.* London: Jackson, Walford and Hodder, 1865.

——. *Sermons Preached in The King's Weigh-house Chapel, London, 1829–1869.* London: Macmillan & Co, 1869.

——. *The Best of Both Worlds: A Book for Young Men.* London: Edward Knight, 1895.

Blouin, Barbara, Katherine Gibson, and Margaret Kiersted. *The Legacy of Inherited Wealth: Interviews with Heirs.* Prince Edward Island: Trio Press, 1995.

Blue, Ron with Jeremy White. *Splitting Heirs: Giving Your Money and Things to Your Children Without Ruining Their Lives.* Chicago: Northfield Publishing, 2004.

Brill, Hal, Jack Brill, and Cliff Feigenbaum. *Investing With Your Values: Making Money and Making a Difference.* Gabriola Island: New Society Publishers, 2000.

Brown, Fredda Herz. *Reweaving the Family Tapestry.* North Charleston: BookSurge, LLC, 2006.

Brown, Fredda Herz and Dennis T. Jaffe. "Overcoming Entitlement and Raising Responsible Next Generation Family Members." *Relative Solutions*, 11–28. http://www.relativesolutions.com/assets/20090929125417_28_ ARTICLE.pdf.

Bruner, Robert F. and Sean D. Carr. *The Panic of 1907: Lessons Learned from the Market's Perfect Storm.* New York: John Wiley & Sons, 2007.

Buffone, Gary. *Choking on the Silver Spoon: Keeping Your Kids Healthy, Wealthy and Wise in a Land of Plenty.* Jacksonville: Simplon Press, 2003.

Burke, Melissa and Ellen Rogin. *Great with Money: The Women's Guide to Prosperity.* Northfield: Two Tangle Productions, 2008.

Carlock, Randel S. and John L. Ward. *Strategic Planning for the Family Business, Parallel Planning to Unify the Family and Business.* Hampshire: Palgrave Macmillan, 2001.

Collier, Charles. *Wealth in Families.* Boston: Harvard University Press, 2006.

Condon, Gerald M. and Jeffrey L. Condon. *Beyond the Grave: The Right Way and the Wrong Way of Leaving Money to Your Children and Others.* New York: HarperCollins Publishers Inc., 2001.

Courton Brown, Michelle, Dennis Collins, Joel L. Fleishman, David Ford, Peter Goldmark, Anna Faith Jones, H. Peter Karoff, Scott Mc Vay, Steven A. Schroeder, M.D., Bruce Sievers, and Adele Simmons (Edited by H. Peter Karoff). *Just Money: A Critique of Contemporary American Philanthropy.* Boston: TPI Editions, 2004.

Curtis, Gregory. *Creative Capital: Managing Private Wealth in a Complex World.* Bloomington: iUniverse, 2004.

Daniell, Mark Haynes. *World of Risk: Next Generation Strategy for a Volatile Era.* Singapore: John Wiley & Sons, 2000.

———. *Strategy: A Step-by-Step Approach to the Development and Presentation of World Class Business Strategy.* Houndsmills, Basingstoke, Hampshire: Palgrave Macmillan, 2004.

———. *The Elements of Strategy: A Pocket Guide to the Essence of Successful Business Strategy.* Houndsmills, Basingstoke, Hampshire: Palgrave Macmillan, 2006.

———. *Strategy for the Wealthy Family: Seven Principles to Assure Riches to Riches Across Generations.* Singapore: John Wiley & Sons, Inc., 2008.

Daniell, Mark and Karin Sixl-Daniell. *Wealth Wisdom for Everyone: An Easy-to-Use Guide to Personal Financial Planning and Wealth Creation.* Singapore: World Scientific Publishing, 2006.

Davis, William. *The Rich: A New Study of the Species.* London: Icon Books, 2006.

Dembo, Ron S. and Andrew Freeman. *Seeing Tomorrow: Rewriting the Rules of Risk.* New York: John Wiley & Sons, Inc., 1998.

Dominguez, Joe and Vicki Robin. *Your Money Or Your Life: Transforming Your Relationship with Money and Achieving Financial Independence.* New York: Penguin, 1999.

Domini, Amy. *Socially Responsible Investing: Making a Difference and Making Money.* Chicago: Kaplan Business, 2000.

Doud Jr., Ernest A. and Lee Hausner. *Hats Off to You: Balancing Roles and Creating Success in Family Business.* Glendale: Doud/Hausner and Associates, 2000.

Dungan, Nathan. *Prodigal Sons and Material Girls: How Not to Be Your Child's ATM.* New York: John Wiley & Sons, Inc., 2003.

Evensky, Harold R. *Wealth Management: The Financial Advisor's Guide to Investing and Managing Client Assets.* New York: McGraw-Hill, 1997.

Family Office Exchange. "Securing the Future: Managing Threats and Opportunities Through Effective Risk Planning," Family Office Exchange White Paper, 2009.

Family Office Exchange. "Recasting the Central Role of the Family Office," Family Office Exchange White Paper, 2006.

———. FOX Investment Survey Results, 2008–2009. FOX Member Research, www.familyoffice.com.

Farkas, Charles M. and Philippe De Backer. *Maximum Leadership*. New York: Henry Holt & Company, 1996.

Fithian, Scott C. *Values-Based Estate Planning: A Step-by-Step Approach to Wealth Transfer for Professional Advisors*. New York: John Wiley & Sons, Inc., 2000.

Fleishman, Joel L. *The Foundation: A Great American Secret*. New York: Public Affairs, 2007.

Fleming, Quentin J. *Keep the Family Baggage out of the Family Business, Avoiding the Seven Deadly Sins that Destroy Family Businesses*. New York: Simon & Schuster, 2007.

Frank, Robert. *Richistan: A Journey through the 21st Century Wealth Boom and the Lives of the New Rich*. London: Piatkus Books 2008.

———. "New IRS Unit Targets Wealthy Tax Dodgers," *Wall Street Journal*, November 5, 2009.

———. "America's Top 50 Philanthropists Gave Less in 2009," *The Wealth Report*, February 8, 2010.

Freed, Rachael. *Women's Lives, Women's Legacies: Passing Your Beliefs and Blessings to Future Generations*. Minneapolis: Fairview Press, 2003.

Friedman, Thomas L. *Hot, Flat and Crowded*. New York: Farrar, Straus & Giroux, 2008.

———. *The World Is Flat: A Brief History of the Twenty-First Century*. New York: Picador, 2007.

Frisch, Ephraim. *An Historical Survey of Jewish Philanthropy*. New York: MacMillan, 1924.

Frumkin, Peter. *Strategic Giving: The Art and Science of Philanthropy*. Chicago: University of Chicago Press, 2006.

Gabe, Grace and Jean Lipman-Blumen. *Step Wars: Overcoming the Perils and Making Peace in Adult Stepfamilies*. New York: St. Martin's Press, 2004.

Gallo, Eileen, Jon Gallo, and Kevin Gallo. *Silver Spoon Kids: How Successful Parents Raise Responsible Children*. New York: McGraw-Hill, 2001.

George, Bill. *Authentic Leadership: Rediscovering the Secrets to Creating Lasting Value*. San Francisco, Jossey-Bass, 2003.

Gersick, Kelin E., John A. Davis, Marion McCollom Hampton, and Ivan Lansberg. *Generation to Generation, Life Cycles of the Family Business*. Boston: Harvard Business School Press, 1997.

Gersick, Kelin E., et al., eds. *Generation to Generation: Life Cycles of the Family Business*. Boston: Harvard Business School Press, 1997.

Gibson, Roger C. *Asset Allocation: Balancing Financial Risk*. 3rd ed. New York: McGraw-Hill, 2000.

Gladwell, Malcolm. *Outliers: The Story of Success*. New York: Little, Brown and Co., 2008.

Godfrey, Joline. *Raising Financially Fit Kids*. Berkeley: Ten Speed Press, 2003.

Godfrey, Neale S. *Money Still Doesn't Grow on Trees: A Parent's Guide to Raising Financially Responsible Teenagers and Young Adults*. Pennsylvania: Rodale, 2004.

Godfrey, Neale S. and Carolina Edwards. *Money Doesn't Grow on Trees: A Parent's Guide to Raising Financially Responsible Children*. New York: Simon & Schuster, 1994.

Gough, Leo with the Citibank Asia Wealth Management Team. *The Citibank Guide to Building Personal Wealth*. Singapore: John Wiley & Sons, Inc., 2005.

Gray, Lisa. *The New Family Office: Innovative Strategies for Consulting to the Affluent*. London: Euromoney Institutional Investor, 2004.

Greycourt & Co., Inc. "Is It Different This Time?" White Paper No. 46, 2009.

Gryskiewicz, Stanley. *Positive Turbulence*. San Francisco: Jossey-Bass Publishers, 1999.

Haman, Edward A. *The Complete Living Will Kit*, Naperville: Sphinx Publishing, 2006.

Hamel, Gary and C. K. Prahalad. *Competing for the Future*. Boston: Harvard Business School Press, 1994.

Hamilton, Sara. "The Challenges of Shared Ownership," in *A Family's Guide to Wealth: Insights from Thought Leaders and Pioneers*. GenSpring Family Offices, LLC, 2009.

———. and Joline Godfrey. "Preparing the Next Generation for the Responsibilities of Ownership." Family Office Exchange White Paper, 2007.

Hauser, Barbara R. *International Family Governance: Avoiding Family Fights and Achieving World Peace*. Rochester: Mesatop Press, 2009.

Hausner, Lee. *Children of Paradise: Successful Parenting for Prosperous Families*. Irvine: Plaza Press, 2005.

Hesselbein, Frances, Marshall Goldsmith, and Richard Beckhard. *The Leader of the Future*. San Francisco: Jossey-Bass, 1996.

———. *The Organization of the Future*. San Francisco: Jossey-Bass, 1997.

Howe, Neil and William Strauss. *Millennials Rising: The Next Great Generation*. New York: Vintage, 2000.

Hughes Jr., James E. *Family: The Compact Among Generations*. New York: Bloomberg Press, 2007.

———. *Family Wealth – Keeping It in the Family: How Family Members and Their Advisors Preserve Human, Intellectual and Financial Assets for Generations*. New York: Bloomberg Press, 2004.

———. "A Reflection on the Roles and Responsibilities of Each Family Member as an Owner of the Family Enterprise in a Family Governance System", unpublished online article, http://64.71.40.26/jamesehu/Articles/Owner.pdf.

Iannarelli, Cindy. *101 Ways to Give Children Business Cents at Home, Work and Play*. Bridgeville: Business Cents Resources, 1998.

Ibbotson, Roger G. and Gary P. Brinson. *Global Investing: The Professional's Guide to the World Capital Markets*. New York: McGraw-Hill, 1993.

Institute for Philanthropy. "Giving in the Recession: Tough Times Call for Smart Giving," June 2009. http://www.instituteforphilanthropy.org/cms/pages/documents/Giving_in_the_Recession.pdf.

Jaeger, Lars, ed. *The New Generation of Risk Management for Hedge Funds and Private Equity Investments*. London: Euromoney Institutional Investor, 2004.

Jaffe, Dennis T. *Working with the Ones You Love*. Newburyport: Red Wheel/Weiser, 2007.

———. *Stewardship in Your Family Enterprise: Developing Responsible Family Leaders Across Generations*. Omaha: Pioneer, 2009.

Jaffe, Dennis T. and S. H. Lane. "Sustaining a Family Dynasty: Key Issues Facing Complex Multigenerational Business- and Investment-Owning Families," *Family Business Review* 17, no. 1 (2004), 81–98.

Jaffe, Dennis T. and Fredda Herz Brown. "From Entitlement to Stewardship: How a Prosperous Family Can Prepare the Next Generation," *The Journal of Wealth Management* 11, no. 4 (Spring 2009), 11–28.

Jaffe, Dennis T. and James A. Grubman, "Acquirers' and Inheritors' Dilemma: Discovering Life Purpose and Building Personal Identity in the Presence of Wealth," *The Journal of Wealth Management* 10, no.2 (Fall 2007), 20–44.

J.P. Morgan. "Wealth Preservation: The Spending Rate Matters More Than The Asset Allocation," J.P. Morgan Private Bank White Paper, 2006.

Kansas, Dave. *The Wall Street Journal: Complete Money & Investing Guidebook*. New York: Three Rivers Press, 2005.

Kaplan, Robert S. and David P. Norton. *The Balanced Scorecard*. Boston: Harvard Business School Press, 1996.

Kaye, Kenneth. *Family Rules: Raising Responsible Children*. Bloomington: iUniverse, 2005.

———. *The Dynamics of Family Business: Building Trust and Resolving Conflict*. Bloomington: iUniverse, 2005.

———. "Trust in the Family Enterprise," 2010. http://www.kaye.com/fambz/Trust2.pdf.

Kaye, Kenneth and Nick Kaye. *Trust Me: Helping Our Young Adults Financially*. Bloomington: iUniverse, 2009.

Kloman, H. Felix. *Mumpsimus Revisited: Essays on Risk Management*. Bloomington: Xlibris Corporation, 2005.

Kochard, Lawrence and Cathleen Rittereiser. *Foundation and Endowment Investing*. New York: John Wiley & Sons, Inc., 2008.

Kochis, S. Timothy, and the partners and staff of Kochis Fitz. *Wealth Management: A Concise Guide to Financial Planning and Investment Management for Wealthy Clients*. Chicago: CCH Inc, 2003.

Kocis, James M., James C. Bachman IV, Austin M. Long III, and Craig J. Nickels. *Inside Private Equity: The Professional Investor's Handbook.* New York: John Wiley & Sons, Inc., 2009.

Kolva, Judith. "Family Stories: An Unrecognized Asset," Fox Resource Library, 2009.

Lampedusa, Giuseppe Tomasi di. *Il Gattopardo (The Leopard).* New York: Pantheon, 1960.

Lansberg, Ivan. *Succeeding Generations: Realizing the Dream of Families in Business.* Boston: Harvard Business School Press, 1999.

————. "The Tests of a Prince," *Harvard Business Review* (September 2007), 92–101.

Le Van, Gerald. *Raising Rich Kids.* Bloomington: Xlibris Corporation, 2003.

Levy, John L. *Inherited Wealth: Opportunities and Dilemmas.* North Charleston: BookSurge Publishing, 2008.

Link, E. G. "Jay". *Family Wealth Counseling, Getting to the Heart of the Matter, A Revolution in Estate Planning for Wealthy Families.* Franklin: Professional Mentoring Program, 1999.

Linksy, Marty, Ronald Heifetz, and Alexander Grashow. *The Practice of Adaptive Leadership.* Boston, Harvard Business Press, 2009.

Lipnack, Jessica and Jeffrey Stamps. *The Age of the Network.* New York: John Wiley & Sons, Inc., 1994.

Lowenstein, Roger. *When Genius Failed: The Rise and Fall of Long-Term Capital Management.* New York: Random House, 2000.

Macdonald, Ian and Jonathan Sutton. *Business Families and Family Businesses: The STEP Handbook for Advisers.* London: Globe Business Publishing, 2009.

Maginn, John, Donald Tuttle, Jerald Pinto, and Dennis McLeavey. *Managing Investment Portfolios: A Dynamic Process.* New York: John Wiley & Sons, Inc., 2007.

Malkiel, Burton and J. P. Mei. *Global Bargain Hunting: The Investor's Guide to Profits in Emerging Markets.* New York: Touchstone, 1999.

Martel, Judy. *The Dilemmas of Family Wealth: Insights on Succession, Cohesion, and Legacy.* New York: Bloomberg Press, 2006.

Maslow, A. H. "A Theory of Human Motivation," *Psychological Review* 50 (1943), 370–96.

Maude, David. *Global Private Banking and Wealth Management: The New Realities.* New York: John Wiley & Sons, Inc., 2006.

McConnell, Carmel. *Make Money, Be Happy.* Upper Saddle River: Pearson Prentice Hall Business, 2005.

Miller, Danny and Isabelle Le Breton-Miller. *Managing for the Long Run.* Boston: Harvard Business School Press, 2005.

Mobius, Mark with Stephen Fenichell. *Passport to Profits, Why the Next Investment Windfalls Will be Found Abroad–and How to Grab Your Share.* New York: Warner Books, 1999.

Moldaw, Stuart. *A Life Story for My Grandchildren.* Bloomington: Xlibris Corporation, 2006.

Morris, Richard A. and Jayne A. Pearl. *Wealth and Consequences: Ensuring a Responsible Financial Future for the Next Generation.* New York: Bloomberg Press, 2010.

Morris, Virginia B. and Kenneth M Morris. *Standard & Poor's Guide to Money and Investing.* New York: Lightbulb Press, 2005.

Murrah, Jeffrey D. *The True Meaning of Wealth.* Parent University, http://www.pasadenaisd.org/ParentUniversity/parent42.htm.

Nash, Laura and Howard Stevenson. *Just Enough: Tools for Creating Success in Your Work and Life.* New York: John Wiley & Sons, Inc., 2005.

Norris, Floyd, Gretchen Morgenson, and Allen Myerson. *The New Rules of Personal Investing: The Experts' Guide to Prospering in a Changing Economy.* New York: Times Books, 2001.

O'Neil, John and Alan Jones. *Seasons of Grace: The Life-Giving Practice of Gratitude.* Hoboken: John Wiley & Sons, Inc., 2003.

O'Neill, Jessie H. *The Golden Ghetto: The Psychology of Affluence.* Milwaukee: The Affluenza Project, 1997.

O'Toole, James and Walter Isaacson. *Creating the Good Life: Applying Aristotle's Wisdom to Find Meaning and Happiness.* Emmaus, PN: Rodale Books, 2005.

Oechsli, Matt. *The Art of Selling to the Affluent: How to Attract, Service, and Retain Wealthy Customers and Clients for Life.* New York: John Wiley & Sons, Inc., 2005.

Opdyke, Jeff D. *Love & Money: A Life Guide for Financial Success.* New York: John Wiley & Sons, Inc., 2004.

———. *The Wall Street Journal: Complete Personal Finance Book.* New York: Three Rivers Press, 2006.

Owen, David. *The First National Bank of Dad: The Best Way to Teach Kids About Money.* New York: Simon & Schuster, 2003.

Parker, Virginia Reynolds. *Managing Hedge Fund Risk: From the Seat of the Practitioner – Views from Investors, Counterparties, Hedge Funds and Consultants.* London: Risk Books, 2000.

Pearl, Jayne. *Kids and Money: Giving Them the Savvy to Succeed Financially.* New York: Bloomberg Press, 1999.

Perry, Ann. *The Wise Inheritor: A Guide to Managing, Investing and Enjoying Your Inheritance.* New York: Broadway Books, 2003.

Peters, Thomas J. and Robert H. Waterman Jr. *In Search of Excellence: Lessons from America's Best-Run Companies.* New York: Harper & Row Publishers, 1982.

Philanthropic Initiative, The. "Raising Children With Philanthropic Values," February 2009. http://www.tpi.org/resources/primer/raising_children_with_philanthropic.aspx.

Pompian, Michael M. *Behavioral Finance and Wealth Management: How to Build Optimal Portfolios That Account for Investor Biases.* New York: Wiley Finance, 2006.

Pompian, Michael. *Advising Ultra-Affluent Clients and Family Offices.* New York: Wiley Finance, 2009.

Porter, Michael E. and Mark R. Kramer, "The Competitive Advantage of Corporate Philanthropy," *Harvard Business Review* 80, no. 12 (December 2002), 56–68.

————. "Philanthropy's New Agenda: Creating Value," *Harvard Business Review* (November–December 1999), 121–30.

Prahalad, C.K. and Yves L. Doz. *The Multinational Mission: Balancing Local Demands and Global Vision.* London: Free Press, 1987.

Riemer, Jack and Nathaniel Stampfer. *So That Your Values Live On: Ethical Wills and How to Prepare Them.* Woodstock: Jewish Lights Publishing, 1991.

Rogers, Douglas. *Tax-Aware Investment Management: The Essential Guide.* New York: Bloomberg Press, 2006.

Rottenberg, Dan. *The Inheritor's Handbook: A Definitive Guide for Beneficiaries.* New York: Simon & Schuster, 2000.

Salzer, Myra. *The Inheritor's Sherpa: A Life-Summiting Guide for Inheritors.* Boulder: The Wealth Conservancy, 2005.

Schervish, Paul G. *Hyperagency and High-Tech Donors: A New Theory of the New Philanthropists.* Boston: Social Welfare Research Institute, 2003.

Schoch, Richard. *The Secrets of Happiness: Three Thousand Years of Searching for the Good Life.* London: Profile Books, 2006.

Schwab-Pomeranz, Carrie and Charles Schwab. *It Pays to Talk: How to Have the Essential Conversations with Your Family About Money and Investing.* New York: Three Rivers Press, 2003.

Sedlacek, Verna O. "Socially Responsible Investing: More Than Meets the Eye," *Mission Matters.* Commonfund Chronicle (Spring/Summer 2007).

Senge, Peter M. *The Fifth Discipline: The Art and Practice of the Learning Organization.* New York: Currency Doubleday, 1994.

Shaw, John C. *Corporate Governance and Risk: A Systems Approach.* New York: John Wiley & Sons, Inc., 2003.

Shenkman, Martin M. *The Complete Book of Trusts.* 3rd ed. New York: John Wiley & Sons, Inc., 2002.

Shipley, Jill. "Freedom within a Framework: The Key to Raising Responsible Owners of Wealth," White Paper, GenSpring Family Offices, LLC, 2009.

Shook, R. J. *The Winner's Circle IV: Wealth Management Insights from America's Best Financial Advisors.* Cherrybrook: Horizon Publishers Group, 2005.

Spector, Robert. *Family Trees: Simpson's Centennial Story.* Tacoma: Simpson Investment Company, 1990.

Spence, Linda. *Legacy: A Step-by-Step Guide to Writing Personal History.* Athens, Swallow Press/Ohio University Press, 1997.

Stanley, Thomas J. and William D. Danko. *The Millionaire Next Door: The Surprising Secrets of America's Wealthy.* New York: Pocket Books, Simon & Schuster, 1996.

Stoval, Jim. *Wisdom of the Ages.* Mechanicsburg: Executive Books, 2000.

Swensen, David F. *Pioneering Portfolio Management: An Unconventional Approach to Institutional Investment.* New York: Free Press, 2008.

———. *Unconventional Success: A Fundamental Approach to Personal Investment.* New York: Simon & Schuster, 2005.

Taleb, Nassim Nicholas. *Fooled by Randomness: The Hidden Role of Chance.* New York: W. W. Norton & Company, 2001.

———. *The Black Swan: The Impact of the Highly Improbable.* New York: Random House, 2007.

Templar, Richard. *The Rules of Wealth.* Upper Saddle River: Pearson Prentice Hall Business, 2007.

Thaler, Richard. *Nudge.* New Haven: Yale University Press, 2008.

Train, John and Thomas A. Melfe. *Investing and Managing Trusts Under the New Prudent Investor Rule.* Boston: Harvard Business School Press, 1999.

Tremper, Charles. "Securing the Future: Managing Threats and Opportunities Through Effective Risk Planning," Family Office Exchange White Paper, 2009.

Turnbull, Susan B. *The Wealth of Your Life: A Step-by-Step Guide for Creating Your Ethical Will.* Wenham: Benedict Press, 2005.

Udell, Bruce S. *Enjoy Your Wealth and Pass It On: A Blueprint for Family Wealth Enjoyment.* Sarasota: Bruce Udell, 2004.

Wallace, Alan B. *Genuine Happiness: Meditation as the Path to Fulfillment.* New York: John Wiley & Sons, Inc., 2005.

Ward, John L. *Keeping the Family Business Healthy: How to Plan for Continuing Growth, Profitability and Family Leadership.* Marietta: Family Enterprise Publishers, 2007.

———. *Perpetuating The Family Business: 50 Lessons Learned from Long Lasting, Successful Families in Business.* Houndsmills, Basingstoke, Hampshire: Palgrave Macmillan, 2004.

Ward, John L., Amy Schuman, and Stacy Stutz. *Family Business as Paradox.* Houndsmills, Basingstoke, Hampshire: Palgrave Macmillan, 2010.

Weiss, Howard. *The 100-Year Wealth Management Plan.* Boston: Aspatore, 2004.

White, Doug. *Charity on Trial: What You Need to Know Before You Give.* Fort Lee: Barricade Books, 2007.

Williams, Roy and Vic Preisser. *Preparing Heirs: Five Steps to a Successful Transition of Family Wealth and Values.* San Francisco: Robert D. Reed Publishers, 2003.

————. *Philanthropy, Heirs and Values: How Successful Families are Using Philanthropy to Prepare Their Heirs for Post-Transition Responsibilities.* San Francisco: Robert D. Reed Publishers, 2005.

Willis, Thayer Cheatham. *Navigating the Dark Side of Wealth: A Life Guide for Inheritors.* Portland: New Concord Press, 2003.

Zweig, Jason. *Your Money and Your Brain: How the New Science of Neuroeconomics Can Help Make You Rich.* New York: Simon & Schuster, 2007.

INDEX